Southern Arabia

NEW ASPECTS OF ANTIQUITY

Edited by Sir Mortimer Wheeler

Southern Arabia

Brian Doe

8 Colour Plates
134 Monochrome Plates
41 Line Drawings

THAMES AND HUDSON

First Published 1971
Printed in Switzerland by Druckerei Winterthur AG.

ISBN 0 500 39008 8

Contents

GENERAL EDITOR'S PREFACE 7

INTRODUCTION 9

I THE BACKGROUND 13

General history 13

Topography 15

Climate 18

Language 21

Religion 23

Frankincense and myrrh 30

II HISTORY, THE KINGDOMS AND ART 60

The Minaeans 66

The Qatabanians 70

'Ausān 73

The Sabaeans and the Himyar 74

The Ḥaḍramaut 97

Architecture 102

Sculpture 106

Alabaster and pottery 115

Alabaster vessels 115

Domestic pottery 116

Jewellery 118

Coins 118

III THE SITES 123

The First and Second Governorates 123

The Aden area 123

The Third Governorate 142

The Abyan area 142

The Audhilla area 147

The Fourth Governorate 180

The Wāḥidi area of Wadi Maifaʿah 180

The Wadi Jirdān area 190

The Baihān area 215

The Fourth and Fifth Governorates 226

The Wadi Ḥaḍramaut 226

The First Governorate 244

The Island of Socotra 244

NOTES 251

SELECT BIBLIOGRAPHY 254

BIBLIOGRAPHY 254

LIST OF ILLUSTRATIONS 259

INDEX 262

General editor's preface

SOUTHERN YEMEN – Aden and the adjacent former Protectorate – is grouped in this book as Southern Arabia in an attempt to avoid the embarrassment of political boundaries which have varied without precise or lasting definition through the centuries. In spite of dynastic and other fluctuations this vast region of hills, valleys and often more traversable coastlands has possessed a certain functional unity in two main aspects. First, with Somaliland across the Gulf of Aden, it produced the two principal gum-resin perfumes of the ancient world, the frankincense and myrrh which were essential for religious and healing rites in and beyond Egypt at least as early as the Old Kingdom. Secondly, it was a hinge in the long-distance commerce between East and West; an exchange and mart where goods brought by monsoons from India and East Africa could be bartered for onward transit by land and sea to the Mediterranean or to the harbours of western India. Apart from its resins it was primarily a middle-man region rather than a creative centre of original production and artistry.

This is not to say that it lacked a measure of originality in its languages and craftsmanship. Even its ancient (as indeed its more modern) architecture can on occasion claim something of a monumental efficiency for which alien and particularly Egyptian inspiration may sometimes be suspected. Too little work has yet been done on this, either by discovery or by analysis, to discriminate foreign influence and more native contributions. Indeed, the whole of Southern Arabia awaits intensive and intelligent exploration. Meanwhile, down to – indeed especially down to – the present day irreparable damage and other loss are being incurred as the result of deliberate plunder or less methodical spoliation. Here is one of the regions of the world where the partial impact of Western values has with rare exceptions been on the whole more deleterious than salutary.

A part of the purpose of the present book is to delay these processes of deterioration by indicating something of the very considerable potential of the region as an area worthy of the controlled cultural interest and attention which other parts of the Arabian Middle East have for some time attracted both extraneously and increasingly from their own nationals. In the present situation my friend the author would be the last man to describe his book as anything more than an introductory sketch of the scene in which he spent a decade, first as government architect and subsequently, at his own volition, as the Director of the young Department of Antiquities at Aden. His tour of the latter office began in 1960, and all too many of the following years were complicated and frustrated by violent insecurity. That in the circumstances he was able to achieve as much as he did by visitation and collection is matter for congratulation. He was not indeed readily deterred. In 1966, when the trouble was at its height, the present General Editor recalls how, after formally laying the foundation-stone of a much-needed if not altogether timely Museum at Steamer Point, he and Brian Doe drank warm champagne together within the circle of an armed escort whilst the dedicatory brass plate, put up that morning, was being removed from its wall for continuing security! It is greatly to be hoped that, when political equilibrium is fully established, the work of cultural conservation may be resumed in the 'Doe' spirit, and that a new appreciation of the value and dignity of their past through many millennia may inspire the emancipated inhabitants of Southern Arabia to cherish their heritage for their greater glory and incidentally, in these modern days of far-flung tourism, for their greater profit.

MORTIMER WHEELER

Introduction

Southern Arabia provides a new field in the archaeological world in two respects; first, because the area is still largely unknown and absolutely anything found, be it ancient site or artifact, is of accumulative historical or archaeological significance; secondly, because the area of study is vast and there is very little preliminary information to go on. Local inhabitants can often produce a few potsherds or lead one to a few tumbled stones which at first sight may be of any age and often prove to be comparatively modern. Nevertheless information of this kind must always be followed up for it can lead to the finding of important sites or cast a new light on an area thought to have nothing to offer. The collection of information in this way frequently means extensive travelling by land through rough terrain. This often requires the arranging of escorts for unreliable districts and the frequently difficult provision of fuel and food, and above all plenty of water. A knowledge of the good wells is always necessary.

Elsewhere archaeologists may be armed with the technical aids of modern science and accompanied by specialized technicians, but in Southern Arabia the bulk of the work of archaeological survey has normally to be carried out with the least possible equipment, for the explorer must travel light. Here it is a deep knowledge of the country and terrain and of the present-day people that immediately contributes most to the study of the past.

The field archaeologist, that lone person, must be able to assess the approximate significance of artifacts and other material as he finds them, in desert or wadi, and for this he must have a constructive imagination. It is one thing to stumble on a ruin with a wall around it but it is quite another to find an inscription with an unknown town name, and from local knowledge of the country actually to discover the place referred to, perhaps with ancient fields now oversilted, and former irrigation sluices now merely small piles of seemingly insignificant stones. Flat-topped mounds or tells may indicate the whereabouts of a long-dead town, and water-catchment systems, cisterns and wells may show where an ancient community lived and its extent. Fortunately waterholes in use today were often used in antiquity, for in this type of country there has been little change through the centuries.

Old methods of irrigation for arable land, the use of floodwaters and of sluice diversions to spread the water over the widest possible area, continue to this day, although well systems are now often assisted by deep-bore diesel pumps. The old method of dispersal of fresh silt brought down by floodwaters still survives with the use of wooden scoops dragged by bullocks. This system has in the past resulted in the fields rising so far above the wadi bed that they have become unworkable. Thus ancient fields can sometimes be identified by their higher level, with a ground pattern of interlaced old water-channels,[1] and nearby one might expect a ruin-site of reasonable importance. Geographic location with suitability for defence and its relationship to an ancient caravan route may also be useful pointers. The finding of a pre-Islamic inscription or votive tablet can be the highlight of such a survey. Also, whilst driving or walking, the scanning of the rock walls of a wadi for a graffito or drawing must become part of the explorer's second nature.

Southern Arabia is one of the few regions of Western Asia which present a new challenge to the archaeologist; not least, a physical challenge, the ability to prepare camp at the end of an exhausting journey along dusty, bumpy tracks and to begin work immediately on survey, for often time at the destination is very short. When long distances have to be covered, an intimate knowledge of the terrain and also of the tides, for the beach is frequently used for travel, is absolutely necessary. As a matter of pride as much as of personal comfort, one tries not to be a nuisance to the authorities. For this reason when travelling known routes, messages are sent ahead with an estimated time or date of arrival at a certain place. Usually more than one vehicle is used, so that the party may expect at least to remain mobile.

In such territory it is also the simple things that delight – the partaking of midday meals on white, glaring sand sitting in the only patch of shade, usually an *ilb* tree; the evening bathe when on the beach, not going more than a few feet because of sting and whip rays or basking sharks; and feeling the fatigue, as well as the day's grime, wash away; to view the magnificent sunsets and finally to sleep under the brilliant stars set in black void, and feel the cool night breeze – and to wake with a start in a hasty torchlight check of jerrycans to make sure that it really was petrol you poured into the tank!

The purpose of this work is to introduce the early history of the people of South-western Arabia to a wider range of readers than has been covered by previous specialized publications on individual aspects. It is to those readers who are interested in this distant land and who wish to learn something of the early culture, trade, art and architecture of its ancient peoples that it is particularly directed.

Although the historical remarks concern the whole of ancient Southern Arabia, the bulk of the evidence presented is drawn from the extreme south which is the area of the author's experience.

The book is divided into three main parts, the first two of which describe the place and the people. The third part is solely concerned with descriptions of some of the ancient sites known to the writer. The sites are identified on the map (p. 17) and are listed as far as possible so as to progress from west to east.

I wish to express indebtedness to my friends and colleagues, R.D. Barnett, A.F.L. Beeston, G.W. Van Beek, W. Dostal, G. Lankester Harding, Miss M. Höfner, A.K. Irvine, A. Jamme, T. Johnstone, W. Phillips, Miss J. Pirenne, J. Ryckmans, R.B. Serjeant and H. von Wissmann who have through their academic work identified themselves with Southern Arabia; and in Aden to M. and Mme A.B. Besse, whose help and hospitality to visiting scholars is so well known, to Officers and members of the Royal Air Force, the British Army, the South Arabian Army and to Officers of the old West Aden Protectorate and High Commission Office and other Government Departments, who made so many of the visits up country at all possible.

Generally the transcriptions of important place names are retained as they are usually spelt, instead of the direct transliterations based on early South Arabian inscriptions. For instance <u>Dh</u>ufar instead of Ḍufar or Ẓufar and Shabwa instead of Šabwat. Although this will appear technically inconsistent to the epigraphist, it is thought that it will help to locate place names more easily.

The dates provided for historical events relating to the South Arabian Kingdoms and their rulers, as well as for structures and texts included in this book are generally in accordance with the longer chronologies based upon the following foreign synchronisms:

(a) the Assyrian texts which mention the Sabaeans Yt‘’mr (714 BC) and Krb’l (685 BC), although the justification for their inclusion in the early dynasty of Saba’ remains not proven.

(b) the expedition of Aelius Gallus to Arabia Felix and Marib (25–24 BC).

(c) the *Periplus of the Erythraean Sea* (now dated to the early third century AD).

(d) the an-Namāra epitaph (328 AD).

St John's College,
Cambridge

D.B. D.

I

The Background

General history

From the earliest historical times South-west Arabia was inhabited by some half-dozen main groups of people who formed themselves into individual states or kingdoms. The history of these kingdoms is one of constant warfare and changing frontiers, first one state holding the supreme power, then another. To complicate the story even further, there are great gaps in our knowledge so that only the broad outlines emerge.

In the midst of this continual anarchy, however, one theme seems to have remained fairly stable and that was the trade carried along the camel-caravan routes from South to North Arabia. This trade began with frankincense, the famous aromatic resin which was produced in Arabia and found a market among the Egyptians, who needed it for their religious rites. The Egyptians sent out trading expeditions by sea for this commodity, and we learn that they visited the 'Land of Punt'. This may have been Somaliland although the best frankincense was known to have come from Dhufar on the coast of South Arabia. One of these expeditions is shown in reliefs on the walls of the temple of Queen Hatshepsut at Deir el-Bahari in Egypt. After the domestication of the camel and its consequent use as a beast of burden, it was found much more economical to transport this growing trade overland, and from the tenth century BC it was possible for camel caravans to carry merchandise from the Indian Ocean as far north as Gaza on the Mediterranean.[2] The frankincense was joined by rich merchandise and luxury goods from Africa, India and the Far East, which were brought by sea to Aden and to Qana' near Bir 'Ali to start on the long journey northwards. By levying taxes and tolls the agrarian states and tribes astride the caravan roads grew wealthy. They realized that encouragement of trade was more remunerative than attacking and robbing the caravans. They became the middlemen in a great commercial industry which attracted the attention of the civilizations from the Euphrates to the Nile, and cultural influences passing down the trade-routes resulted in the growth of fine cities and temples and vast irrigation schemes to help feed an expanding population. With the new prosperity came greed for more territory to embrace a greater part of the trade-route system. Thus the history of the kingdoms and supporting tribes mentioned in the inscriptions is often one of conflict and conquest. Surprisingly, the continual struggle for ascendency does not appear to have affected trade, and this seems to indicate the existence of a very stable mercantile organization.

The kingdom that first controlled the inland part of the trade was the powerful Kingdom of Saba', from its capital at Marib. At another time it was the Kingdom of 'Ausān that was foremost in the trading world. It is thought to have covered most of the coastline of South-west Arabia, and was important for its close trading links with the African coast.

In the late fifth century BC, the Kingdom of Saba' over-ruled most of the coastal states and conquered 'Ausān (RES 3945). At the same time Saba' seems to have encouraged the development of a trading colony on the Abyssinian coast.[3] Only after Sabaean power weakened did the other tribes come into their own as fully independent kingdoms.

The Kingdom of Qataban was the next to rise to power, while the kingdom of Maʿin, which lay to the north, also grew in importance and took part in breaking the power of the Sabaeans. With Qataban reigning supreme, a new state of Himyar came into being and set out in its turn to conquer the country. The kingdom of Ḥaḍramaut took the opportunity at this time of conquering part of Qataban themselves; Timnaʿ, the capital, was destroyed about AD 100, and the whole frontier line of Ḥaḍramaut was pushed westwards. However, Himyar had already overrun the coastal areas and amalgamated with part of Saba'. This was later known as the kingdom of Saba' and Dhu Raydān, with their capital city at Ẓafar, near the present-day Yarim.

The Sabaeans of the traditional dynasty in the north then reasserted their independence, and this formation of a second kingdom of Saba' and Dhu Raydān with their capital at Marīb attacked the Himyar. They then attacked and conquered most of Ḥaḍramaut, when the port of Qana'[4] was taken and Shabwa, the capital, was sacked. It is probable that, as a result of this, Shibām became the site of a new capital city situated farther east in the Wadi of Ḥaḍramaut.

In the third century AD, South-west Arabia was invaded by the people of Abyssinia,[5] referred to by the South Arabians as the Habašat,[6] and for a while a large part of the country on the west coast was under their rule.

It is possible that as a direct result Christianity was first introduced into South-west Arabia, and in about AD 360 the Himyar king was baptized.[7] After this conversion the Abyssinian troops were withdrawn but Christianity among the Himyar was not strong, and we find that at the beginning of the next century the ruler 'Abukarib 'As'ad adopted Judaism. The non-Christian tribes of Himyar began to persecute those who retained their faith, but, when a large number of Christians were martyred at Najrān, the Abyssinians returned to South-west Arabia to support their faith.

The settlement of the Abyssinians this time lasted until after the birth of Muhammed. At the invitation of the Himyar they were finally driven out by the Persians, who wanted to control the South Arabian coastline with the Red Sea trade, and they succeeded in crushing those who had owed allegiance to the Abyssinian king at Aksum. This Persian satrapy in South-west Arabia collapsed before the rise of Islam in the seventh century AD.

Topography

Southern Arabia may be described as a mountainous country with narrow wadis expanding into arid level desert. Agricultural areas are to be found in the wadis wherever the seasonal floods can be controlled and the fresh silt collected. One of the greatest problems has always been the provision of water, primarily for drinking, and wells and catchment areas are guarded jealously by the tribesmen, especially in the more remote districts.

The area of Southern Arabia extends from the Red Sea with a southern coastline to the Dhufar region. The terrain along this coast consists generally of varying widths of sandy plains along the eastern front backed by massive rock outcrops and ranges of mountains. Many of the rock outcrops visible from the sea are the remains of ancient volcanoes, such as Jabal Kharāz, seventy miles west of Aden, which threw its lava and ash over an area of some fourteen miles in diameter.

Figs 1, 2
Plate 45
Fig. 7

The rocks of Aden are the remains of smaller volcanoes,[8] and Aden is probably unique in that the walls of the ancient crater have provided a natural security for inhabitants from early times. About 130 miles eastwards from Aden are the remains of vast black lava flows which spread

Plate 46

over the countryside and volcanic craters. Between Bal Ḥāf and Bir ʿAli and extending into the mountains there are large lava fields formed by comparatively recent eruptions.

Plate 45

Geographically, Aden is situated at the mouth of a wide wadi which lies due north, and below the surface of this sandy delta area of Laḥej underground streams of fresh water flow, disappearing into the sea.

Probably the most important wadi used as a communication into the interior is the Abyan delta area some forty miles east of Aden. Here is one of the largest agricultural areas where the floodwaters are still being controlled for irrigation. North of this area the granite mountains extend into jaggy peaks dispersed by narrow wadis. About twenty miles inland is the great Kaur range forming a plateau at an average height of 7000 feet above sea-level. The climate here is good for growing crops and every wadi has its tilled areas in stepped terraces, revetted with stone walling.

The third great wadi along this coast is the Wadi Maifaʿah. Again it has a wide sandy delta area which extends inland some fifty miles, where narrow rocky cliffed wadis form the tributaries from the catchment areas. Eastwards and roughly parallel lies the fertile Wadi Hajr which has a continual stream of fresh water from springs high up in the mountains.

East of the mountainous area of the Yemen and north of the mountains of this area lies the vast desert sea called the Ramlat Sabatain which extends as far east as the mouth of the great Wadi Ḥaḍramaut. The northern side of this desert extends into the Empty Quarter desert, which lies beyond, into the centre of Arabia.

The area of the Ḥaḍramaut is in the form of a vast flat rock plateau or jōl interspersed with innumerable eroded clefts and wadis or valleys which are tributaries of the main Wadi Ḥaḍramaut. Here the flat mountain tops contrast with the jagged range after range of rock outcrop at the western end of Southern Arabia.

The Wadi Ḥaḍramaut continues eastwards in a vast arc until, renamed the Wadi Masailah, it finally reaches the sea. The rocky coast extends beyond here to Ras Fartak. In the deep bay beyond lies the frankincense region.

Fig. 2

At D͟hufar within the Qamr Bay the Qara mountain range forms a backcloth to the level coastal region. This was the place where rare frankincense of the best quality was found to grow naturally. Thus D͟hufar and its port of Sumhurum and Moscha in ancient times were of great

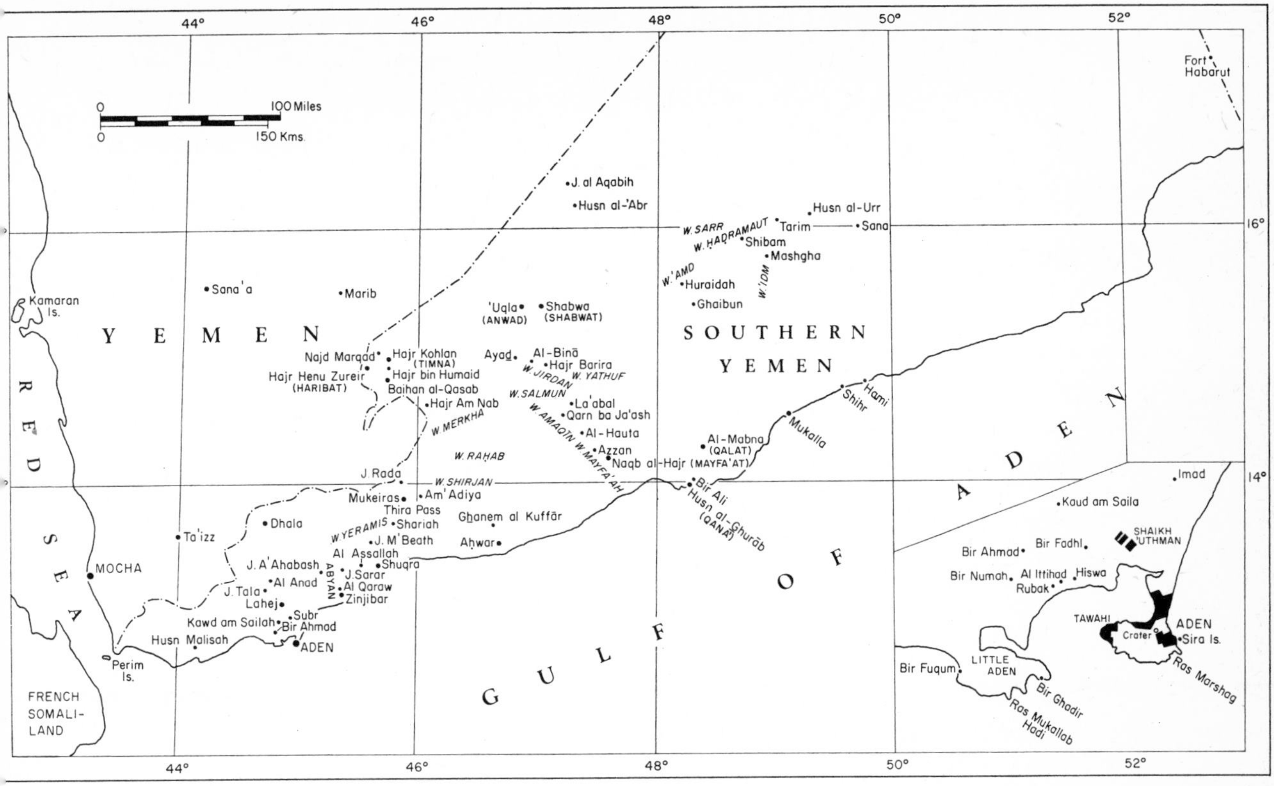

1 *A general map of South-west Arabia*

importance. North of the Qara Mountains, the sand sea of the Rub' al-Khali or Empty Quarter formed a natural protective barrier.

Much of Southern Arabia, its towns and villages and the countryside of wadis or valleys and forbidding bleak mountains and rocks, the steppe land and desert waste, is relatively unknown. This is not surprising, for there are many difficulties in the path of the would-be traveller, not the least of which are the immense distances to be covered and the attendant problem of fuel and supplies, but also the security of an area in which it may not be advisable to travel in certain stretches without prior approval or without an escort. This precludes the traveller who wishes to wander and see for himself in much of the western area; conditions for travel are usually easier in the eastern areas.

From Aden most of the traffic to the states or Governorates starts from the tracks along the beach, although the immediate countryside may be reached through Shaikh ʿUthmān and along the tarmac road to Al-Ḥauta, Laḥej, capital of the Abdali State. The routes northwards to Dhala and Musemeir as well as the northern Yemen border and town of Kirsh all pass through Laḥej.

Climate

It seems possible that Southern Arabia was not a more fertile land at the time of the ancient tribes. This is shown by the number of rain-water ways, catchments and irrigation schemes which would probably have been inundated by a wetter and more temperate climate. There is also no evidence that present living conditions and aridity are so very different from that of about three thousand years ago. Agricultural life from the second millennium BC appeared on the well-watered high ground in the south-west of Arabia, and the ruins of irrigation schemes found there indicate experience and a high standard of technical ability.

In this dry climate the existence of settled peoples and expanding population depends entirely on irrigation to raise their standard of living above that of the nomad. Possibly by trial and error, or on knowledge gained from the more advanced countries of the north, the problem of water conservation, the development of a system of irrigation and the prevention of erosion from flash-floods or *sails*, was met and solved by the use of dams, canals and sluice gates, a form of river-valley civilization. The South Arabians must, however, be credited with the development of *sail* irrigation – the economic use and speedy distribution of flood-water. The development of this form of irrigation, together with the use of the camel as a domestic and load-bearing animal, may have increased the settling of areas hitherto thought impossible and too isolated for agriculture. Localized climatic changes, too, particularly near Aden, may have occurred where large areas were denuded of bush and timber by inhabitants for building and boat construction, charcoal and wood fires.

The present-day climate from October to April during the north-east monsoon period is usually cool but in the summer months there are hot sandy winds, usually from the north and landward side. The winds in the Aden area almost cease during the months of May and September when there is a change in the monsoon winds. Then the humidity is felt and it is hot and oppressive. The hottest months are usually June and July.

The rainfall in the Aden area has been recorded only since 1860, and the amount fluctuates from year to year. Captain F. M. Hunter[9] records that in 1870 8.03 inches fell while in 1871 only 0.24 inch was measured. It is significant that he reports that the great water-cisterns of Crater, since they were repaired in 1858, were filled on two occasions only, in 1864 and 1870. To the writer's knowledge they were last filled to the brim in 1953.

Present records of rainfall in Southern Arabia show Aden, Mukalla and Salalah on the coast, not the mountain area, as being the driest areas.

Average rainfall for these places below 100 feet above sea-level are:[10] Aden 1.6; Mukalla 2.8; Salalah 3.8.

Mukeiras at just about 7,000 feet has an average of 9.5 with the wettest months between July and September, when 3.8 inches has been recorded for August. The wettest area is Dhalla, roughly the same distance inland although at 4,580 feet above mean sea-level. The annual average is recorded as 15.0 inches with July and August showing as much as 4.2 and 4.5 inches respectively. In both these places there is also a marked increase in the rainfall during April and May.

Over Southern Arabia there are two distinct seasons associated with the south-west and north-west monsoons, well known by the early South Arabian sailors, which may also be defined as the Hot and Cool seasons.

The south-west monsoon, as it travels across the Abyssinian highlands and the Horn of Africa before traversing the Gulf of Aden, loses its moisture in the rains of Abyssinia, and the air is subsequently warmed and dried off the coast of Somalia. This dry and hot air-flow spreads over the Gulf of Aden, reaching Aden about the end of May, spreading towards the eastern coast of Arabia about three or four weeks later. The south-west monsoon usually recedes towards the end of September and is quite different from the wet south-west monsoon which spreads over most of India.

Across the Gulf of Aden the dry air is cooled at a low level, but after striking the coast it receives a surface heating which lifts the air over the mountains and escarpments. This gives rise to thunderstorms in the mountains of the Yemen, and in the hills of the western regions and the jōl of the Ḥaḍramaut the south-west monsoon is wet. These inland storms are sometimes sudden and violent, causing immediate floods when dry wadis become raging torrents. These floods or *sails* are controlled to irrigate the land in agricultural areas but more often the floodwaters subside into subterranean storage.

Unlike the central deserts, these south-western mountains receive rain at certain seasons of the year, and the water flowing down the mountain valleys is eagerly awaited by people who live in the lower coastal plain; for here the rain falls less readily, although springs are not unknown.

The same south-west monsoon, reaching the eastern coastline beyond Ras Fartak from mid-June to mid-September, does not get warmed but retains moisture from its cooling passage over the sea. Consequently, when it reaches the coast here, fog and low stratus clouds are usual. There is often a persistent drizzle with damp fog, especially on the slopes of the ranges of mountains a few miles inland from the coast, where cumulus clouds develop.

In the Dhufar (Salalah) region it is precisely this climate which is beneficial for the frankincense, which grows wild.

Average temperatures for this period from June to September differ according to the area and mean height above sea-level. On the coast, Aden's average maximum temperature is 96° to 98°F and at Salalah it is 81° to 84°F. Inland, the altitude is a principal factor in determining the average daily maximum temperature. At Mukeiras, about 7,000 feet, it ranges between 75° and 78°F, while at Dhala about the same distance inland but 2,000 feet lower, the temperature ranges between 78° and 92°F.

At Baihān, which lies some 150 miles inland on the southern boundary of the sand sea, the average maximum temperature is between 96° and 102°F.

The variations of temperature between night and day are 14°F at Aden, between 7° and 10°F at Salalah; Mukeiras is about 20°F, Dhala 26°F, and Baihān has about 32° variation.

The north-east monsoon is usually between November and April and cold air from the north extends southwards over the Persian Gulf to the Arabian coast, although it reaches Aden a little later than the eastern coast area. There are often showers and squalls at the eastern end but, although these are not prominent characteristics at the western end of the coast, the Red Sea may provide local variations.

Usually the daily maximum temperature is about 15°F below the summer temperature with appropriate variations affected by altitude at the inland places.

The period of transition between the monsoons usually lies about May for the change from north-east to south-west monsoon. This time is a period of light and variable winds with scattered thunderstorms. The north-east monsoon then usually takes place during October or November.

Sand or dust storms are likely to occur often over sandy or dust areas during the south-west monsoon or summer months. This usually means that visibility is reduced to between a quarter and three quarters of a mile and the air is full of fine dust carried to a great height. The first sign is an approaching wall of dust-laden air which may be several thousand feet in height lifted by the strong rising currents and stirred by a fairly strong wind. Blown sand at low level can occur in both seasons but it is more frequent during the summer. Ground visibility may be reduced to the limits of a sand storm but this depends on the strength of the gusts.

Language

The early South Arabian language has been well recorded by metal plaques and carved stone inscriptions used as official and religious documents, as well as by pecked graffiti on rock surfaces. Its alphabet of 29 letters consists, like other Semitic forms, of consonants.

The writings on the rock face at the turquoise mines in Sinai date from 1850 BC and these graffiti provide the bridge between the Egyptian hieroglyphs and the Phoenician alphabet.[11] This Sinaitic alphabet, as well as the Phoenician when communicated southwards, was developed by the early South Arabians into the well-proportioned rectilinear characters of the archaic form. The process of this development into sophisticated letters with their apparent Graeco-Hellenistic character is not yet decided. It is of great interest that several early South Arabian inscriptions using these characters have been found south of Kuwait. However, forms graphically related to the Sinaitic form, as represented by the Liḥyānite inscriptions of Dedān, modern Al-ʿUla, and the Thamudic graffiti writings and the Ṣafaʿ graffiti of the same region, developments of the Liḥyānite script, are also represented on the rock faces of Southern Arabia.

The Minaeans opened trade relations to the north, and this proved so successful that the capital of the Liḥyānites at Dedān was controlled by Maʿin, and Minaean inscriptions have been found there as well as hybrid Minaeo-Liḥyānite texts.[12]

Plate 7

Fig. 16

The earliest Sabaean inscriptions found, thought to be of the seventh century BC, are often boustrophedon, but all later inscriptions read from right to left. One of the problems is still to find the reason for the sudden appearance of the well-cut geometric letters in inscriptions at such an early date, with no apparent signs of their development.

Generally the inscriptions found can be located to the area from which they originally came, and for the epigraphist there are ways of showing the period of the inscription by the gradual changes in the form of the characters.

Plates 76, 123, 124, 128

Apart from the official inscription tablets, usually blocks of fine limestone or alabaster, there are also graffiti of a more sophisticated nature to be found on rock surfaces, and these, usually constituting a formal document, portray the more normal South Arabian characters. Pecked and inscribed graffiti are often to be found in great quantity on smooth rock surfaces throughout Southern Arabia. These are sometimes given the name of Thamudic and appear to show the type of inscribed characters first discovered in the area of Thamud, although there are epigraphic differences.[13] However, here they do not necessarily illustrate part of the actual development of the South Arabian alphabet, but merely indicate the standard of craft and knowledge of the inscriber. They usually consist of a proper name accompanied by a drawing or symbol.

Plate 84

The decipherment of some of the earliest inscriptions found was made by Emil R. Rödiger of Halle in 1837 and by H.F. Wilhelm Gesenius in 1841,[14] when they interpreted the inscription at Naqb al-Hajar. The first comprehensive work on South Arabian grammar was published by Maria Höfner in 1943 and A.F.L. Beeston has continued the study.[15] From the inscriptions collected in the areas of the different kingdoms, it is possible to note that the languages of the Minaeans, Sabaeans, Qatabanians and Ḥaḍramaut were similar but with differing dialects. The Sabaean dialect in particular contains features which suggest a North Arabian origin. The symmetrical geometric characters took a long time to develop from earlier forms, and affinities seen to Greek characters may indicate a parallel development also with direct Greek influence. The earlier forms of the incised characters are usually of rectangular shape and of simple geometric classical design, often without serifs. One is almost forced, by this obvious Greek influence, to consider a much later date for the early inscriptions. The period between the sixth and fifth centuries BC seems more in accord with the evidence available. The problems regarding the origins of the alphabet have been well discussed by J. Pirenne.[16] In a much later form, which is especially noticeable in the last Sabaean period of the dual monarchy of Saba' and Himyar, the characters lose their simplicity and serifs are added. Later still, in the fourth to sixth centuries AD, they take decorative forms with accentuated serifs and sometimes distortion of the letter. Inscriptions of this latter period have, in addition, been found in which the characters were not incised, but the interstices were cut away to leave the characters raised from the surface.

Plates 57, 75, 120

Figs. 20, 24

No early South Arabian script has been found on perishable material, and normal transactions or literary achievements, if recorded on leather or fabric, have entirely disappeared. However, painted inscriptions and drawings have been found executed in red ochre, probably mixed with a resin, on the smooth faces of large boulders, normally in a position protected from the sun.

Plates 91, 93

Religion

Early religious belief in Southern Arabia is illustrated by arrangements of stones. These usually consist of settings of prominent stones planned either as an enclosure which embraces the deity-stone or as alignments, apparently on astral bodies. These megalithic structures are to be found in the more isolated areas. One found in the Mukeiras region is close to the edge of the Khaur range and south of the site of Am Adiya. It consists of a perimeter of stones each some two feet in diameter with a fifteen-foot-high boulder on the northern side, dominating the enclosure.

Plate 66

Another planned layout of stones is to be found in the Wadi Sarr near Shibām. Here the central structure is a square enclosure formed of upright limestone slabs, with recumbent slabs forming a kerb. Inside the south-west corner of this enclosure is a dolmen-like structure, and similar structures may have stood at each corner. There are also ten large stones and stone circles; standing stones bear graffiti, as well as an engraved, three-line, crenellated design. The age of this particular complex is unknown, and stone and chert artifacts do not provide conclusive evidence. The graffiti indicate that they were *in situ* in the period of the early South Arabian script.[17]

Near the low rocks of Afalil in the Ramlat Sabatain north-west of Shabwa, H. St John Philby noticed a 'curious grouping of great basalt boulders, very suggestive of a primitive sun temple. The rocks form a circle of some size with a central aisle, lined with boulders, leading up to a large "altar stone" at the western end'.[18] Whether this arrangement was the work of man or of nature, Philby was not sure. He found flakes of obsidian and flint and thought he could see traces of ancient fields nearby.

Plate 78
Figs 25, 26
Other early structures are to be found in the main wadi some twenty miles north of Aḥwar. Here at Ghanem al-Kuffār are the remains of several stone cairns some twelve to fifteen feet in diameter and, with each, long alignments of stones extending in different directions. These were typically rows of small stone groups about two feet high. On one stone circle, built of vertical slabs, are graffiti drawings, and nearby pecked graffiti in early South Arabian script. On the hill ridges of wadis in the Ḥaḍramaut and particularly in the area of Al-ʿAbr, and as far south as

Fig. 39
Wadi Jirdān, there are large cairns, generally some fifteen feet in diameter, usually with a row of smaller cairns, some two to three feet high, often placed so as to be silhouetted against the sky. There seems no doubt that these are burial cairns or ossuaries with a line of small cairns which may indicate the importance of the deceased. Cairns of a similar variety have also been observed in the Wadi ʿIdm (ʿAdim),[19] but they have not been scientifically examined.

On the summit of the main ridge of Ruwaik and also on the ridges and hillsides at ʿAlam ʾAswad and ʿAlam ʾAbyad, Philby saw many pill-box-shaped stone cairns spread over neighbouring hills and he estimated that there were thousands, forming a vast necropolis. The design of the tombs was circular, built of flat slabs of untrimmed natural limestone varying in size and thickness, and the largest noticed was ten feet high and twenty-five feet in diameter. The entrance was a narrow corridor about five feet wide above ground level, leading to a central chamber about five feet across roofed with overlapping masonry slabs.[20]

Plates 67–69
North of Mukeiras on a site straddling the track to Al-Mathan are several large cairns of similar construction averaging some fifteen to eighteen feet in diameter and about five feet high. On rock surfaces nearby are early South Arabian graffiti.

Triliths set up in long rows were reported by Bertram Thomas in the wadis north of Dhufar; each consisted of three small stones about eighteen inches high with a capping stone. Parallel to the lines of triliths and about nine feet distant were small conical heaps of stone. Their function has not been satisfactorily explained although they are probably associated with religious rites or tribal ceremony.[21]

If these structures illustrate a primitive and presumably earlier form of religious belief, a later stage of development, with elaborate rites and a pantheon of astral deities and sophisticated temple-design, may be thought to reflect the wealth and prosperity of the people associated with the trading caravans.

In the Wadi ʿAmd near the town of Ḥuraiḍah in the Ḥaḍramaut, Dr Gertrude Caton-Thompson excavated cave tombs in the scree slopes edging the wadi. These tombs, which had been used as ossuaries, are the only cave tombs to have been investigated archaeologically. They are of particular interest as they had undoubtedly been connected with the rectangular stone temple a short distance away in the main wadi.[22] *Fig. 40*

The South Arabians before Islam were polytheists and revered a large number of deities. Most of these were astral in concept but the significance of only a few is known. It was essentially a planetary system in which the moon as a masculine deity prevailed. This, combined with the use of a star calendar by the agriculturists of certain parts, particularly in the Ḥaḍramaut, indicates that there was an early reverence for the night sky.

It would seem that the religious cult, the temples, ritual and power of the priest rulers were the outcome of a sedentary way of life, the agriculturists-cum-merchants relying on the trade caravans.

Amongst the South Arabians the worship of the moon continued, and it is almost certain that their religious calendar was also lunar and that their years were calculated by the position of the moon. The national god of each of the kingdoms or states was the Moon-god known by various names: ʾIlumquh by the Sabaeans, ʿAmm and ʾAnbay by the Qatabanians, Wadd by the Minaeans, and Sin by the Ḥaḍramis. The Sun-goddess was the moon's consort; she was perhaps best known in Southern Arabia as D͟hat Hamym, 'she who sends forth strong rays of benevolence'. Another dominant deity was the male god known as ʿAt͟htar corresponding to the Phoenician ʿAs͟htarte.

There were many gods of tribes and places, and irrigation deities in addition to this astral pantheon. The god ʾIl, worshipped in the north, was also included in names by the South Arabians, although the word ʾIl was used frequently to mean merely a god or deity.

Temples dedicated to the gods abound in Southern Arabia. The gods owned land, flocks and herds, administered by the temple priests. The temple was thus supported by tithes and dues levied on the tribesmen, to whom the sacred ground of the temple complex was the centre of the community. Official enactments and laws were all declared in the name of the gods and any transaction, the building of houses, terraces for vineyards and plantations, reservoirs and irrigation works were all confided for protection to the gods and the temple.

Understandably the priests wielded great authority and power in their capacity as both secular and religious rulers. It appears that after the fifth century BC the duties of priest and ruler in Saba' were separated and instead of being known as a Mukarrib or priest-king, the title changed to Malik or king.[23]

Classical writers were impressed by the temples and palaces which epitomized the wealth of the early South Arabians.[24] The temples were the finest structures of the community, and on these the utmost care in construction and finish was lavished. Generally they were of rectangular plan, oriented with the corners pointing to the cardinal points. Some were roofed, but many were open to the sky within a perimeter wall. The most *Fig. 4* famous open temple was that of ʾAwwām situated near Marib, which is the exception for it has a massive oval or kidney-shaped plan and a high perimeter wall of fine ashlar masonry enclosing a religious enclave. The Plates 105, 108; main temple at Timnaʿ in Baihān is in the centre of the city and here *Fig. 36* the rectangular forecourt of the temple building is approached by a Plates 116–118 magnificent broad staircase. The main temple found at Shabwa, ancient capital of the Ḥaḍramaut, appears to have had a portico of four Plate 118 circular columns; but if this is so it must have been unique, for the usual column in Southern Arabia was a square monolith having a capital decorated with three or four rows of dentils supporting the entablature.

The gods of the temples were asked for favours and blessings – for those who needed good health, fertility of land, forgiveness for past happenings, and for penitants generally. Within the sanctuary burnt offerings and blood sacrifices were made. Oracles were sought over an altar and delivered by a priest in the name of the god of the temple. A thanksgiving sacrifice was then made first with bowing and prostrations in several directions. Then upon the sacrificial altar the blood of lambs was offered.[25] The oracle could be consulted only on certain days in specified months. In the case of the desired oracular response not being received the sacrifices were repeated.

Confessions of sins or law-breaking, whether ritual, legal or moral, required public repentance and the performing of penance. Often, and as a simple act of piety, a person would dedicate himself or herself or the children to the service of the gods and the temple.[26]

In all cases the burning of incense played an important part in the religious ceremony, both in the temple and on the little altars in the home. Votive offerings would be inscribed with the offerer's name and dedicated to the god of the temple. These included stelae, sculptured heads representing the dedicant or offerer, incense altars and, in rarer cases, statuettes and figurines. The quality of such offerings, both in alabaster and bronze, varied considerably.

Plates 18, 19, 22, 23

Burials were made in various ways and include simple stone-lined graves covered with a cairn of stones, excavated tombs in the scree slopes at the sides of wadis with concealed entrances, and mausolea with chambers for the reception of the bodies. Having a belief in an after-life, the dead were usually buried with material objects which they had required during life. These included jewellery, pottery and alabaster vessels, stelae, money and figurines. Finds of this nature often provide the only evidence of living standards. Very little is known, however, of pagan Southern Arabian mythology or theology. It is of great interest to realize that the pagan stone structure known as the Ka'bah with its stone images and statues was venerated at Mecca, the sanctuary to which annual pilgrimages were made before, no less than after, the rise of Islam.

The spread of Christian teaching in Arabia and Abyssinia was due to the efforts of missionaries sent in the fourth century AD from Constantinople and Tyre.[27] In Abyssinia this was mainly the work of Bishop Frumentius, while in Southern Arabia Bishop Theophilus Indus, who was sent by Constantine II, led an Embassy with gifts for the King of Himyar. The number of converts in Southern Arabia was considerable and among the most important proselytes was the Himyar king, thought to be T̲h̲a'ran Yuhan'im, at Ẓafar near Yarim. Bishop Theophilus was allowed to build a church at Ẓafar, another one at Aden[28] in about AD 342 and there was possibly yet a third at Sohar in Oman.

Another important convert was at Aksum in Abyssinia where King Ezana was christened about AD 350.[29] It may have been on account of the Roman Emperor's role in the conversion of the Himyar monarch that Ezana decided to abandon any further policy of interest in Arabia and concentrate his expansionist activities within Ethiopia itself. Ezana's troops probably left Arabia before AD 361[30] although a garrison may have remained behind.

In Arabia, Najrān – an ancient pagan pilgrim centre – became a Christian stronghold. Situated in a fertile district and on the trade route, it was a wealthy and politically advanced city. It may have been during this time that the direct trade route from the Ḥaḍramaut and Shabwa northwards through Mushainiqa to Najrān was opened as an indication of the friendship that existed between the pro-Christian Ḥaḍramis and the Christians at Najrān, as well as by-passing the Sabaean trade centres.

This spread of Christianity naturally aroused opposition in some quarters of Arabia. One answer was the support given to the rival Judaism, whose religious centre was at Medina. This rivalry supported by the competition between Byzantium and Persia was to be a continual source of contention in Southern Arabia during the following years. Here was an area in which major powers were pitted against one another and the South Arabians played their part in the game of political intrigue.

King D̲h̲u Nuwas Yusuf was known as 'Lord of the Curls' and until recently Yemeni Jews commemorated this characteristic by wearing a long curl on the side of the head. The last of the elected kings of Himyar, he came to the throne in AD 522 and was thought to be a descendant of King 'Abukarib 'As'ad, one of the traditional heroes of the Himyar and, like him, also Judaized. Opposed to the fragmentation of Southern Arabia by the contending religious factions he attacked Christian Himyar. During the summer of AD 523[31] probably in reply to these attacks the Abyssinians sent troops to form garrisons in South-west Arabia. Gathering Bedouin to his banner, D̲h̲u Nuwas attacked Ẓafar in the highlands, the ancient capital of Himyar (D̲h̲u Raydān), a stronghold of Christianity, and the church of Theophilus Indus was destroyed. From Ẓafar the troops of D̲h̲u Nuwas advanced swiftly into the western Tihama, destroying Muza and its church.

The Christian centre of Najrān was the next objective. Here the leading member of the community was Arethas but whether he was Bishop or

Governor is uncertain. Tradition has it that so fanatical were the people of Najrān that they made everyone within the city precincts acknowledge Christ. It is understood that when Dhu Nuwas arrived before Najrān he offered Arethas and his people the choice between Jewry and death. When they did not recant he ordered vast trenches to be dug and filled with timber, which the Christians were made to stand upon as the faggots were fired. H. St John Philby suggested that it was from this incident that Najrān was afterwards called 'Ukhdūd' or 'The Trenches'.

This act prompted the Abyssinian King Ella 'Asbaha to prepare an avenging army of 70,000 strong during the winter of AD 524–525 and with the help of Byzantium he launched an expedition against Arabia the following May.[32] The first clash between the two armies resulted in the Himyar retreating to the hills, but the Abyssinians followed this up with an even more determined attack, and completely routed the Himyar. Dhu Nuwas was killed, for he is said to have spurred his horse into the sea, rather than submit to the foe.

Before the autumn of that year the King of Abyssinia had chosen a Christian Himyar noble, Sumyafaʿ 'Ašwaʿ, to rule as a tributary king over South-west Arabia. Sumyafaʿ 'Ašwaʿ reigned about five years and was killed in AD 530.[33] It is probably his death and not that of Dhu Nuwas which is referred to in the inscription known as CIH 621 at Husn al-Ghurāb, the fortress rock at Qana' in the bay of Bir ʿAli. This is dated as year 640 of the late Sabaean era. However, the dominance of Abyssinia is shown by the appointment of Abraha, who had been in charge of the latest expedition to Southern Arabia, as ruler. One of the first tasks was the construction of a large church at Sanʿa in the mid-sixth century AD, at a time when Bishop Gregentius was appointed from Alexandria to a see at Ẓafar.

Against this rise of Christianity, Persian and Himyar interests continued to encourage the Jews, for a religious war splitting the country provided ideal conditions for Persia to unify it and take control.

Abraha's new church at Sanʿa became a greater attraction than the pagan shrine at Mecca. When the church was 'defiled' by those who saw that Sanʿa might displace Mecca as a pilgrim centre, Abraha used this incident as an excuse to march on Mecca and it is suggested that this attack was also directed against Persians who were settling there in increasing numbers.

This expedition, described in the *Qur'ān*, took place about the year of Muhammed's birth (AD 570), generally remembered as the 'year of the elephant'. The story suggests that after defeating a Himyar chief, the force attempted to enter the town to destroy the Kaʿbah, but the leader's elephant refused to move forward and this contributed to the failure of the expedition. During the return journey most of the army is supposed to have suffered from disease and Abraha is thought to have died soon afterwards, for he was 'smitten with a plague so that his limbs rotted off piecemeal'.

Shortly after this Persia was invited by the anti-Christian Himyar to help finally oust the Abyssinians from Southern Arabia. Persians overran the country and for a short time it became a Persian satrapy.

The moment was now ripe for a change. The economy of the country was precarious, the trade routes were falling into disuse, for the area was by-passed by direct sea trade. Tribal life and prosperity were completely disrupted, religious aspects were brought into disrepute and the tribes were broken up into rival factions for there had never been national stability, and without political organization anarchy prevailed. It was a situation that could not continue and the time, in Southern Arabia at least, was ready for a new era and a new religious and temporal leader.

Frankincense and myrrh

The wealth of Southern Arabia depended on trade, largely with countries bordering upon the Mediterranean Sea. The principal export was incense, required above all by Egypt for religious rites. In one way and another, Southern Arabia thus became a 'hinge' in the commercial system of the ancient world between East and West.

Fig. 2

The earliest references to the use of myrrh and frankincense in rituals occur in inscriptions in Egypt during the Vth and VIth dynasties.[34] Overland expeditions went to the incense land after the twenty-eighth century BC[35], although it seems possible that supplies of incense were brought to the upper Nile by traders from Punt or Somaliland. Egypt had at this time little contact with the peoples east of Sinai and it seems that a series of defensive posts, probably constructed before 2500 BC as a barrier along the line of the present Suez Canal, kept out the nomad Bedouin or Semites.

This restriction, however, also cut off direct contact with the rest of the Fertile Crescent except through the Phoenician traders.[35] The discovery of copper and turquoise in Sinai led to the conquest of the Sinai Peninsula by the Egyptians, their seizure of the mines that had been worked by the early Semites, and the establishment of Egyptian garrisons there. A road was opened across the peninsula to enable the troops to move more easily and to connect with the main trade routes from Arabia.

The use of incense in the religious ceremonies of burial began when the art of embalming was evolved, though it was not in general use for about another 1000 years, when incense became more readily available and cheaper.

From the second millennium BC the Egyptians had a regular trade with Somaliland and probably with the South Arabians who then controlled the incense. Their route was along the western shores of the Red Sea to Quṣeir or Myos Hormos and northward along the Nile from Coptos.

Egyptian records are silent for about 150 years from 1730 BC. This was no doubt due to the assault of the northern Hyksos, who broke through and ruled the area until the Egyptians and mercenaries from Thebes liberated the Delta area before 1580 BC. After this Amenhotep I developed a regular navy, first to clear the Red Sea of pirates and raiders who had for a long time terrified the coast towns and traders, and also to survey Egypt's coastal areas.

Early in the fifteenth century BC[36] an expedition with a large fleet was arranged and sent by Queen Hatshepsut down the Red Sea to the 'Land of Punt'. This trip is fully described in reliefs on the walls of her temple at Deir el-Bahari, from its beginning in Egypt to the return with the treasures including ebony, ivory, gold, cinnamon, apes' skins and people from Punt. They appear to have brought back myrrh as well as incense trees from Somaliland or Arabia to plant in the Nile valley, but the trees apparently did not grow successfully in Egypt.

King Solomon's merchant fleet, built and manned by Phoenicians, sailed from the port of Ezion-Geber for trade with Ophir, probably Somaliland and Southern Arabia, at the beginning of the first millennium BC, although his ships took about a year and a half to complete the round voyage.

Religious ceremonies throughout this part of the Middle East entailed the burning of incense in temples, from Karnak to Nineveh. Moses told the Israelites in the wilderness 'take ye every man his censer and put incense upon them' and later with the plague he told Aaron the High Priest to 'take his censer and carry it quickly among the congregation, and make atonement for them ... and he stood between the dead and the living and the plague was stayed' (*Numbers* xvi). The instructions of the Israelites regarding the making of the temple incense-burner (*Exodus* xxx) are well known. The reliefs of Nineveh furnish frequent illustrations of the offerings of incense to the Sun God and his consort. The Kings of Assyria united in themselves the royal and priestly offices, and on the monuments they erected they are generally represented as offering incense to the Tree of Life.

According to an inscription, the Assyrians under Tiglath Pileser III toward the end of the eighth century BC penetrated down the trade route, pushing the South Arabians back. This had no permanent disrupting effect and the trade routes continued to flourish, and tribute to be paid.

The religious use of incense in ancient Persia was such that the Arabs brought one thousand talents of frankincense every year to Darius as tribute. According to Herodotus, frankincense to the amount of a thousand talents' weight was offered every year during the feast of Baʿal on the great altar of his temple in Babylon.[37]

Both frankincense and myrrh are gum resins. Frankincense varies in colour from pale yellow to green and yellowish brown and it is translucent when first gathered. When burnt it first produces a sooty smoke but smouldering it produces a pleasant aroma. Myrrh is red-brown in colour; its smell is not so delicate when smouldering on charcoal.

Commercial frankincense comes from a tree which, without a central trunk, has the characteristics of a large bush of an average height of eight to ten feet. This is the variety known as *Boswellia sacra*. Another variety of the same genus is *Boswellia carterii*, which has a central trunk and the characteristics of a small tree. Myrrh is obtained from a tree with a central trunk known as *Balsamodendron myrrh*. Both resins were obtained by cutting and peeling the bark for several inches during the summer. This allowed the gum to form globules which hardened and were then collected during autumn and stored in special buildings. By the winter season the harvest was completed and the gum was shipped.

The best frankincense is to be found growing naturally in quantity only in the unique climatic conditions of the Dhufar region of South

Plate 115

1 A carved limestone slab with rectilinear recessed panel designs. The dentils in the side panels and the representation of hooves as feet confirm the correct position of the slab. The inscription at the bottom, between the hooves, is reversed and is a late addition. Possibly the design was copied from wooden furniture and may have been intended for a stone chest or bench seat. Whilst the provenance of this piece is unknown similar slabs have been found at Marib, whence this may have originated

2 A carved limestone architrave, or lintel, from Husn al-ʿUrr. The fish decoration ($4^1/_2$ ins in length) is the only example known to the author and, by analogy with other decorative panels from the site, may be assigned to the third–fourth centuries AD. This single example cannot confirm Christian influence in the Ḥaḍramaut although the period saw the conversion of some Himyar to Christianity

3–6 Examples of carved architectural elements. *Above, left*, an intertwined grape vine design on an architrave from Husn al-ʿUrr, which shows two human figures climbing the vine tendrils. The design on the other face, *above, centre*, has two figures dressed in long robes, the smaller of which appears to be holding a child. Near the top of the design is an ibex standing behind crossed tendrils. *Above, right*, another architrave from the same site has an involved tendril decoration with vine leaves and grapes. *Left*, a limestone capital with acanthus leaf decoration beneath which is a crouching ibex flanked by bucrania panels. Unlike Hellenistic acanthus patterns the leaves of the lower level do not cover the leaf joints of the upper row. Although the capital was found in the Wadi Harib it is thought to have been brought from Marib

7, 8 Two variant representations of the ibex, a common motif in South Arabian art. *Above,* crouching ibexes with curled, over naturalistic, horns set in rectangular panels form a border to an inscription in clear-cut letters. *Below*, a very typical horizontal frieze of ibex heads, bordered by recessed panels at each end, which was probably a sill or lintel

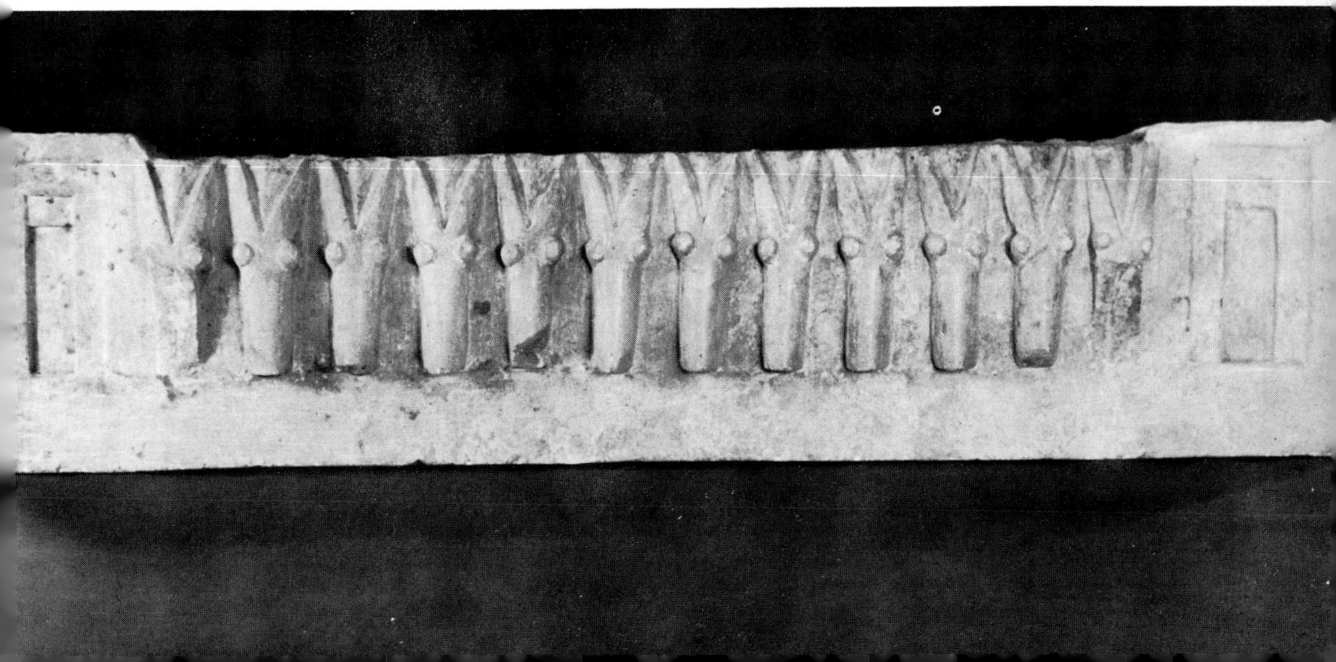

9, 10 Examples of good quality marble carving. *Above*, part of a decorative panel, probably a tympanum, from Marib. A triangular frieze of vine tendrils and grapes surrounds a central, seated female figure. Outside the frieze a winged griffin with serpent tail climbs upwards with, on its back, a cherub holding a dagger in his right hand. This design was used as a postage stamp by the Yemen Republican Government. *Below*, a portion of a marble entablature, or frieze, probably from Marib, has the crescent and orb of Venus as a central motif flanked by crouching ibexes.

11–13 Three carved decorative friezes with antithetical designs. The first two came from Baihān but probably originated in Marib. *Above*, a central bull's head is flanked by a winged, anthropomorphic creature with human head and bull's body. *Right*, rampant ibexes flank a palm tree and each turn their heads to face a naturalistic 'tree of life'. *Below*, winged griffins flank a more stylized 'tree of life'. This design, or with winged sphinxes, is found used as a central motif on lintels and also on inscription tablets and it is not restricted to limestone or alabaster; it also occurs cast in bronze as a marginal decoration for inscription plaques. A long time lag is indicated from its possible Assyrian-Mesopotamian origin in the latter cases as the palaeography of these inscriptions is of the late period, third–fourth centuries AD

14 The great temple enclosure of the moon god 'Ilumquh, chief deity of Saba', at Marib. It was known to the Sabaeans as 'Awwam, and later as Maḥram Bilqis. This view shows the entrance hall leading to the temple enclosure. It consists of a great court with a peristyle verandah entered through a portico of eight monoliths which once supported an entablature

15 The Marib Dam showing the interior of the northern sluices, the overflow and the entrance to the long canal and additional sluices

16 The great wall of the temple of ʾIlumquh at Ṣirwāḥ with its fine ashlar masonry and a dedication to the deities. There is much re-used and modern material at this point, part of the village within the walls

17 A general view of the temple of al-Masajid which lies south of Marib. The formal porticos, with the limestone monoliths, contrast strongly with the random stone walling of the side walls

18, 19 A series of alabaster heads. They were either used as votive pieces made in honour of the gods and dedicated in the temples or as memorial stelae in honour of the deceased. The group above could be of either category, those below are stelae plaques of the type that usually carry the name of the dedicant inscribed upon it, as the example on the right

20 A full length female figure plaque inscribed with the name T<u>H</u>LSM <u>D</u> (of the clan) RA'N

22, 23 Various types of stelae. *Above, left,* a stele base with the name of the dedicant <u>D</u>RA'M <u>D</u>KRN in letters standing forward in relief from the surface. *Right,* a plain alabaster shaft with concave top, inclined sides and in one piece with the base, inscribed HWFʿ AM YLGB. *Below, left,* a more primitive form of votive sculpture, though not necessarily an earlier type, with the eyes symbolizing the dedicant and his name, <u>T</u>WBT <u>H</u>ZF, below. *Right,* the bull's head on this stele symbolizes the moon god 'Ilumquh and the name of the dedicant, 'ALN'AD 'ABYD, is inscribed below

21 A naturalistic left hand holding a stylized bird, possibly a dove. It is a motif frequently found in Coptic sculpture

25 This free-standing alabaster female statuette exhibits a simplicity of technique and the style and the expression portrays a high standard of art and craftsmanship. Of unknown provenance it is thought to have come from Marib

24 A finely carved, naturalistic, alabaster head of a female child which is probably a portrait. It is not known if it was part of a votive stele or of a plaque depicting the goddess D̲at Ḥ̣MYM

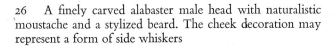

26 A finely carved alabaster male head with naturalistic moustache and a stylized beard. The cheek decoration may represent a form of side whiskers

27 Two unglazed wavy-rim bowls of the type made in Baihān in the first–second centuries AD

28 Clay short-stemmed goblet from Al-Qaraw, Abyan

29 Unglazed bowl with horizontal pierced lug handle from Al-Qaraw, Abyan. It has the Himyaritic letter Ḥ scratched on its surface

30, 31 Examples of Qatabanian domestic pottery, typical of sites in the Wadi Baihān area. *Above, left*, a stemmed, light brown slipware bowl with horizontally pierced lug handles and, *above, right*, a small, dark grey, handled jug in a hard, well-fired clay. It was probably used for oils. *Below*, two small, ring-based jars with lug handles, *left*, with a light buff slip and, *right*, a dark red slip

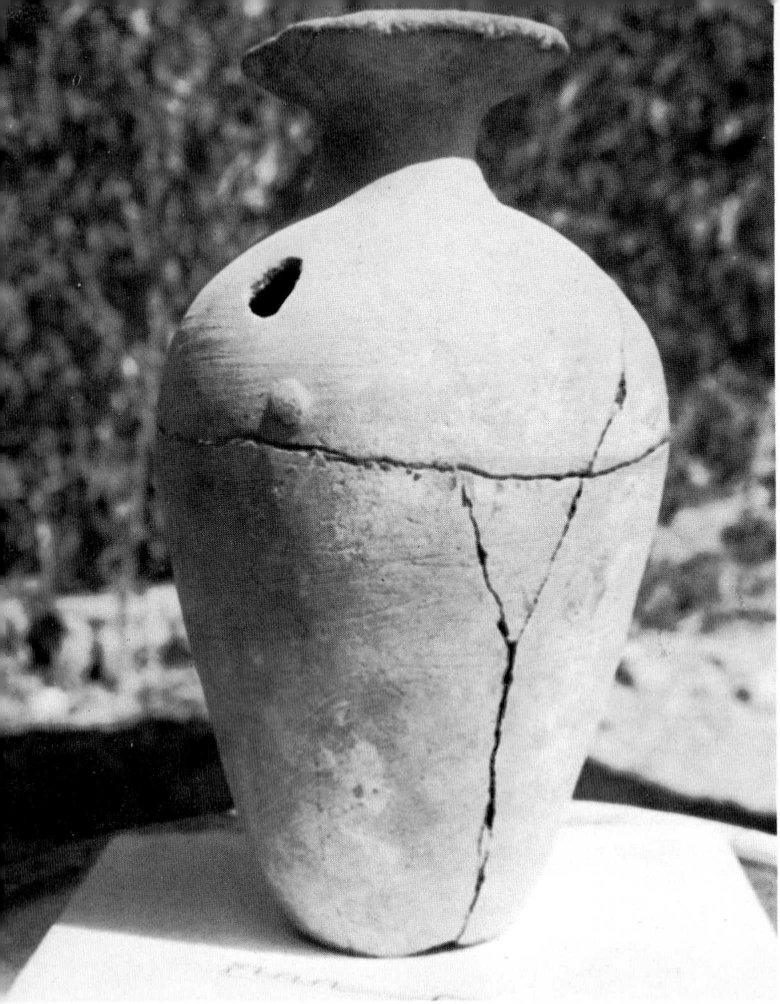

32 An unglazed jar from the Wadi Jirdān near the site of Hajar al-Barīra. The high neck and prominent rim are unusual in this area. The base, now broken, was originally curved and there are four prominent, raised dots on the upper part of the body

33 These two-handled jugs were found during engineering excavation about 15 ft below the surface at Bir Nasir, south of Ṣubr in Laḥej. The surface itself was strewn with sherds of the type found at Ṣubr. Unusual in their shape they are also curious in the very thick body, as seen in the broken specimen

34, 35 These examples of green glazed jugs and bowls, both forms of pleasing shape, were found near Shaikh ʿUthmān. They date, in all probability, from the second–third centuries AD

36 A bronze, seated statuette of the Lady Bara'at found by the expedition of the American Foundation for the Study of Man in a house excavated near the South Gate of Timnaʿ

37 A selection of alabaster jars from the Muncherjee Collection in the Aden Museum. The veined alabaster may have been imported into Southern Arabia although the jars appear to be of local craftsmanship. Of particular note is the jar, back right, with a crouching lion handle to the lid and the jar on the left with ibex handles

Arabia, on the coastal plain and slopes of the Qara range of mountains and prolifically at about 2000 feet above sea level. This area, called S'kl in ancient times, was once part of the kingdom of Ḥaḍramaut. The *Periplus* refers to the frankincense country as being located in a deep bay called Sachalites and it was shipped from the port of Moscha at Khor Ruri, east of present-day Salalah.

In Somaliland lies the only other place where frankincense grows naturally. This area, topographically similar to Dhufar, is some miles east of the coastal town of Berbera inland on the plateau. According to the *Periplus* (paragraphs 8–12), the ports used for the export of frankincense were Malao (possibly Berbera), Mundus, Mosyllum and the Market of Spices. Myrrh too was exported from Somaliland from the same ports as frankincense and also seems to have grown inland from Berbera. It seems likewise to have grown in South-west Arabia in the mountain area inland from the port of Muza and also north of Aden and Abyan. Pliny lists myrrh as coming from the kingdoms of Southern Arabia except Saba'. 'There are a great many varieties, the first among the wild kind being the cave-dwellers' myrrh, next, the Minaean [Maʿin], which includes the Astramitic [Ḥaḍramaut], Gebbanitic [Qataban] and Ausaritic ['Ausān] from the kingdom of the Gebbanitae; the third quality is the Dianite, the fourth a mixture from various sources, the fifth the Sambracene from a seaboard state in the kingdom of the Sabaei [Tihāma] and the sixth one called Dusirite.'[38]

A unique white myrrh was also obtained through the town of Mesalum identified with Al-Aṣṣallāh in Abyan.

Frankincense resin, well known for its perfume when burnt during religious rites, was also known for its healing properties; it stopped bleeding and haemorrhages and was used as an antidote for poisons.

Myrrh was used as a perfume in the temple and as a base for anointing oils, but its principal use seems to have been in the manufacture of cosmetics or ointments. It was also used extensively in medicine for poultices and ointments to relieve inflammation and to heal wounds. In Egypt, myrrh was specifically used in the process of mummification.[39]

Thus the incense gums, both frankincense and myrrh, held a religious significance and were also of great importance in the life of the people of the ancient Near East and Mediterranean. This was a need for which the South Arabians strove to provide. With so large a market it is easy to understand that much of the early history of Southern Arabia shows a dependence on the incense trade.

By the first millennium BC, the peoples of Southern Arabia were no longer nomads in the true sense and tribes had already achieved and developed a sedentary culture. This has been shown by archaeological evidence in Baihān and in the Ḥaḍramaut, and by the organization behind the visit of the Queen of the South to Solomon to arrange the agreement for the incense-trade and other commodities from the East.[40]

At first, the precious incense was possibly carried from Dhufar by camel caravan and also in small coastal boats up the Arabian Gulf where the sea lanes were well known, to the distribution centre of Gerrha. A coastal trade was also conducted with India in exchange for cinnamon and spices. Due, however, to the various upheavals and intermittent warfare in Mesopotamia, this Gulf trade fell into a decline and other routes had to be found. Although the southern coast was known to Arabian trading fleets it was then too hazardous to sail the small South Arabian boats up the uncharted Red Sea. This factor was the beginning of the famous overland incense routes of Southern Arabia which were recorded by classical authors.

Fig. 2

The early trade routes on the west side of Arabia were aligned on the already existing arduous tracks of the salt trade leading from the mines bordering the desert Ramlat Sabatain. Donkeys and mules were used as beasts of burden and trade caravans were small, slow and irregular, due to the frequent need to stop for water. At this time the camel was thought too important a creature for the purpose of carrying merchandise. The tamed camel was for use only in warfare, as in the Midianite camel attacks on the Israelites. The donkey was, however, eventually superseded by the camel which appeared on the historical scene as a 'domesticated' animal and a beast of burden sometime after the eleventh century BC.[41] The camel was mentioned by an Assyrian king, Tiglath Pileser I (1115–1074 BC), as a 'Beast of the Sealands', and this suggests that camels were then something of a novelty. They may have been introduced to Arabia as early as the second millennium BC and it is thought that they were introduced into Egypt by the Persians in the sixth century BC.

There is no doubt that the advent of the camel caravan system revolutionized the trade and communications of Arabia. Now for the first time straight routes could be planned without meandering from water hole

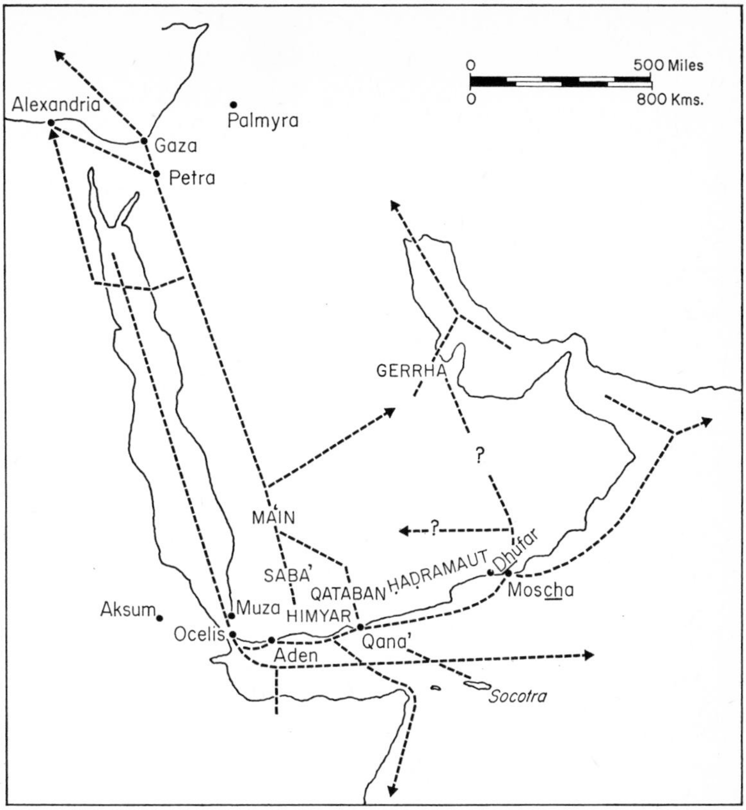

2 Diagramatic sketch of mainland and sea trade routes from Arabia to India and to the north as well as the direct route by sea from Suez to India. Hypothetical land routes leading from Dhufar westwards along the edge of the desert and also northwards across the Empty Quarter through the legendary 'lost city' of Ubar are also indicated

to water hole, and the pace of trade quickened. As the trade caravans became more organized, the routes became safer. In the early stages the caravans were under the constant threat of attack by brigands, but with the increase in the value of the trade, the marauding tribes changed their tactics and instituted a regular toll system. The caravans then passed through their territory safely. As time went by, all along the trade routes towns and cities sprang up fed by the wealth of the commerce that passed through their gates. Around these cities, wherever possible, stretched cultivated fields of barley, wheat and millet bordered by waving date palms. These cities were often large enough to form a kind of city state and a number of the city states would link themselves together within a protective federation as security against the nomadic hordes which still roamed the desert.

Of the incense-bearing country itself Pliny says: 'About the middle of that country are the Astramitae [Ḥaḍramaut], a district of the Sabaei, the capital of their trade being Sabota [Shabwa] situated on a lofty mountain;

and eight days' journey from Sabota is a frankincense-producing district ... The forests measure ... twenty schoenus [about 5 miles] in length and half that distance in breadth.'[42]

The trees themselves were jealously guarded. The privilege of tending them and gathering the incense was the preserve of three thousand families only, who carefully wrapped the whole process in an aura of religious mystery which helped to maintain its high price.

'The members of these families are called sacred and are not allowed to be polluted by ever meeting women or funeral processions when they are engaged in making incisions in the trees in order to obtain the frankincense, and that in this way the price of the commodity is increased owing to the scruples of religion.'[43]

The trade routes for the carriage of incense extended like a large network over Southern Arabia. It is probable that with the shifting political powers over the years, first one trade route was the principal one, then another, due to the constant struggle for control of the incense trade by the various South Arabian kingdoms. The frankincense from D͟hufar was generally carried along the coast on inflated skin rafts and small boats to the port of Qana', whence it was transported overland to Gaza for further distribution and processing.

In addition to the incense the caravans carried luxury goods from the eastern countries, spices including cinnamon from India and silks and fine cloths and precious stones landed at South Arabian ports.

There appear to have been at least two main routes leading inland from Qana' to Shabwa. Probably the main route led past Mayfa'at (Naqb al-Hajar) through Wadi Amaqīn and Wadi Jirdān passing Hajar Barīra, the customs post and garrison at the mouth of the wadi.

The Wadi Hajr, probably the river Prion of Ptolemy, was also a route through the mountain pass at the Wadi Mabnaʿ. Here there was a customs post between the Himyar and the Ḥaḍrami, on the boundary created during the first war with Ḥaḍramaut when they had captured Qana' possibly in the first century AD. This was the great wall and gateway of Qalat. Every alternative wadi opening was sealed off with masonry walls, forcing the traveller to pass the gate in a massive stone wall some six hundred feet long and fifteen feet high leading to a two-hundred-foot pass between mountainside and wadi. From here the route eventually led over the mountains, through the Futura Pass to Shabwa.

Both these routes converged on Shabwa where there was a very strict customs due imposed by the priests. 'Frankincense after being collected is conveyed to Sabota [Shabwa] on camels, one of the gates of the city being opened for its admission; the Kings have made it a capital offence for camels so laden to turn aside from the high road. At Sabota a tithe estimated by measure and not by weight is taken by the priests for the god they call Sabis ...'[44]

On the western side of the Ramlat Sabatain, Timnaʿ was another important customs post and distribution centre. The kingdoms of Qataban, Ḥaḍramaut and Maʿin formed a rough triangle with Saba' to the west and most of the goods channelled north passed from Ḥaḍramaut and Qataban on through Sabaean and Minaean hands. Thus a caravan arriving from the east or from Mayfaʿat (Naqb al-Hajar), capital of lower Ḥaḍramaut, and passing direct into Qatabanian territory would enter the Wadi Baihān from the desert track. After being checked and paying toll charges at Timnaʿ, it would continue. One alternative route was through the pass now known as Najd Marqad which lies to the north-west of Timnaʿ, close to the sand sea. Whether goods from the south went always by the same route is not known, for the axis used may have changed from time to time for various reasons.

Imports from East Africa and Somaliland, usually through Aden, involved the internal caravan routes from Abyan to Aqaba ʿUrr (ʿUrr Basileon guarded this pass into Upper Yafaiʿ), al-Baidha, Miswara, once capital or important city of ʾAusān, and Mark͟ha, probably the site known as Hajar am-Nab, also a city of ʾAusān, and on to Baihān. Ptolemy mentions another route, Aden to Bana (Abyan) – ʿUrr Basileon Madhij – Sarw and Shabwa, capital of Ḥaḍramaut.

There was yet another main route which extended from Muza, the port of Himyar, to Sawara, seat of the King of Maʿafir [Maphoritae], and Ẓafar, capital of Himyar. Muza was also an important port for the export of myrrh.

It may be wondered why the expensive caravan trade, with tolls exacted throughout the length of the route, was able to last about fifteen hundred years; the reason may be that the alternative method by sea was equally slow and not as regular. The Red Sea was always notorious for its dangerous reefs and currents, as well as the home of innumerable nests of pirates, ready to plunder any defenceless vessel. This meant that ships had to travel in fleets for mutual protection. The ships themselves were tiny and frail by modern standards and as much as possible they crept along the coastlines, afraid to lose sight of land. They did not have much room on board for provisions, so had to make frequent and often long stops on shore for fresh supplies. The boats had flat bottoms, which enabled them to be navigated in shallow water or drawn up on the beaches, but made them unsuitable for stormy weather out at sea.

In spite of these difficulties, however, sea trade in the northern Red Sea increased as navigational skills improved, knowledge of the Red Sea coast grew and it was gradually found that to carry goods by sea was cheaper than by camel-caravans on land. The Egyptians, Phoenicians and later the Greeks were the chief promotors of this sea trade. To facilitate this, the Pharaoh Necho (612 BC) started to clean out and restore the Nile Canal[45] which had fallen into disrepair. This canal was later completed by the Persians but it silted up during the time of the Ptolemies in the third century BC. A new course was then cut leading to the neighbourhood of Suez. The canal was used again in medieval times but it was finally abandoned on account of the high cost of maintenance in the eighth century AD by the second Abbasid Caliph, Al-Mansur, who hoped incidentally to cut off a possible line of attack from the Fatimi insurgents of Mecca and Medina.

The Pharaoh Necho is also remembered for his plans for circumnavigating Africa, the coast of which was then thought to continue westward from Cape Guardafui. For this, he built two fleets and had them manned by Phoenician crews for their voyage of discovery. One fleet was sent to the Mediterranean and the other down the Red Sea and the East Coast of Africa.

Under the Ptolemies Egyptian trade in the Red Sea was carefully fostered, and apart from re-cutting the canal from the Nile, they constructed and rebuilt ports on the coast at Myos Hormos, Berenike and Cosseir, and restored connecting roads to shorten the sea journey.

Merchandise from India, the Far East and Arabia was brought by boat to these ports from Leuke Kome (Al Hawra or Yanbo al-Bahr) on the eastern shores of the northern end of the Red Sea and the head of the caravan routes. However, the sea traffic between India and Arabia remained the monopoly of those who had always sailed there and knew the navigational secrets of the Indian Ocean. The Ptolemies in no way wished to interfere with this arrangement, although Ptolemy Philadelphus sent a representative to visit Socotra (Dioscorida) which was supposed by him to be ruled by a Sabaean king.

On the African coast, however, they founded agencies and colonies, one of which was at Adulis (Zula), and they encouraged the Greek traders and merchants who established a trade between the Gulf of Aden and the Mediterranean, despite the hazards of the monsoon winds which initially remained a dangerous mystery.

When the Arabs first understood the pattern of the monsoons and were able to utilize these strong winds to navigate between Arabia and India is not known, but it is certain that this trade began early. Classical writers mention merchandise such as cinnamon being obtainable in Arabia. This can have come only from India, which means that the trade between these two countries had been established at least before the turn of the era. At this time it is probable that the flat-bottomed coastal boats gave way to a type more suitable for deep water travel. Possibly the design of the large *sambuk*, still built in Aden, is the nearest present-day approach to these new ships.

The South Arabian kingdom of Saba', which was the first to dominate the incense trade and was greatly responsible for the rapid expansion of South Arabian trade in about the sixth to fifth centuries BC, was said by the writer Agatharchides to have sent out merchant colonists to India itself. The South Arabians thereby must have established a much more efficient and regular trading system with India than one which could have been operated by individual ship's masters.

It is thought that the South Arabians also formed trading colonies on the coast of Ethiopia[46] to stimulate exports from that country. The spices and other luxuries which came from India and the Far East, together with ivory, frankincense and gold from the African Coast, formed a rich stream of merchandise passing through South Arabian hands. The peoples of the Mediterranean countries for whom this trade was intended firmly believed that Southern Arabia was itself the origin of all these commodities, an illusion which the South Arabian middlemen were careful to maintain.

According to Herodotus, Arabia was the only country which produced frankincense, myrrh, cassia, cinnamon and gum mastic, and the trees bearing the frankincense were guarded by winged serpents or snakes, small in size and of varied colours.[47] This illustrates the aura of mystery which surrounded the production of the incense and helped to keep the secrets of this valuable trade.

The virtual monopoly of this trade from India and the Far East remained in South Arabian hands until the beginning of our era. The ports on the south coast of Arabia which served as the entrepôts were Mocha (Muza), Aden (Eudaemon Arabia), Husn al Ghurāb (Qana') and Dhufar (Moscha).

About the turn of the first centuries BC–AD, however, the pattern of the monsoon winds in the Indian Ocean became known to the Greek and Roman merchants. A Greek called Hippalus is credited with the discovery of the secret, and after this the Greeks and the Romans were able to cross the Indian Ocean themselves. Thereafter the Arabian merchants lost some part of their profitable position as middlemen. A ship was able to leave Egypt early in July for Okelis or Aden and then, helped by the late south-west monsoons, arrive in India in September. Here it spent about two months during business transactions before it started the return journey in November. Blown by the north-east monsoon it put into Aden and then returned up the Red Sea. The merchandise would reach Alexandria about February.

One of these early merchant mariners wrote *The Periplus of the Erythraean Sea*[48] which included a compilation of detailed information on the coastal towns of Arabia along the route to India. The following list of ports and their principal imports and exports is mentioned:

Muza (Mocha)	*Imports:* purple cloth, clothing, saffron, muslins, blankets, fragrant ointments, wine and wheat. *Exports:* myrrh and alabaster.
Cana (Qana') which has trade with Egypt	*Imports:* wheat, wine, clothing, copper and tin. *Exports:* frankincense, aloes, alabaster.
Dioscorida Island (Socotra)	*Imports:* (from Muza) rice, wheat, cloth, female slaves. *Exports:* tortoise shell, Indian Cinnabar (Dragon's blood).
Moscha (Dhufar)	*Imports:* cloth, wheat, sesame oil. *Exports:* frankincense.

The *Periplus* describes these South Arabian ports in the following words:

'21 ... in a bay at the foot of the left side of this gulf there is a place by the shore called Muza, a market town established by law ... And the whole place is crowded with Arab shipowners and seafaring men, and is busy with the affairs of commerce ...
22 ... Three days inland from the port is a city called Saua ... And there is a vassal chief named Cholaebus who lives in that city.
23 ... And after nine days more there is Saphar [Ẓafar] the metropolis in which lives Charibael, lawful king of two tribes, Homerites and those living next to them the Sabaites; through continual embassies and gifts, he is a friend of the Emperors.
24 ... The market town of Muza is without a harbour but has a good road-stead and anchorage because of the sandy bottom thereabouts, where the anchors hold safely ...
26 ... beyond Okelis, the sea widening again toward the East and soon giving a view of the open Ocean after about 12,000 stadia there is Eudaemon Arabia, a village by the shore, also of the Kingdom of Charibael, and having convenient anchorages and watering places, sweeter and better than Okelis.

It was called Eudaemon because in the early days of the city when the voyage was not yet made from India to Egypt, and when they did not dare to sail from Egypt to the ports across this ocean, but all came together at this place and received the cargo from both countries, just as Alexandria now receives the things brought back from abroad and from Egypt.
27 ... After Eudaemon Arabia is a continuous length of coast and a bay extending 2,000 stadia or more, along which are the Nomads and Fish Eaters living in villages.

Just beyond the cape projecting from this bay there is another market town by the shore, Kane [Qana'[of the kingdom of Eleazus, the frankincense country ...

Inland from this place, lies the metropolis of Sabbatha, in which the king lives. All the frankincense produced in the country is brought by camel to that place to be stored, and to Kane in rafts held up by inflated skins after the manner of the country and in boats ...'[49]

The result of direct trading was an immense increase in the amount of goods purchased by the Romans and Greeks from India; the shipments came more regularly and probably took less time, as the goods were less frequently trans-shipped. Some of the middlemen's profit was also saved and there were cheaper Chinese brocades and embroidered fine cloths from India to adorn more and more of the ladies of Rome, although Pliny deplored the amount of money spent on these luxuries. 'And by the lowest reckoning India, China and the Arabian peninsula take from the Empire 100 million sesterces every year – that is the sum which our luxuries and our women cost us; for what fraction of these imports, I ask you, now goes to the gods or to the powers of the lower world?'[50]

The South Arabians naturally did not welcome this intrusion and the loss of their monopoly, and attacks were made on passing vessels in the Gulf of Aden to frighten the merchants. By the time of the *Periplus*, Aden had been destroyed, possibly in intertribal warfare, and Okelis was used as a watering place instead, although its water was not as sweet as that of Aden. Aden was later rebuilt, but did not regain any importance as a trade centre for several hundred years. The Himyar, who were the last of the South Arabian kingdoms to hold a dominating position, had their capital at Ẓafar, and used the nearest port of Muza, near the present day Mocha, for their trade.

It may have been at this time, shortly after the destruction of Aden, that the Qamr traders from the Comoro Islands near the coast of East Africa[51] came for a short period to make a trading station there, connecting with Mahrah coast settlements.

Some of the trading by the Himyar had been with the East Africans. The *Periplus* describes the African coast to Zanzibar as under some ancient right and subject to the Himyar who send many large ships, using Arab captains and agents who are familiar with the whole coast and who intermarry with the natives and understand their language; and the East African coastline was governed by a Maipha chief (Maʿafir in the extreme south-west), thus signifying that there was a South Arabian control of the area.

South Arabian trading overseas by the time of the *Periplus* was nevertheless dwindling. The Greek traders appear to have concentrated their efforts on the Abyssinian coast and signs of their culture spread inland from the port of Adulis.

With the assistance of Byzantine ships the Abyssinians later attacked the Himyar in force and finally overthrew them in about AD 525.[52] Their occupation of the coast of South-west Arabia automatically transferred the control of the sea-trade at the mouth of the Red Sea to Abyssinia, although this fact is thinly camouflaged by the religious aspect of the war against Judaism and paganism.

With increased knowledge of the shipping lanes the sea began to play a much larger part in the distribution of luxuries, and the camel caravan stations inland suffered accordingly. In addition, they were affected by a gradual reduction in the need for incense.

The signs of poverty were already evident. One of these was the collapse of the great dam wall at Marib. There was a diminishing need for such vast irrigation works for the settled people were drifting away and the agricultural areas were no longer needed. The first significant break in the dam masonry is recorded in the fifth century AD and a further break was repaired (CIH 541) by order of the Abyssinian ruler Abraha. But various repairs at the sluice gates were not sufficient. Due to lack of maintenance and cleaning out and the consequent silting up in the latter half of the sixth century AD, the great dam wall was flooded and smashed. The waters spilled over the countryside washing away the cultivations of centuries, before soaking away in the sands of the Ramlat Sabatain.

The Persians were ready to control the Red Sea trade and were able to assist militarily with the final expulsion of the Abyssinians. Southern Arabia thus, for a short period, became a Persian satrapy in the late sixth century AD.[53]

Between then and the coming of Islam the land routes finally ceased as a factor in the international trading scene. In AD 628 the Persian satrap Bādhān embraced Islam, and this was a prelude to the final collapse and the coming of the Dark Ages in South Arabia.

II

History, the kingdoms and art

Our first knowledge of the history of Southern Arabia comes from the records and chronicles of early travellers and historians. The classical authors, including Herodotus born about 485 BC, Strabo born about 63 BC, Pliny born about AD 23 and Claudius Ptolemy who wrote in the mid-second century AD, all mention South Arabia, as does the unknown author of the *Periplus of the Erythraean Sea*. There are also allusions to the pre-Islamic period in the *Qur'ān* and the Old Testament. In the Bible there is mention of the trading fleets of Solomon (*Kings* I, ix, 26); also a description of his well-known meeting with the Queen of Sheba when she visited Jerusalem, which crystallizes the story of the new caravan-route system.

She came, it says, 'with a very great company, and camels that bare spices, and gold in abundance and precious stones'. (*Chronicles* II, ix, and *cf. Kings* I, x.)

Apart from these early histories, very much more of pre-Islamic Southern Arabia has been revealed by inscriptions on stone slabs and rock faces found in the country itself. The scholars and travellers, T. Arnaud, J. Halévy and E. Glaser, in the nineteenth century were among the first to explore the country for inscriptions. They recorded as many of them as they could and were also among the first to draw the attention of the academic world to the archaeological evidence of the early kingdoms of Southern Arabia in the Yemen.

Eduard Glaser visited Marib in 1888 and his collection of texts of early South Arabian inscriptions is renowned. It is important and of interest to read of his aspirations and approach to his travels in Southern Arabia.[54]

'*And when the Queen of Sheba heard of the fame of Solomon concerning the name of the Lord, she came to prove him with hard questions.*'

'So begins the biblical account (*Kings* I, ix) of a journey undertaken by the Queen of Sheba to the Judaean capital. This simple yet enchantingly romantic description of the journey made by a Sabaean queen to Northern lands has inspired not only poets and historians of every age but the simplest reader of the Holy Scriptures. How then could I, who have made exploration of the Sabaean countries my life work, remain indifferent to its inspiration? From the very day I set foot on Arabian soil all my schemings and strivings were concentrated on reaching Marib, the 'Metropolis Sabaeorium' of Strabo, the 'Regia Omnium Mariaba' of Pliny, to see this ancient capital of the Sabaean Empire, admire the remains of its glory and lift the veil which shrouds its legendary past with dementing obstinacy.

True, long before me two Europeans had trod the historic ground of the Sabaean capital – the Frenchman Thomas Arnaud, in 1843 and, twenty-seven years later, his learned compatriot, Joseph Halévy. But the circumstances in which they travelled allowed neither of these courageous men to search unhindered for stone witnesses of the past. Arnaud, though summoned to Marib by the reigning prince, the Emir Shariff Abdul Raḥman, brought back only forty-four inscriptions (most of them fragments and brief texts) whilst Halévy, disguised as a Jerusalem Jew, succeeded in obtaining only thirty-five, most of which had already been copied by Arnaud. There was, therefore, ground for hope that a newcomer might discover inscriptions which had escaped his predecessors. Not for the world would I have it believed that this implies any reproach of those who preceded me; the two Frenchmen have a right to the fullest measure of gratitude from the contemporary world and posterity.

Success frequently depends upon the season of the year, the political conditions prevailing in the country visited, on personal contacts, on the traveller himself and on the methods chosen by him. That it was given to me to collect three hundred and ninety-one inscriptions[55] in Marib, does not signify that my achievement should rank higher than Arnaud's or Halévy's. It is due to circumstances and chance and, maybe, to a considerable knowledge of the country.'

Since Glaser's time considerable work by scholars specializing in South Arabian epigraphy has greatly increased our knowledge of the names of the ancient kingdoms and tribes, the relationship of ruling families, the deities worshipped and the prevailing customs. The sequence of events, however, often remains a matter for conjecture. Assistance in dating inscriptions may be obtained palaeographically but the work of archaeologists and historians is considerably helped when an event with a verified date can be linked with an internal incident. The visit of the Roman Legion which, in 25–24 BC at the command of Augustus, penetrated to the defended southern kingdoms is such an incident. Here, as Strabo states, Ilasaros defended Mariaba against the soldiers of Aelius Gallus. Ilasaros has since been identified as 'Ilšaraḥ son of Sumuhʿali Yanuf of the tribe of 'Rymn (RES 4085) of the kingdom of Saba'. Similarly, the certain dating of the *Periplus* (generally but not universally accepted as the beginning of the third century AD) would do much to settle the disputed chronology of South Arabian dynasties by fixing a date for the reigns of Charibael, King of the Sabaeans and Homeritae, and of Eleazus, King of the country of Sabbatha. Both these monarchs are mentioned in this document, and they have been identified as possibly Karib'il Watar Yuhanʿim, King of Saba' and Dhu Raydān, and 'Il ʿazz Yalit, King of the Ḥaḍramaut respectively.

The study of inscriptions is nevertheless only one side of the research. Field archaeology, the survey of sites, the collection of artifacts and the digging of test pits is also necessary. Excavations at sites in Southern Arabia have not been numerous but each has added to our knowledge and understanding of the past. These include the expedition of H. von Wissmann and C. Rathjens who excavated the temple of Huqqa, north of Sanʿa in the Yemen, in 1932;[56] Gertrude Caton-Thompson who excavated the moon temple and tombs at Ḥuraiḍah, in the Ḥaḍramaut, in 1937;[57] and the American Foundation for the Study of Man under W. F. Albright and Wendell Phillips in 1950–52, which excavated a portion of Timnaʿ in Baihān, the ancient capital of the Kingdom of Qataban, notably the temple and the south gate and buildings nearby together with several other adjacent sites.[58] Work was also started by this expedition at the temple of 'Awwām, dedicated to the Moon-god 'Ilumquh at Marib, the old capital of the Kingdom of Saba'.[59]

The results of such excavations have done much to enlighten us regarding the way of life in ancient South Arabia. We know the type of pottery vessels used for cooking and drinking, the methods of constructing roads, mountain passes and dwellings, and the design of public and private buildings. It has been possible to trace vast irrigation systems and to study the development of works of art in bronze, precious metals and stones and to relate the design-motifs and architectural features. Many of the architectural refinements and the trabeated masonry construction reflect Mediterranean workmanship. The artistry portrayed by religious carvings, votive offerings and so on, mirror unmistakably Hellenistic or Roman originals.

The bulk of our present knowledge of site location has been gained through the activities of officials and travellers, notably Captain S.B. Haines and Lieutenant Wellsted, of the Indian Navy, who, as officers of the survey ship *Palinurus* in 1834–36, were occupied in the detailed survey of the South Arabian coastline. From these surveys and from expeditions into the interior an accurate knowledge of the places and people of the tribes was acquired. Lieutenant Wellsted was interested in antiquities and he is credited with copying the Husn al-Ghurāb inscription for the first time as well as preparing an accurate site description of Naqb al-Ḥajar. Baron von Wrede in the 1840's found the wall and inscription of Qalat north of Bir ʿAli, and later Colonel S.B. Miles, Wyman Bury and Harold Jacobs blazed many new trails. The work of H. von Wissmann and C. Rathjens in the Yemen has been already referred to, but the former's work and surveys in the Ḥaḍramaut with D. van der Meulen are also very well known. Captain Hamilton, later Lord Belhaven, known for his excavation at Shabwa also travelled widely over the country. Colonel Lake, by his travels on foot, prepared maps with accurate place names in the western area. H. St John Philby, Ahmed Fakhry, Harold Ingrams, Doreen Ingrams, Freya Stark and R.B. Serjeant all belong to that select group who have travelled widely in Southern Arabia and have recorded their findings for others to follow. As a result of their observations, many ancient sites have been mapped and rock carvings and graffiti recorded. The last few years have fortunately seen an increase in our knowledge of the sites and their locations, which at one time seemed destined to remain mere dotted indications on the map, have in some cases been verified.

In 1959 and 1960 G. Lankester Harding carried out a survey of Southern Arabia and estimated its archaeological potential. His report[60] presents in one volume brief descriptions of most of the known sites. In 1961 the Smithsonian Institution sponsored a small expedition under G.W. Van Beek to survey sites in the Wadi Ḥaḍramaut with the intention of listing them and obtaining surface material. Our knowledge of sites on the edges of the jōl has increased enormously as a result, and we now consider it quite likely that man once hunted there with his flint weapons some 15,000 years ago. Among many sites discovered was a large flint factory where the cliff top was strewn with flint fragments and waste.

From Aden, the Department of Antiquities persevered with a more detailed programme of survey covering the known sites and, wherever possible, explored the possibilities of new ones. Surveys carried out by the Department included Naqb al-Hajar, the walled fortress city of Mayfaʿat in the Wadi Maifaʿah, and at Husn al-Ghurāb with Qanaʾ, ancient port of the Ḥaḍramaut, situated near the modern village of Bir ʿAli. The sites of Hajar al-Barīra and Al-Binā in the Wadi Jirdān have now been plotted and the irrigation and *sail* channels surveyed.

Many sites and numbers of graffiti on rock faces have been visited and recorded. Sometimes the ruin is not at all ancient and the graffiti turn out to have been scribbled by a bored lorry driver, but gradually the information expands. One of the great problems in Southern Arabia is the length of time taken in journeying over extremely rough ground, and also the remoteness of some of the sites. The time spent on the site is often far less than the time spent on travel. This is not the place to mention security risks, but it is a fact that, when visits are not advisable to certain areas, it may be a long time before a hurried site drawing during a former visit can be amplified.

Potsherds have been carefully collected from each location where they were present because pottery, as a material, is virtually indestructible and remains long after all other obvious signs of earlier habitation have disappeared. It is ideal for the purpose of comparison and dating and it is hoped that some kind of pottery sequence may soon be established which will assist in the identification of period and cultural influences.

Already through the study of pottery and marble fragments it has been possible to link the Abyan area with a period much earlier than other evidence had shown. The recent discovery of two pre-Islamic inscriptions[61] there appears to confirm this opinion. The first inscription consists of a single word SMHʿLY, which is known from the inscriptions at Marib to be a royal Sabaean name. The second is a seven-line fragment written in the script of the late Sabaean period and bearing a symbol which has appeared elsewhere as an emblem of the Moon-god ʾIlumquh. Although these new discoveries still offer no conclusive evidence, one cannot help speculating upon what may appear next in the area and hoping that yet another aspect of ancient Southern Arabia may be revealed.

Fig. 16

Plate 57

THE KINGDOMS

The Sabaeans, always referred to by the classical writers when describing this country, continued as the dominant kingdom throughout the history of Southern Arabia before Islam. Names of the rulers of the traditional dynasty of the Sabaeans are known from the eighth century BC. They are thought to have originated in the northern regions and settled in the area of Marib, whereas the other kingdoms seem to have already inhabited the southern regions, and from inscriptions we learn that down to the first century BC the kingdoms of the south included also Maʿin, Qataban and ʾAusān as well as Ḥaḍramaut. However, after the second century AD we find only Sabaʾ, Himyar and Ḥaḍramaut as states of importance. For this reason the Sabaeans and Ḥaḍramaut are described in the second half of the chapter.

During the later period, after the first century AD, the continuous thread of action seems to be linked with the growth of Himyar and other tribes of Southern Arabia, who rose against the authority of the established kingdoms. The new tribal onslaught made their internicine battles pale by comparison.

By the first century AD the ruler confederation of Sabaʾ consisted at one time not only of the traditional dynasty at Marib but also the western highland clans. These were Banu Bataʿ with their capital at Hazim, the Hamdan of the large tribe of Samʿi with their capital at Nā-ʿit and the tribedoms of Gurat centred on their capital of Kanin to the west of Samʿi territory and Marṯadum of Šibam ʾAqyān nearer to Marib. Sanʿa, the present capital of Yemen, was within this territory.

Thus one finds Sabaean tribal leaders assuming the title King of Sabaʾ and reigning at the same time although there was always one central steadfast dynasty of the Kings of Sabaʾ at Marib.

Unrest amongst the southern South Arabian tribes grew into a revolution reacting against the kingdoms, first against Qataban and Ḥaḍramaut and then Sabaʾ. It is probable that the name Himyar was used as the designation of the ruling tribal confederation which included tribes as they were absorbed during the period of tribal strife. Finally, when the Sabaeans were concerned with their frontier on the north and the control of the old Minaean territory, the Himyar seized their opportunity and spreading through the coastal territory to the borders with Sabaʾ eventually established themselves with a centre at Ẓafar.

The use of the title *King of Saba' and Dhu Raydān* in inscriptions is confusing because this title appeared in two of the provincial dynasties of chiefs in the Sabaean highlands west of Marib. It was also used at the same time by Kings in Marib as well as in Ẓafar, and in the later periods only by these kings although inscriptions show that the Sabaeans often referred to the Himyar as the Dhu Raydān.

Occupation of Marīb by the Himyar no doubt originally brought about the title of King of Saba' and Dhu Raydān. After the Himyarites had occupied Marib this first time they called themselves Kings of Saba' and Dhu Raydān and on recapturing Marib the Sabaean ruler there assumed the additional title of Dhu Raydān. This does not however show a unification between the two states but only a claim on both sides.

Eventually Marib was captured and became the second capital of Himyar and seat of the Kings of Saba' and Dhu Raydān, initiating a period known as the latest Sabaean era. The revolution had led to the virtual political control of south-west Arabia by the Himyar, a probable reason for all the people of Southern Arabia before Islam often being referred to as the Himyarites.

The Minaeans

'The Minaei, through whose territory the transit for the export of the frankincense is along one narrow track. It is these people who originated the trade and who chiefly practise it and from them the perfume takes the name of "Minaean".' (Pliny, *Natural History*, Bk. XII, xxx 53, xxxi 56.)

The Minaean capital was at Qarnāwu in the southern Al-Jauf, and from inscriptions we learn of the town of Yṯl and that another important town was Našq.[62] Their territory was thought to have extended at one time from the Yemen to the Ḥaḍramaut.

Of this juxtaposition of the Kingdom of Ma'in and Ḥaḍramaut, Pliny says: 'Adjacent to the Astramitae [Ḥaḍramaut] is another district, the Minaei ...'[63] 'Adjoining the Astramitae in the interior are the Minaei ...'[64] This seems to refer to direct traffic between the two kingdoms, along the route from Shabwa through Al-'Abr to Qarnāwu passing Ruwaiq and 'Alam 'Aswād and 'Alam 'Abiaḍ, the latter a route, which, owing to its scarcity of water, could only have been used by camels. The Minaeans, and for that matter the Sabaeans also, must originally have utilized and adapted the knowledge of the caravaneers of the ancient salt trade from the mines on the south border of the Ramlat Sabatain. The incense was carried on to the Hejaz, from there to Yaṯrib (Medina), on to Elath on the Gulf of ʿAqaba and finally to Gaza and to Maʿan near Petra, where there was a trading colony. Possibly the Minaeans traded in incense alone, but it was apparently the Sabaeans who, by extending their trade to India and Africa were to transport through Maʿin the luxuries of the East to wealthy Greeks and Romans.

Very little is known of Maʿin, and except for information gleaned from inscriptions copied by Joseph Halévy and by Eduard Glaser, we have only the references of classical writers. Our present knowledge of the historical position of the Minaeans in pre-Islamic Arabia is shown by F. V. Winnett[65] and this is based on the Liḥyānite and Minaean inscriptions found at Al-ʿUla'.[66] The explorer, H. St John Philby, fortunately visited Najrān, and provided a description, but we have no similar record of Qarnāwu.

We know from Strabo, quoting Eratosthenes, merely that they were contemporaries of the Sabaeans, Qatabaneans and Ḥaḍramis, and that their city was Karna (Qarnāwu), about the early third century BC. Another report quoting Artemidorus says that the Minaeans and the Gerrhaeans brought their load of aromatics to Palestine.[67] There may have been a direct trade through Gerrha with the Gulf and possibly India and the East, by-passing the south-western trade-routes. This implies that D͟hufar sent frankincense either direct to Gerrha, or through western Ḥaḍramaut and Maʿin for onward shipment. Gerrha was probably one of the earliest outlets from D͟hufar. Strabo also says that the journey between Ḥaḍramaut and Gerrha took forty days,[68] suggesting that the Gerrhaeans also visited Ḥaḍramaut.

The Wadi Najrān, north of the capital, was the home of a large, partly independent, trade centre and agricultural community, for water was plentiful and the fifteen-mile-long valley was well irrigated and fertile. The city of Najrān[69] may have been called Ragmat, and the ruins of the metropolis are now known as al-Uk͟hdūd after the trenches or banked fields filled with burning faggots for the Christian martyrs in the early sixth century AD. There is little doubt that with the possession of a pagan

Ka'bah, Najrān must have ranked with Mecca as one of the important centres of religious pilgrimages in ancient times. The twelve-acre castle or citadel contains the remains of many walls which help to indicate the forms of the buildings, some of them probably belonging to the Palace. One of these structures was thought by Philby to have been an early domed building, possibly the Christian church or cathedral, around which the ground was paved with large slabs of stone. The castle seems to have been surrounded by a moat, and the city of over seventy acres extends along the southern side of the wadi. On the level, plain side of the wadi the boundary lines may have been dictated by marsh or lake with dykes to prevent flooding. Inscribed on stone in the temple group at the northern side of the city is the apotropaic formula to Wadd 'Ab.

The ancients readily assumed a connection between the Minoans and Minaeans. According to Pliny the island nations of the Minaei and Rhadamaei (Radman?) derived their names from Minos and Rhadamanthus (the legislators of Crete) and their fabled origin from Crete.[70]

In Greece there is a tradition of an Arab colony settled by Cadmus in Euboea. An altar dedicated to Wadd' the Moon-god, is known to have been found on the island of Delos; this Minaeo-Greek inscription has been dated to the latter half of the second century BC.

Agatharchides in the mid-second century BC, writing of the Dedabae (the tribe of Debai) in the Hejaz, stated that they were particularly friendly towards the Peloponnesians and Boeotians on account of a tradition of former connections. H. von Wissmann says, 'Might the descendants of isolated Greek colonists in this area have united with a purely nomadic race to form one (Debai)?'[71] According to Agatharchides, the Dedabae lived in the coastal area in the fourth century BC near the Wadi Baid, where there was gold. Diodorus Siculus in the second half of the first century BC remarks on the mining of pure red gold,[72] and Ptolemy also mentions a 'Thebai-polis' probably at Wadi Dhahaban, a name derived from *Dhahab* (gold). Wissmann further suggests that Ptolemy's 'Baitheo basileion' on the Wadi Baish indicates a border town on the northern boundary of Saba'.[73] That trading existed from some considerable time between the people from islands near Greece and the Arabians, from about 300 BC onwards, seems possible but there is no concrete evidence for this early connection.

At Minaean trading posts, especially the Liḥyānite capital Daydān (Dedān) and the ruins of Al-ʿUla' and at the one time Nabataean centre of Al-Ḥijr, modern Mada'in Saliḥ, are pre-Islamic monuments and tombs hewn in the solid rock. Their decorations show an affinity with the carvings at the rock city of Petra, and probably Nabataean craftsmen worked here in the early part of the first century AD.[74] The Nabataeans maintained a trade centre here after the Minaeans had lost their trading rights to the neighbouring kingdoms of Saba' in the south.

Information on the rulers and the internal history of Maʿin is scanty. W. F. Albright[75] dates the beginning of the earliest known dynasty at about 400 BC, and from an inscription from the West Gateway at Qarnāwu (RES 2774) assigns a king of Maʿin to about the third quarter of the fourth century BC.[76]

The name of the first known king was 'Ilyafaʿ Yathaʿ, who was the son of Yd'ᶜL, king of Ḥaḍramaut, who also ruled Maʿin. After Hufnu Dharih, his eldest son, the second son called 'Ilyafaʿ Riyam, who was king of Ḥaḍramaut also,[77] reigned over Maʿin.

This indicates an early trade alliance between the two peoples and the personal relationship between the rulers of Maʿin and Ḥaḍramaut serves to confirm that at one time they maintained a common front against Saba'.

Maʿin apparently reached the height of its power in the first half of the third century BC. Their trading colony at Dedān (Al-ʿUla') must have been in control of the northern part of the incense route at this time. It seems also that the Minaeans controlled the coastline – the ancient area of gold mines such as those of the Wadi Dhahaban, associated with Maʿmala (a mine or place of work) which was dependent on Maʿin;[78] once possibly the Hawila of *Genesis* x and also part of the Ophir of Solomon.

There is a possibility that the end of the independence of Maʿin in 115 BC[79] may have coincided with the appearance of the new 'Sabaean' era of Himyar.[80] King 'Ilyafaʿ Yašur II, possibly the last King of Maʿin, was a vassal of Šahr Yagul Yuhargib, King of Qataban after about 75 BC.

According to the account of the expedition of Aelius Gallus in 25–24 BC '... the Minaei have land that is fertile in palmgroves and timber, and wealthy in flocks ...'[81] The description of the invasion by Strabo mentions the ruler of Najrān, who fled, but the seat of the Kings of Maʿin, the city of Qarnāwu are not mentioned. It seems, however, that the towns of Ma'in were then held by Saba' as outposts.

In the middle of the second century AD, Ptolemy in his *Geography* VI. 7. 23 refers to the Minaeans as 'a great people'. Although Ptolemy was probably basing his remarks on earlier sources, this is the last literary reference and nothing more was heard of them until their stone inscriptions were found and copied in the nineteenth century AD.

The Qatabanians

'The Gebbanitae with several towns of which the largest are Nagia and Thomna, the latter with sixty-five temples, a fact which indicates its size.' (Pliny, *Natural History*, Bk. VI, xxxii 151–154.)

Plate 106

The Qatabanian kingdom was for centuries a neighbour south-west of Saba' and the capital city was Timna', now also known as Hajar Quḥlān (Koḥlān) in the Wadi Baihān. During this time the adjacent Kingdom of 'Ausān also controlled much of the coastal trade. 'Ausān was conquered by Saba' in the fifth century BC under the Mukarrib, Karib'il Watar, and placed under the control of Qataban whose own status then was a subservient kingdom of Saba', supporting a section of the trade route.

However, with 'Ausān, Qataban grew in strength and conquered Saba' and, taking control of the whole south-west, isolated Saba' from the source of trade although the caravans still passed through Saba' and Ma'in. This was the most powerful period for Qataban although with Saba' sited on the fringe of this activity little imagination is needed to visualize the occasional clash of arms for the defence of boundary rights.

In Baihān today are the remains of some of their constructions and public works. The Mablaqa Pass or *Aqabat* across the mountains to Wadi Ḥarib presents a great engineering feat. It seems likely that this pass was constructed for the incense trade and international communication crossing the kingdom. This was not the only lateral access, for between the Wadis Baihān and Ḥarib on the fringes of the open desert stands the walled pass and customs-post of Najd Marqad through which camel caravans passed.

Plates 112, 113

Land irrigation in Wadi Baihān was based on a main canal which has been traced down the Wadi from beyond Baihān al-Qasab with many sluices and gates for control of the floodwater into side channels. A date in the fifth century BC[82] has been given for the construction of the main canal, and an inscription of about the first century AD intimates that this irrigation system was then still maintained.

The earliest buildings on the site of Timnaʿ cemetery on the rock outcrop known as Haid bin ʿAqil, belong to the period of the mukarribs, the religious and secular leaders in the fifth century BC. The walled city of Timnaʿ with the great temple and its entrance court and rows of columns must have dominated the area. It seems likely that the walls and the south gateway of the city of Timnaʿ were built by these early rulers and, judging from the massive masonry walling of the main temple, it is possible that the foundations of this were also laid out at the same early date.

The ruler of Qataban, Mukarrib Yadaʿ ʾab Dhubyān, ordered one of the earliest inscriptions to be cut on the South Gate of Timnaʿ. Another group of kings headed by ʾAbšibām included Šahr Ghaylān, who also had several inscriptions cut on the South Gate describing the laws of the city.[83] Šahr Hilāl Yuhanʿim likewise ordered inscriptions to be cut on the South Gate and he is best remembered for his inscribed monolith or stele south-west of the main temple.

W. F. Albright gives a list of rulers[84] which is particularly helpful about the mukarribs and kings of Qataban. J. Pirenne in *Le Royaume Sud-Arabe de Qataban* (1961) discusses the date links with Sabaʾ and proposes a later date sequence. However, the earliest known rulers of Qataban listed by Albright are the Mukarribs Sumhuʿalay Watar and Hawfiʿamm Yuhanʿim whom he puts at about the sixth century BC.

The kingdom of Qataban was a strong power controlling the coastal trade[85] which from about 350 BC extended from the Red Sea port of Okelis to Abyan. It seems to have lost supremacy about the end of the second century BC, for after this time a large area of the Qatabanian country was controlled by Himyar. This territory had originally been taken from Sabaʾ by the conquests of Yadaʿ ʾab Yagil (RES 3858) although there were several wars which led to a victory by Sabaʾ under Yathaʿ ʾamar Bayin about 285 BC.[86] It seems that Qataban was able to recapture the country, for in the second century BC, using the title of Mukarrib, Yadaʿ

'ab Dhubayān bin Šahr mentions all the territory again (RES 3550, RES 4328, RY 390). This ruler may have also called himself king (RES 3878) after the rise of Himyar although probably mukarrib was the title retained for the outermost tribes.[87]

It is possible that in the first century BC Hawfʿamm Yuhanʿim, King of Qataban, was followed by Šahr Yagul Yuhargib, who is mentioned in the inscriptions regarding the building of a house called Yafaš in Timnaʿ. However this ruler is also called mukarrib in the inscription built into a wall at al-Wuste.[88]

When Maʿin was attacked and conquered by Saba', the last king of Maʿin was the vassal of Šahr Yagul Yuhargib (RES 3021),[89] and he in turn was obliged to deal with the attacks of the expanding tribe of Himyar. Extending from the Yafaʿ country the Himyarites spread and enveloped the country to the south and west from Jabal Kharāz to Wadi Maifaʿah. Thus Qataban found that she had lost complete control of the coastal trade.

During the first century AD, Warawʿil Ghaylān Yuhanʿim is found to have struck coins bearing his name.[90] The royal mint used the name of the palace Ḥarib just as the coinage of Himyar carried the name of the palace Raydān.

Plate 44

The date of the end of Qataban as an independent kingdom and the destruction of Timnaʿ have not been decided finally. On the basis of potsherds at Timnaʿ its destruction has been placed at around AD 10.

H. von Wissmann says that the destruction must have taken place between AD 90 and 100, in the time of Šahr Hilāl Yuhaqbid,[91] and Timnaʿ was mentioned as a capital city of the Gebbanitae (Qatabanians) in the first century AD by Pliny.[92]

Timnaʿ was certainly destroyed when the capital of Qataban seems to have been moved south to the site of Hajar bin-Humaid. Here the royal palace of Nabaṭ Yuhanʿim, son of Šahr Hilal, was called Ḥarib;[93] but the ancient name of the site is not yet known.

King Yadaʿ 'ab Ghaylān, son of the Ḥaḍrami conqueror of Qataban, then founded and walled a town named Dhu Ghaylān, which is thought to be on the opposite side of the main wadi from Hajar bin-Humaid, near the mouth of the Wadi Mablaqah where an inscription was found,[94] and Ḥaḍramaut continued to occupy the area for a long period until they in turn were driven out by the later kings of Saba' and Dhu Raydān.

'Ausān

The kingdom of 'Ausān was for a long time a subservient kingdom held by Qataban from the end of the fifth century BC. However, it had once flourished as a great trading country which extended by Bab al-Mandab along the coast to Aḥwar and inland as far as the borders of Qataban south of Baihān. The central part of the kingdom seems to have been the highland bordered by Baihān, Wadi Markha, Nisāb and, in the south, 'Aud, and the Kaur Range, dropping 3000 feet to the plains of Dathina.

The capital city is thought to have been Miswar (mentioned in the inscription RES 3945, *Glaser* 1000A), a fortress south of Wadi Baihān, and Wadi Khaura, or perhaps at Hajar am Nab, the extensive ruins in Wadi Markha.[95] Plate 101

The wealth and power of 'Ausān as one of the greatest trading kingdoms which rivalled Saba' was probably built on an extensive trade with the East Coast of Africa as far south as Pemba and Zanzibar. This commercial power may be reflected in the mention of the 'Ausanic' coast in the *Periplus of the Erythraean Sea*[96] which was written some five hundred years after the conquest of 'Ausān by Saba'.

How long 'Ausān had been trading to build up such a reputation is not known. It is suggested that whereas Saba' had been primarily concerned with the land routes for trade to the north, 'Ausān may have been the feeder to this route from the sea trade with Africa; but from a subservient position it had grown too powerful and independent for Saba' to ignore as a possible threat.

The last king of 'Ausān as an independent kingdom was Martawa. He was the ruler of 'Ausān and all its dependent states at the time of the conquest of his kingdom by Karib'il Watar, the last mukarrib or priest king and first king of Saba' in about 410 BC. The temples of the fortress Miswara were destroyed or removed, the land-owning nobles were killed and the towns and cities of 'Ausān and Datinat (Dathina) and Tafid (Abyan) were burnt and plundered. Dahas (Yafaʿ) and Tubanaw (Laḥej) suffered the same fate. All the cities along the coast were likewise burnt and the oasis of Abyan and Laḥej was ravaged. Some 16,000 men were killed and 40,000 captured during this war.[97]

The states of Dahas and Tubanaw were then incorporated into the Kingdom of Saba' and, shorn of its coastal regions, the central kingdom of ʾAusān was allocated to Qataban, then itself a vassal state of Sabaʾ, which was thus in supreme control of the trade through Southern Arabia. With the addition of the trading establishments and colonies on the coast of Africa and Abyssinia, Sabaʾ had a complete monopoly on the luxury goods from the east and south desired by the great powers of the Mediterranean and the Fertile Crescent in the north.

At Naʿmān[98] north-west of Miswara was apparently a shrine or temple to Wadd, the national god or deity of ʾAusān. Here Yaṣduq'il Farʿam Šarahʿat as King of ʾAusān maintained an altar where sacrifices were made. This indicates a connection with the Kingdom of Maʿin, which worshipped the same moon-god. Another inscription mentions the votive offering (Mʿmr) or altar (of incense) of the same king, and refers to the oblation of offerings at this altar by the Kings of ʾAusān as commanded by their deity Wadd.[99]

Burial gifts which apparently surrounded one of the Kings of ʾAusān, ʿAmyathaʿ, in his tomb are kept in the Aden museum.

The alabaster statuettes of members of the royal family who ruled ʾAusān and their inscriptions collected from the same area show the possibility of a dynastic series.[100] Two of these statuettes depict an unusual wig head-dress with a serrated fringe. Yaṣduq'il Farʿam Šaraḥʿat is shown wearing a costume of Greek Cypriote type[101] whereas Yaṣduq'il Farʿam and Maʿad'il Salhan both wear a *lunghi* skirt similar to the present-day South Arabian dress.

Plate IV
Plate V

The Sabaeans and the Himyar

'The Sabaei [Sabaeans] are the most wealthy, owing to the fertility of their scent-producing forests, their gold mines, their irrigated agricultural lands and their production of honey and wax.'
'... the Homeritae [Himyar] are the most numerous tribe ...' (Pliny, *Natural History*, Bk. VI, xxxii, 159–162.)

The Sabaeans are the best known of the ancient tribes of Arabia and in the latter part of the second or early part of the first millennium BC seem to have settled on the Marib plains, with the Minaeans as northern trading neighbours. Here they first made their capital at Sirwāḥ (al-Khariba), a fortress-site in the hills south of Marib.

Plate 16

It is not known for certain if Marib was already in existence at the time. The mythical Lukmān bin Ad is supposed to have constructed a dam to control irrigation in 1700 BC. If this is factual, it would appear that an agricultural community had a centre here to which the Sabaeans later moved and made their capital.

From the beginning of the first millennium BC the Sabaeans ruled part of the trade-route, and they seem to have gradually gained control of the whole trade. One of the indications of this was the recognition of the Sabaean Kingdom by an early record linking Southern Arabia with the north found in the annals of Tiglath Pileser III (745–727 BC) when the Sab'ai sent him a tribute of gold, camels and spices.

However, Sargon II (722–705 BC) reports that in 715 BC[102] he received from Yitha''mar, a Sabaean ruler, gifts such as gold, precious stones, herbs, horses and camels. Yitha''mar was probably one of the early mukarribs of Southern Arabia, and Karib'il, a later mukarrib, also sent gifts to Sennacherib about 685 BC. During this period the hereditary leaders were known as the mukarribs or priest kings but after the fifth century they lost their religious title and inscriptions refer to the ruler as malik, the South Arabian name for king. The mukarrib Karib'il Watar who reigned about 450–410 BC, also describes himself in an inscription (RES 3945) by the title of malik. This fact suggests that he was one of the last priest rulers of Saba' to assume a temporal role.

Tradition tells us that Bilqis, the Queen of Sheba, lived at Marib about 950 BC. If the story of her meeting with Solomon is to be believed,[103] this points to the Sabaeans trading on their own behalf long before the Minaeans. The Sabaeans arranged a ceremonial visit to Solomon, the largest trader in goods from Ophir, probably present-day South Arabia and East Africa, as an advertising campaign. Everything could be canalized to him through their hands, if it could be shown to be a more regular and cheaper method than carriage by his merchant fleets, or the trade-route from the Persian Gulf. There is unfortunately so far no evidence that the Sabaeans then lived so far south as Marib and no archaeological evidence of this early date for the city. Whether there was a more personal relationship between Solomon and Bilqis must also be left to conjecture.

However, ready markets were found and the fame of the Sabaeans as traders grew. With their improved status and wealth they rebuilt and developed Marib which was well placed at the junction of trade routes from Baihān and Ḥaḍramaut and the southern ports of Qana', Aden and Muza (near Mocha).

A description of Marib by Artemidorus says '... the city of the Sabaeans, Mariaba, is situated upon a well-wooded mountain ... the masses engage partly in farming and partly in the traffic in aromatics, both the local kind and those from Ethiopia; to get the latter they sail across the straits in leather boats.'[104]

So fertile was the district of Marib that a legend persists that the whole land was under cultivation from Marib to the Ḥaḍramaut. With control of floodwaters from the wadis irrigating the land on the north-west of Ramlat Sabatain, it is simple to see the origin of the story.

Fig. 3 The most famous construction at Marib is the wonderful dam with its perfectly dressed masonry barrages, portions of which still remain, fifty *Plate 15* feet high, as a lasting monument to fine craftsmanship. The dam wall was first just a huge bank of earth about 1800 feet long, faced later with stones set in mortar on the upstream side. This distribution system probably was completely rebuilt in fine-cut masonry by the mukarribs between the eighth and seventh centuries BC, and spillways and sluice-gates for irrigation were cut into the mountainside. Distribution of water was by controlled flooding through massive sluice channels into the two main crop growing areas known as the north and the south gardens.

Fig. 4 Another remarkable building at Marib is the temple of 'Awwām dedicated to 'Ilumquh the Moon God and chief deity which is also known as the Maḥram (or Ḥaram) of Bilqis, Queen of Sheba. It consists of a massive wall thirteen and a half feet thick of rubble stone with ashlar-faced masonry. The original height is not known, except that it must have been more than thirty feet, as indicated by remaining portions. It encloses an oval or kidney-shaped area approximately 1000 feet in circumference with a long diameter of 375 feet and a width of 250 feet. In all probability it was built in the eighth to sixth centuries BC, though this may well have been on top of earlier foundations.

Plate 14 Of particular beauty at the Marib temple is the fifth-century entrance-hall, which was lined internally with square columns forming a peripheral *Fig. 5* verandah or loggia. The design of the mausoleum-capitals appears similar to those of the temple at Huqqa of about the third century BC,[105] and consists of very simple incisions in the column-head, forming three rows of shallow dentils. The geometric motif is also seen continued in the

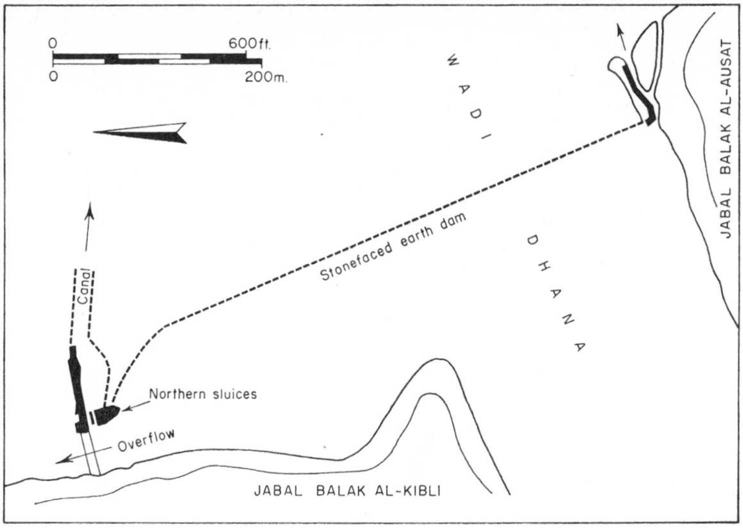

3 The Marib Dam – a sketch layout based on the survey by E. Glaser and the plan by R. le Baron Bowen

4 The oval temple of 'Awwām at Marib from the survey drawing by F.P. Albright. Its plan may have been dictated by the shape of an early hauta *or religious sanctuary. The formal entrance court is one of the finest examples of Southern Arabian architecture. On the east side is the small columned mausoleum which was also excavated by the American Foundation in 1951–52*

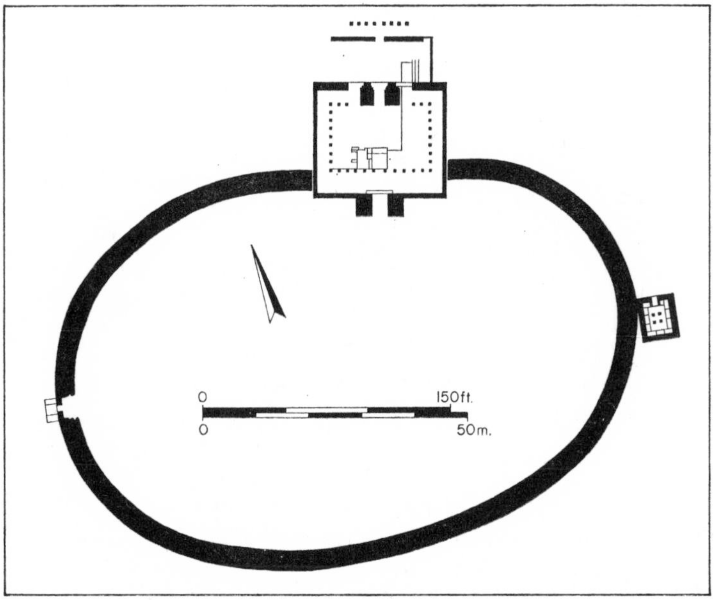

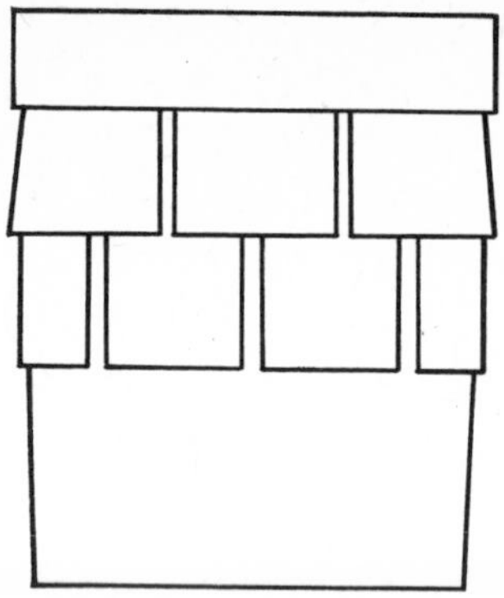

5 A measured drawing of a column capital from the mausoleum surveyed by F. P. Albright. The thickness of the abacus seems to have been used as the module of measurement

panels round the peristyle verandah. There is evidence that bronze was used as a covering for the steps and doors in the peristyle entrance hall.[106]

The emergence of Himyar as a power has plausibly been associated with the start of the Late Sabaean era in 115 BC (or 109 BC) and their future role was to hold the control of Southern Arabia, for they became involved in the struggle with the traditional dynasties of the kingdom of Saba' centred on Marib. It is, therefore, important to consider the Himyar at the same time as the Sabaeans. There is reason for assuming that the tribe of Himyar was originally under the rule of Qataban, for the surname 'children of ʿAmm' was used by the Himyar, and ʿAmm was the name of the Moon God and national God of the Kingdom of Qataban. The earliest literary mention of Himyar is in Pliny in a list of Southern Arabian tribes,[107] but it has been suggested that the expansion of Himyar coincided with the direct sailing of ships for the first time from Egypt to India.[108] This was also a time when the Kingdom of Qataban seems to have lost control of the coastal areas which had been held since about the fourth century BC. Coinciding with the rise of the Himyar the Sabaeans of Marib seem to have taken the border fortress towns of the Minaeans, ensuring their stability in the northern front. The towns visited in 25–24 BC by Aelius Gallus and the x Legion included Negrana (Najrān) from which the king had fled and Našqm, then a stronghold of Saba'. According to Pliny they were probably destroyed by the Romans but Qarnāwu, the seat of the King of Maʿin, is not mentioned at this time.

However, when Aelius Gallus visited Marib he came upon 'Ilšarah (Ilasaros) who was the leader and prince of the distinguished Sabaean tribe of the Raymanitae ('RYMN) who controlled the Marib district.[109]

The recorded account of Aelius Gallus which says 'The Homeritae are the most numerous tribe'[110] confirms the view that long before this the

Himyar who lived in the Yafaʿ area north of Abyan were growing powerful and were probably preparing an attempt to overthrow the coastal areas of Qataban. The Yafaʿ of today certainly consider they are of pure Himyar descent and their mountainous country has been identified as an area known as Dahas in the time of the last mukarrib of Sabaʾ.

When the Himyar had consolidated and formed themselves into a kingdom they made their capital at Ẓafar, in the mountains near the present-day Yarim. The most important hill-fortress or palace of the ruler there was called Raydān, and currency later minted there used this name. It is thought that the name Raydān was borrowed from the dominating rock of Jabal Raydān in Qataban, a feature well known to the Himyarites, who had been friendly with the Qatabanians, situated at the southern end of Wadi Baihān, not far from the modern Baihān al-Qasāb. The name was incorporated in the royal title, 'King of Sabaʾ and D̲h̲u Raydān'. During the wars between Sabaʾ and the expanding Himyar we find ʾIlšarah Yaḥḍib, who was a military official or Kabir before he was crowned, fighting against Himyari forces.[111] It is noticed that in inscriptions the Sabaeans referred to their adversaries as Himyar or D̲h̲u Raydān.[112] In an inscription (CIH 365) the Himyar are shown to have fought the Sabaeans of the traditional dynasty of Marib, the great clan of D̲h̲u K̲h̲alil to which the earlier Mukarribs and kings had belonged. Defeat of the traditional Sabaean ruling clan gave victory to the Himyari ruler D̲amarʿali Yuhabirr and he took the title 'King of Sabaʾ and D̲h̲u Raydān', although from epigraphic evidence we know that later he was forced out of Marib by Wahabʾil Yaḥuz, King of Sabaʾ. Plates 103, 104

However, after the destruction of Timnaʿ, the rulers of the Sabaean dynasty of Gurat fought against Yadaʿʾil, King of Ḥaḍramaut, and Nabat, King of Qataban.[113] Shortly afterwards Karibʾil Bayin of the Marib traditional dynasty was also at war with Yadaʿʾil Bayin of Ḥaḍramaut. Peace seems to have arrived for a short period, when ʿAlhān Nahfān of the Hamdanid dynasty of Nāʿit unified Sabaʾ. He formed an alliance with Yadaʿ ʾab Ghaylan of Ḥaḍramaut (CIH 155) and later with Gadarat, ruler of Aksum, and Abyssinians then settled on the Red Sea coast of Arabia. At this time, ʿAlhān's son, Šaʿirm ʾAutar, served with him but later, when ruling alone, Šaʿirm ʾAutar fought against Gadarat for the coastline and adjoining country of Sabaʾ. He later extended his activity to pursuing the Abyssinians of Habašat in the south as well as the northern region where he reached as far as the central kingdom of Kinda on the route to Gerrha. After this he attacked the Ḥaḍramaut (CIH 334), conquering Shabwa then under ʾIlʿazz and sent another force through Qataban, which was looted, and to Qanaʾ the main port of Ḥaḍramaut. Thus most of the country was dominated. At this point their temporary alliance with Himyarite forces forced the Abyssinians away from Ẓafar, which they had occupied, and out of the Himyar country; then suddenly the Sabaean Hamdanid dynasty of rulers ceased.

One of the Himyar rulers, T͟haʾran Yaʿūb Yuhanʿim, sent representatives to a ceremony at ʾAnwad near Shabwa given by the king ʾIlʿazz Yalit of Ḥaḍramaut (RES 4909). In the late third century AD the Himyar under Šammar Yuharʿiš took Marib and the highlands, only to be driven out later by ʾIlšarah Yaḥḍib and his brother Yaʿzil Bayin.

The expansion of the Kingdom continued from the end of the third century AD with the subduing of the western coastal region now known as the Tihāma. Šammar Yuharʿiš who later extended the forces of Himyar[114] had a long reign and, with help from the Abyssinian ruler, controlled a vast area. Not only did he reconquer Marib but he also conquered a great part of the Kingdom of Ḥaḍramaut, just as Šaʿirm ʾAuter before him, and then gave himself the long title of 'King of Sabaʾ and D͟hu Raydān and Ḥaḍramaut and Yamnat'. The name 'Yamnat' possibly always refers to the southern part of Ḥaḍramaut. He also captured territory lying further north and had a war with the tribes of Tihāma. Šammar Yuharʿiš was a contemporary of Marʾalqays b. ʿAmrū, the 'king of all Arabs' who died in AD 328, and is commemorated in an epitaph erected at an-Namāra in Syria (RES 483). Part of the inscription refers to wars in the south when he reached Najrān, and the town of Šammar.

Marib eventually became the seat of the Himyari kingdom of Sabaʾ and D͟hu Raydān and then ʿAmdān Bayin controlled the whole territory. Coins from his mint in Raydān with the head on the obverse and reverse have been found both on the Somali coast and also within a few miles of Aden.

In the mid-fourth century AD, the Bishop Theophilos, sent by Constantine II, converted the Himyar ruler, thought to be T͟haʾrān Yuhanʿim, to Christianity. His grandson, ʾAbūkarib ʾAsʿad who was converted to Judaism when he visited Yat͟hrib, present Medina, called himself king of the ʾAʿrab of ṬWD^{m} (Central Arabia) and the Tihāmat (lowlands on the

38 A bronze statuette of a male standing figure, of unknown provenance. It could be either an imported work or by a Hellenistic craftsman working in Southern Arabia and modelling it on a Greek original

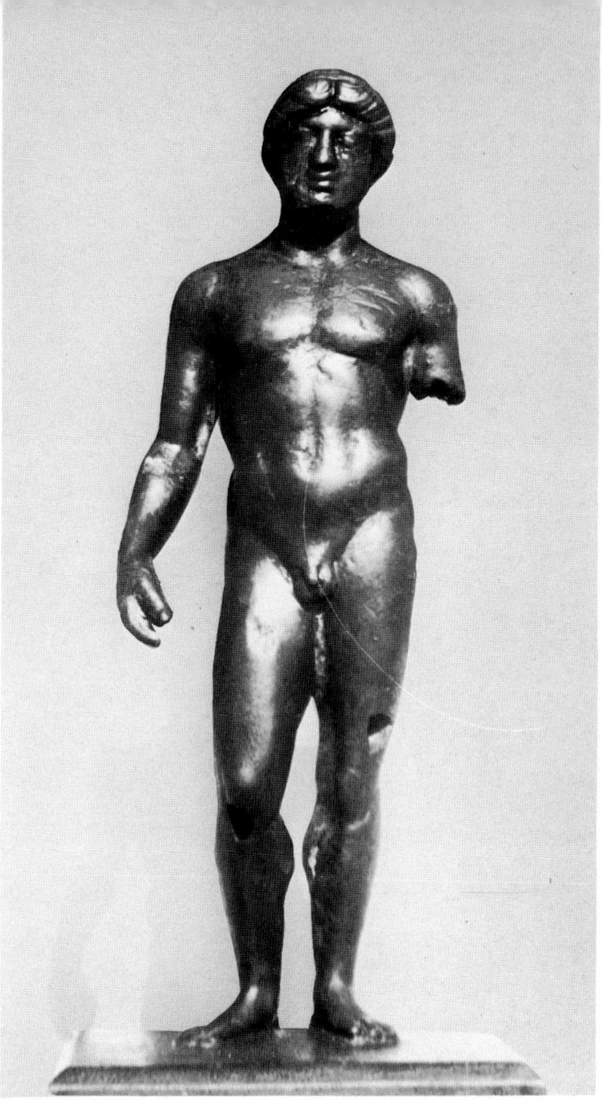

39 A bronze plaque with nine lines of cast text and one line of incised text on the lower frame. In the middle of lines seven and eight is represented a crouched camel. Found at Timnaʿ it is dedicated to a Qatabanian deity D̲u-SMWY and it gives the name of the temple at Timnaʿ as Ẓ̱RBN, the only identification so far, although not positively associated, with the main temple there (Ry. 367)

40 An over life-size bronze figure of Dhamar Ali. Despite its present damaged condition it is an outstanding piece and unique both for its size and technical accomplishment. It still manages to convey an idea of arrested movement, almost as if in oratory, with the raised left arm

41 A bronze, seated cherub which appears to have been fitted at one time on an inscription stone. The head now merely rests on the torso and its original position is not known. Possibly of the third century AD the piece evidences western influence in its workmanship

42 This finely cast male head may well be a portrait. Despite the formalized treatment of the hair the moustache and beard have been suggested in a naturalistic manner. The sensitivity of the face may indicate the influence of a western artist

43 A Sabaean bronze head, probably female, from San'a. The formalized hair style with its curls and ringlets should be compared with the male head in Plate 42. Both the eyes and the nose betray the influence of western art and, again, it could easily be a portrait head

44 A selection of Southern Arabian coins with Athenian tetradrachms of the Old and New Style (lines one and three, left) for comparative purposes as their prototypes. A full description of the pieces appears on pp. 121–2

46 An early Admiralty Chart of Aden and its vicinity shows well its situation within the crater of an ancient volcano

45 View of the Red Sea and the Gulf of Aden taken from the Gemini II spacecraft on its three-day flight, 12–15th September, 1966

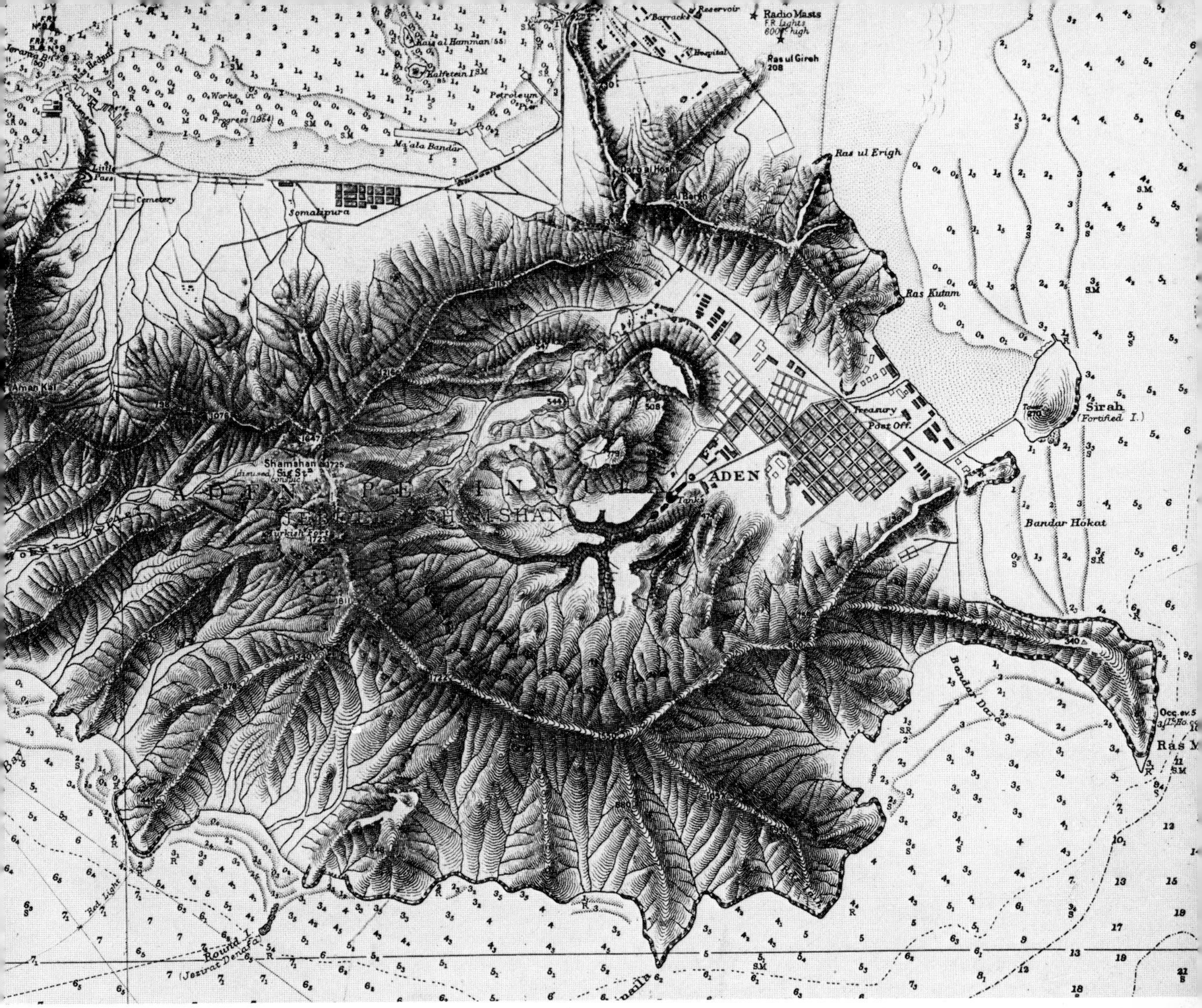

47 The 'Turkish Road' at Aden. This partly paved track leads across the plateau area within the confines of the rim of the ancient volcano of Jabal Shamsan. The track starts above the ridge of Khusaf Valley in Crater and extends to the northern rim summit, about 1,700 ft above sea level. The paved portion, which averages about 10 ft in width, climbs from the plateau to the col between the sixteenth century Turkish fort and the nineteenth century signal station

48 The Tawīla Tanks are a series of cisterns served by catchments and lie in a rock cleft on the south-west of the town of Crater. It is thought that these cisterns were built, or at least repaired and the rock surfaces replastered during the period of Persian control in the sixth–seventh century AD. This small cistern, not directly connected with the main cisterns, lies on the north-east side and is completely plastered and stepped. Its domed entrance porch is a unique feature here

49, 50 The pottery kilns and some of their products at Al-Mimdara near Shaikh ʿUthmān. Firing usually lasts about four hours, but the temperature reached is not high. Larger vessels are usually coil built not wheel-made and some of the typical products, *below right*, are seen for sale at the local market

51, 52 *Above*, the village of Huweirib, west of Jabel Kharāz and north from Husn Malisah. The river boulder walling of the local saint's tomb is typical of the area. *Below*, Husn Malisah, a group of circular and rectangular structures of random size walling on a rock outcrop on the western side of Jabal Kharāz

53 Al-Anād, a rectangular structure of massive masonry that was used as the foundation of a mud brick palace, now eroding away. One stone has a pre-Islamic graffito. The basic structure was probably once part of the early dam of Laḥej

54 A thick layer of potsherds about 6 ft down at Ṣubr. They are of the same type as the surface sherds with the exception of a distinctive form of incense burner

55 Mid-Acheulean quartzite hand-axes from near Jabal Tala, probably the first prehistoric site of this period recognized in Southern Arabia

56 Modern decorative wall painting on one of the small houses at Bir Aḥmed. This type of decoration is found between Hiswa and Laḥej. It is carried out by the womenfolk using limewash on the smoothed mud plaster surface. Often the most important items of the house are depicted. Here we see the portable radio, thermos flask, kettle and hookah shown on the bed and also a pair of scissors, sweeping broom and a female figure with a shopping basket

57 An inscription stone found near Jabal Al-ʿAḥabāš, Abyan. The script is of the latest period of the Sabaean era and the text mentions SLḤN, the name of the royal palace of Marib

58 The exterior of the eastern gate of the inner compound wall of the fort on Jabal Sarar, Abyan. Recesses in the abutments show that timber bars were placed across the opening

59 Jabal Am'abeath in the Wadi Yeramis. This is another example of a fortified hill-top with an external perimeter wall and inner defences with a *husn* at the highest point. The masonry is similar to that of Jabal Sarar

60 Raudha is a small, still used, medieval stronghold on a rock outcrop in the Wadi Yeramis. It is possible that the massive masonry structure on the left (western) end is of much earlier construction

61 The ruins of the mosque at Al-Aṣṣallah with, in the foreground, the stone water channel leading to it from the well

62 The deserted medieval village of Am-Shabuh. There is a large cemetery on the west and a well is located in the valley nearby

63 A pre-Islamic graffito inscribed on a stone on the rock outcrop of Haid Laḥmur. Remains of walling and part of a structure, possibly a fortification, are visible above it

64 Graffiti inscriptions and some drawings of camels in the Wadi Doḥ, south east of Haid Laḥmur. There are local traditions of camel breeding and such graffiti are common on the flat surfaces of rocks

65 The top of the paved pass, the *Aqabat* Thira, about 7,000 ft above sea level. The Thira pass was an important road in early times leading to the Mukeiras area from the coast, either from the Wadi Yeramis or the *Aqabat* ʿArqūb

66 Jabal Radaʿ, north of Mukeiras, is of interest for its alignments of stones (a semicircular group in the foreground), pre-Islamic inscriptions and medieval building remains. The latter are often re-used older material. On the great rock itself, in a cleft, is a local saint's tomb illustrating the continuity of the site's sanctity

Red Sea coast) in addition to the former titles. He was regarded as one of the greatest of the rulers in Arabia before Islam.[115] His son Šaraḥb'il Ya'fur was ruling when the great dam of Marib collapsed and had to be repaired several times, on one occasion by 20,000 men. The further collapse took place in the mid-sixth century AD (CIH 541). It was not long after this that the final destruction took place, when the great agricultural gardens dried up and became one with the desert.

The Ḥaḍramaut

'The Atramitae, whose chief place is Sabota, a walled town containing sixty temples ...' (Pliny, *Natural History*, Bk. VI xxxii 154–156.)

The Kingdom of Ḥaḍramaut (the Hazarmaveth of *Genesis* x) was situated to the east of Qataban.[116] It seems that the inhabitants were amicably disposed to Ma'in on the north-east, for at least one of the Kings of Ḥaḍramaut was a relative of the Minaean ruler.[117]

The full extent of the kingdom seems to have included the frankincense-growing Dhufar (Ẓafar) region in Qamr Bay. It must have been involved in the land trade of frankincense from Dhufar from the very beginning of the westbound axis to the north. The Ḥaḍramaut thus produced the main supply for the trade caravans direct through Shabwa, the capital city, through Qarnāwu (Ma'in) in the district of al-Jauf as well as through Marib.

Shabwa, identified as the Sabota of Pliny[118] who describes it as a city with sixty temples, is situated at the mouth of the Wadi Ḥaḍramaut and faces the Ramlat Sabatain. There are remains of ancient ways or passes leading to Shabwa from the Hajr mountains. H. Ingrams describes one *aqabat* or pass on which he travelled: 'It was about sixteen feet wide and was most clearly built for something more than foot or camel traffic.'[119] Plate 116

The placing of Shabwa so far to the west, away from the well-watered wadi, may, apart from its possession of important salt mines, be explained by its strategic significance. It controlled the entrance into the main wadi from the south and also covered the incense trade on the route from the port of Qana' through to Al-'Abr. Plate 82

The *Periplus* mentions that inland from Cana (Qana') lay Sabbatha (Shabwa) 'where the King lives' and that camels brought frankincense for storage there. Shabwa today in its ruined state does not show much surface indication of former magnificence although four column bases of one large temple dominate the city.

Plate 83

In the south, in Lower Ḥaḍramaut, Mayfaʿat (Naqb al-Hajar) was also an important trade centre, between Shabwa and Qanaʾ the seaport. Built by the Ḥaḍramis and possibly the 'Canneh' of *Ezekiel* xxvii 23, Qanaʾ was one of the most important ports of Southern Arabia. Its ruins are on the isthmus and on the volcanic hill of Husn al-Ghurāb, a magnificent fortress site dominating the bay of the present town of Bir ʿAli.

Plates 81, 82,

Plate 87

The fortress city of Mayfaʿat in the Wadi Maifaʿah lies close to the present-day town of ʿAzzān and tradition suggests this was the home of one of the Magi who brought frankincense to Bethlehem. Its name Mayfaʿat is carved in the main three-line inscription on the South Gateway and it may be identified with the *Maifa metropolis* described by Ptolemy. It was a leading city and probably the capital of the Lower Ḥaḍramaut, an area also known as Yamnat. There is no evidence that it was captured or occupied by the Himyar as an eastern outpost, although we know the walls were strengthened against their attack.

Walled fort sites such as this seem to have been built for the protection of the incense trade and may have also acted as customs posts. From the strategic location of Mayfaʿat on the end of a high promontory it would have been impossible for a camel caravan to pass through unnoticed.

Plates 79, 80

Adolph, Baron von Wrede, who visited this area and the wall of Qalat in 1843[120] said: 'I discovered in the wadi Ubbene [Obne] a Himyaritic inscription on a wall which encloses, as it were the valley.' Here the incense road was a single track in the mountains from which it was impossible to deviate, principally as a means of defence. This inscription on the central gateway bastion of the massive wall describes a state of war between the Himyar and Ḥaḍramaut when the port of Qanaʾ, a vital link with the sea trade for Ḥaḍramaut, was lost. The growing strength of Himyar and expansion over neighbouring territory forced the Ḥaḍramaut from their coastal region, and Qanaʾ then came under the control of Himyar. The building of the boundary wall and gateway of Qalat which controlled the pass shows that despite war, the life-blood of trade was allowed and able to continue.

Plate 80

It is of considerable interest that the Qalat inscription mentions the assistance given in the building of the boundary walls of Mayfaʿat, and it provides a palaeographic comparison for this inscription and the main inscription at Mayfaʿat showing clearly that they are not contemporary.

Pliny the Elder mentions 'Atramitae, a district of the Sabaei, the capital of whose realm is Sabota' (Shabwa).[121] This probably indicates geographical ignorance about Southern Arabia rather than an early occupation of Ḥaḍramaut by Sabaʾ.

The names of some of the rulers of the Kingdom of Ḥaḍramaut are helpfully inscribed on the four rock faces of the large boulders known as 'Anwadm on the south side of the Jabal ʿUqla,[122] which lies some ten miles west of Shabwa. Here are the records of rulers who visited the place and also the names of supporters and friends for several generations the Kings of Ḥaḍramaut gave titles to dignitaries at this group of rocks. However, the inscriptions of Ydʿ 'l Byn, engraved after the part destruction and later repair of the city of Shabwa, do not mention titles, although subsequently his sons did so when they ruled. On the top of the main boulder is a small square masonry building clearly of the pre-Islamic period and, although now broken away, there was once a flight of steps leading to the top of the twenty-foot-high boulder. Plate 120 Plate 119

In these inscriptions several family relationships appear quite clear; but while there are apparently three groups of rulers, it is not possible to link them all with certainty.

One of these rulers, King Yadaʿ 'ab Ghaylān, with his father occupied Qataban after the destruction of Timnaʿ and founded a town called <u>Dh</u>u Ghaylān in the Wadi Baihān. He is also thought to have concluded a treaty with Gadarat, the Abyssinian ruler (Habašat), and ʿAlhān Nahfān, King of Sabaʾ and <u>Dh</u>u Raydān. The king 'Ilʿazz Yalit ʿAmm<u>dh</u>a<u>kh</u>ar,[123] is mentioned in an inscription (RES 3958) found in the Wadi Baihān and he also sojourned at 'Anwad. The visit of the small Himyarite embassy of <u>Th</u>a'rān Yaʿūb Yuhanʿim (RES 4909) to the title-giving ceremony of 'Ilʿazz Yalit must have been a result of a friendly pact with the neighbouring Himyar. 'Ilʿazz Yalit was also accompanied by foreign ambassadors from India (Hind) and Palmyra (Tadmur).

At this time Ḥaḍramaut extended westwards almost as far as Ḥarib in the north. Himyar controlled the southern coast from west of Qanaʾ to the Jabal <u>Kh</u>arāz west of Aden, with their northern boundary touching that of Sabaʾ and the tribes of Hamdan. They were not able to extend eastwards until under Šaʿirm ʾAutar, the Sabaeans attacked Ḥaḍramaut. Strengthening his army by incorporating Himyarite forces (CIH 334) this king was able to attack in two drives, sacking Shabwa the capital, the Wadi Ḥaḍramaut and the port of Qanaʾ. ʾIlʿazz was thus made a vassal of Šaʿirm ʾAutar, who later seems to have assisted Ḥaḍramaut, having then subjected all the states other than those areas controlled by Abyssinians in Habašat.

The voyages of the Greek merchant sailor who wrote *The Periplus of the Erythraean Sea* could have taken place at this time, when Karibʾil, who was noted as King of 'the Homerites and Sabaites', ruled at Ẓafar. Eleazus, called King of the Frankincense Country with Shabwa as his capital of Ḥaḍramaut, can be identified as either ʾIlʿazz Yalit bin ʿAmmdhakhar or ʾIlʿazz Yalit bin Ydʿʾl Byn, or his son ʾIlʿazz (RES 4693 and Hamilton 8).

According to the *Periplus* this was during the rule of Zoscales in Aksum when Ḥaḍramaut covered the whole country from Qanaʾ as far as Dhufar. Inscriptions mentioning ʾIlʿazz, which confirm this, have already been found at Dhufar, carved on the walls of the city of Sumhuram.[124]

Ḥaḍramaut was again attacked and conquered, this time the troops of Šarahʾil and Rabšams, Kings of Ḥaḍramaut (*Jamme* 656), defended their country against the forces of Šammar Yuharʿiš, King of Sabaʾ and Dhu Raydān. The capital Shabwa and the great fertile wadi were captured while another force captured the southern portion of Yamnat with its capital of Mayfaʿat. Although the kingdom of Ḥaḍramaut revived, there were several further expeditions by rulers of Sabaʾ and Dhu Raydān. Shabwa was eventually outflanked by way of Al-ʿAbr, and a king of Sabaʾ and Dhu Raydān reached Maryamat in the Wadi Ḥaḍramaut where the ruins remain beyond the present day town of Saiwūn. This is thought to be the Marimatha mentioned by Ptolemy. The cities of the great wadi were pillaged and from the mid-fourth century AD Ḥaḍramaut probably remained in the possession of the Sabaean-Himyar rulers.

ART

'The chief city of this tribe is called by them Sabae ... This tribe surpasses not only the neighbouring Arabs but also all other men in wealth and in their several extravagances besides ... they have embossed goblets of every description, made of silver and gold, couches and tripods with silver feet, and every other furnishing of incredible costliness and beds encircled by large columns, some of them gilded, and others having silver figures on the capitals. Their ceilings and doors they have portioned by means of panels and coffers made of gold and set with precious stones and placed together, and have thus made the structure of their houses in every part marvellous for its costliness, for some parts they have constructed of silver and gold, others of ivory and the most showy precious stones or of whatever else men esteem most highly.' (Diodorus Siculus, Bk. III 47. 2–9.)

The early South Arabians were active in many artistic fields and their contributions are worthy of study as evidence of their history, religion and way of life.

The sculpture, in particular, has an underlying archaic simplicity of design, combined with a high standard of workmanship, in materials of natural beauty: gold, bronze, alabaster and stone.

Their inspiration, except for items for personal adornment, was often influenced by religious devotions and temple ceremony, and it seems that the art forms of Southern Arabia were the combined result of external influences and local artistic and technical ability. Generally, artistry and function show a substantial measure of uniformity.

This similarity of motif is observed on objects found in Ethiopia on the west and in Dhufar far on the east and confirms the great extent of early Southern Arabian territory. Enough material has survived for us to build up some idea of artistic influences and achievements but the names of artists and their workshops are not yet distinguishable. Often approximate dates can be attributed to works only by palaeographic evidence or other associated material.

The evidence consists generally of architecture, architectural carvings, free-standing sculpture and plaques in marble and alabaster. Works in other materials show the proficiency of the craftsmen in plaques and figurines of bronze, jewellery of gold and semi-precious stones and coinage designs.

Plates III–VI

Plates VII, VIII

Early Southern Arabian pottery forms a large part of the evidence for everyday family life. Being largely a local product it can illustrate varying types of design and manufacture from kilns in the different areas of the country. In most aspects of art and craftsmanship, it is particularly noticeable that there was apparently a uniform progress in style during the period of artistic development. This achievement also reflects the periods of wealth and prosperity of the ancient kingdoms as they rose to power.

Architecture

The best examples of early Southern Arabian architecture consist chiefly of the temples and important civil and domestic buildings which are usually found at the capitals of the kingdoms.

The earliest buildings were frequently constructed of large pieces of masonry roughly cut and accurately placed to form a planned layout. Often the boulders were irregularly cut, as for example the foundation walls with bastions of the main temple at Timnaʿ, which have been dated from the associated pottery to the eighth century BC. Such works show the conception of an overall plan on the part of the architect at an early date.

Skill in building design, as in other forms of art, culminates in religious buildings, for the temple was the focal point of the community. Usually, the development of architectural styles can still be seen from the improvements and additions to an earlier structure. Fully developed pre-Islamic architecture, with its trabeated designs, can often be identified by the precision of the cut masonry walling. This usually consists of fine ashlar limestone blocks, laid dry and with finely cut joints, well boned. These may have plain smooth surfaces, such as the walls of a small building remaining at Timnaʿ near the South Gate, the building of Wadʾab Yafʿan at AmʿAdīya Mukeiras, and in the buildings at Mayfaʿat, the ancient name for Naqb al-Hajar.

Plate II

Masonry blocks are also often decorated with chiselled margins and pecked centre panels, a practice which seems to have been used on important buildings in all the early kingdoms. Various types of marginal drafting and styles of centre pecking have been found in many areas such as the temple at Ḥuraiḍah, the temples at Marib, the main wall at Maʿin and the buildings at Naqb al-Hajar, Baihān and Shabwa. It may be possible to ascribe certain styles to approximate dates by palaeographic evidence. However, this cannot be conclusive, as the various states may have adopted styles at different periods. The motif has clearly developed from a heavier rusticated masonry which was widely used in the Middle East. It is possibly of Assyrian origin and the design extended to the Mediterranean countries during this early period.

A variant of this treatment is the more complicated patterning of raised margins and pecked rectangular panels on flat slabs of limestone.[125] This emphasized a pattern unrelated to the actual joints of the masonry and would have formed a decorative wall pattern reminiscent of original marginally drafted and pecked panel masonry.[126] This technique, probably of a later period, was used when standards of building methods required the use of covering face panels to disguise the actual wall construction.

It is clear that, generally, standards of masonry work were extremely high, with good bonding for walls and, where necessary, dowels and rebates for beam and lintel construction with well-cut arrises and smooth finished surfaces. The use of monolithic columns and lintels for porticos and courtyards is well attested at Marib, Sirwāh, Huqqa and also by the column bases at the main Timnaʿ temple.

A rectilinear or geometric design is the basis for almost all the formal works in masonry and stone carving, and architectural design is strongly reflected on marble, limestone and bronze inscription plaques and decorative mouldings. It also appears in sculptural representations of furniture which seem to have been copied from timber originals.

Panels with this type of design were once thought to represent the façade of a South Arabian house with recessed and panel walls. G. W. Van Beek[127] says there are just not sufficient references to known buildings and that if these panels are inverted they then represent furniture and the roof towers become legs. It is possible that these decorated panels formed sides of sarcophagi, chests or mere benches. Plate 1

The design of recessed panels in representations of furniture is an attractive one. The patterning of light and shade is usually well thought out and, with a little imagination, it is possible to see that such designs seem to be reflected from full-scale building work.

It is interesting to note that carvings of animals' feet or hooves were quite common as part of furniture decoration and bronze hooves to fit the legs of timber furniture have been found, as well as stone carvings between the legs representing turned timber spindles.

The design of architectural detail, the carved entablature, lintels and architraves all seem to be associated with the rectilinear and recessed panel motif. The most common motif seems to have been the panel of horizontal 'louvres' with angled facets slightly raised to obtain maximum reflection from the sun. Below this panel it was usual to incorporate a lower moulding consisting of a row of tegellae or flat dentils, again with raised faces to reflect light and form strong cast shadow.

From the frequent use of this motif, found incorporated in the wall panels at the entrance hall to the Temple ʾAwwām (of Maḥram Bilqis) at Marib, it is possible to suggest a date for the early use of this design from between the fifth and fourth centuries BC.[128] Architectural features such as a rectilinear panel decoration, a style which seems to have been imported from the north and used very frequently by the South Arabians, may be assigned to the period from the end of the fifth century BC to the first or second centuries AD.

Plate 8

Another common design is the ibex head, used as a formalized and continuous horizontal frieze. This motif is usually incorporated in the entablature of buildings. Examples from Timnaʿ leave no doubt that they were used as decoration for the upper section of the entablature, probably in place of the triglyphs and metopes of Greek and Roman entablatures. The same motif is used for the decoration of smaller architectural features and is to be found not only on inset panels, as in the walls of the entrance hall of ʾAwwām (Maḥram Bilqis) at Marib, but also on inscribed marble and decorative plaques. The bucrania motif is sometimes carved on such panels in place of the ibex. Both motifs may have been used in the same way as the Greek 'egg and dart' decorative moulding. End stops to these horizontal designs are usually a pattern of the rectangular recessed panels, their proportion dependent upon the centre decoration.

Plate 7

Another decorative system, this time with the bucranium motif as a frieze, also utilizes the ibex, but in a formalized couchant position carved in low relief on a border architrave surrounding the centre panel.

In 1951, The American Foundation for the Study of Man excavated the great entrance of the Temple of ʾAwwām, some two miles south-east of Marib which was once the capital of the Sabaean kingdom and also the site of the dam renowned in antiquity.[129] We know from inscriptions that the temple was named ʾAwwām and was dedicated to the Moon-god

'Ilumquh, the chief deity of Saba'. The ground plan is kidney- or oval-shaped and the temple wall is well constructed of a fine-cut ashlar masonry shell with a sand and rubble fill. The ashlar stones average 29 cm. in height and vary in length. Their outer surfaces are cut on a curve to match the curvature of the building. The outer wall surface is carefully pecked – the inner surface is left slightly rough as if intended originally as a key for a covering in plaster.

The entrance hall was the only part of the temple entirely excavated. It consisted of a peristyle hall with one large door leading into the temple and a triple door leading to an outer court and building complex which ended in a row of eight pillars. There were also pillars on the east and west sides.[130] On top of each is a small rectangular block which seems to have been to secure the entablature. The pillars stand on plinths – no capitals were found for these pillars.

Capitals for monoliths and columns have been found elsewhere and these again have been cut with care. Some are separate from the column, with a dowel-hole inset in the base. The dentil pattern is used very effectively, and the tegellae cut close together produce a dark shadow. The actual tegellae are cut with the vertical surfaces slightly raised. This refinement was used to catch the maximum reflection from the sun, and the maximum shadow below each row of tegellae. Used thus, as a finial, it must have contrasted with the smooth monoliths and have been brilliantly effective at a distance.

A design used principally for architraves, but also for panels, is the curvilinear and formalized vine pattern. These are a complete contrast to the rectilinear panel design and portray influences which are quite direct and clearly mirror later Hellenistic designs; in particular those to be found in the colonial Roman and later examples of Palmyra.[131]

Several of these design panels were discovered in the Yemen, principally in the Marib area, while in the Wadi Ḥaḍramaut at Husn al-'Urr, door architraves or lintels bearing this same design were also found.[132] Plate 9 Plates 3–5

It is of importance that although this vine-leaf motif has been seen to decorate the frames for incised inscriptions, it is also used with inscription panels where the characters, instead of being incised, are in high relief.[133] This is a characteristic style of some of the inscriptions of the later Sabaean era of the third to the sixth centuries AD, a factor which helps to confirm the late use of this motif.

It seems that during this later period not only do the decorative rosettes and formalized flower and petal designs embellish the wall panels and architraves, but a general artistic decadence seems also to have started. This is to be seen in the northern Yemen area where examples of column bases and capitals were drawn by C. Rathjens at Šibam Kaukaban. Here the monoliths consist of round columns with accentuated double fluting and are also decorated around the base with roulette moulding. The square bases on which the columns stand are embellished with rosettes set in relief. One capital shows an attempt to produce the acanthus leaf design set above a circular decorated neck. Here, however, the detail design of the capital and its length, compared with the total column height, is grossly ill-proportioned.[134]

The effects of this over-decorated and ill-designed material appears not to have percolated into the southern area but stayed in the area of Sanaʿa. This serves to illustrate the strong influence from the northern end of the trade route and the affluence of the Sabaeans towards the end of the great land-trade era. Such over-embellishment of utilitarian features may reflect an easy or even decadent way of life, in contrast to the stark simplicity of the rectilinear forms characteristic of the earlier and more energetic era of trade and commerce.

Sculpture

Most of the sculpture carved by the early South Arabian artists was the result of religious inspiration, and surviving examples are therefore chiefly votive pieces made in honour of the gods and presented to the temples, or memorial stelae in honour of the deceased. Stelae have been found in graves at Ḥaid bin ʿAqil, in the precincts of the temple at Timnaʿ, and also in habitation areas. The stelae vary in form, being either simple

Plates 18–20, 22, 23
Plate III
Plate VI

vertical shafts carved in alabaster, or more elaborate carvings, either of a bull's head symbolizing the moon-god, or a carving portraying the dead person. They were sometimes carved in one piece with the bases, or set separately into a base which could be of a different material; for instance, an alabaster stela set into a limestone base. Frequently only the bases in the cheaper material have survived, as the more valuable alabaster was stolen or re-used in antiquity. Usually, the name of the deceased or the dedicator appears on the base and their survival is fortunate not only because of their artistic merit, but for the names, their distribution and the design of the inscribed characters which tended to show regional variants. Plate 25

Free-standing votive sculpture provides information for costume. Plates III, IV Portrayals of important personages were made with great attention to detail; some of these, mostly male statues, have stylized beards, elaborate hair-styles, wigs and even moustaches. We know that statues were made of Plate 26 members of royal families and kings, confirmed by inscriptions on the bases of some giving the name of the royal house of ʾAusān. Several of these wore moustaches and wigs styled with triangular-shaped fringes, and it is possible that those sculptured portrait heads found which have moustaches indicate high office or blood royal. The sculptors were hampered by the small size of the alabaster and marble blocks available and usually carved away as little as possible. This limited their creative ability and imagination, and the attitudes of statuettes were usually rigid and Plate VI stylized.

Many full-length statues have close fitting garments formed from a single length of cloth, or with a skirt arranged like a simple Arab *lunghi* or futah. Probably the most elaborate dress detail can be seen on the statuette of Yaṣduq ʾil Farʿam Šaraḥʿat, King of ʾAusān. The material has Plate IV, V been cut to hang in a fashion similar to that of Greek drapery from the eastern Mediterranean about the fifth century BC.

Statuettes are also often shown wearing sandals with open toes and leather straps forming the heel and cross straps to hold the foot. There are three variations of cross strap: a single strap extending between the first and big toe, a loop around the second toe and a third type with an additional cross strap over the instep in the manner of the Dorian sandal.

The hands of alabaster statues usually extend forwards at the level of the bent elbow and are carved or bored to suggest that they held a staff, probably in another material. Hamdani in Book VIII of the *Ilklil* remarks on the early Islamic tomb robbers' finds including gold or bronze staffs.

The finding of sculptured hands reliably thought to have come from Marib is probably unique in Southern Arabia. A cupped left hand bears Plate 21 a small bird and a right hand a bunch of grapes. They are finely executed with great attention to the detail of finger-nails and with a most realistic appearance of gripping the object. One of the fingers has a ring carved in one piece with the finger.

From a sanctuary of boy attendants of the goddess Isis at Sheikh Ibada in Upper Egypt have come several similar sculptures in soft limestone.

The holding of grapes and a dove has been associated with the boy-god, Harpocrates, son of Isis, and one piece of Coptic Egyptian sculpture shows the seated figure of a boy dressed in a simple tunic, clasping a bunch of grapes in the right hand and a dove in the left hand, the latter being a frequent symbol in Christian art. A date of about AD 300 has been suggested for this.[135]

There is the possibility here of a characteristic resemblance to the sculpture of Southern Arabia, but even coupled with the grapes and dove which illustrate a link with Coptic art, a direct connection cannot yet be proved. It is a fact, however, that during this period many of the Himyar followed the Christian faith.

Plate 13

Carved friezes have been found which portray interesting mythological beasts and symbolic religious subjects. They serve to emphasize the influence of the countries of the Fertile Crescent and the Mediterranean in artistic matters. There are reliefs of two animals, usually sphinxes in antithesis, facing a central floral design possibly symbolizing the 'tree of life' motif.[136] Such patterns formed the centre part of the frieze and the motif is of Mesopotamian origin.

One particular frieze in low relief found at Timnaʿ, capital of Qataban, in Wadi Baihān, shows standing winged sphinxes eating the fruit of the tree of life. This is a continuous frieze and the sphinxes are standing tail to tail with bodies elevated and front legs braced against the tree. In this case the tree seems to be a formalized date palm.

Plate 12

Another frieze, also found at Timnaʿ, shows ibexes with front legs mounting the thick trunk of a formalized tree, probably a palm but without clusters of dates, while the heads are turned outwards to face a bushy-topped tree. A similar motif also appears in bronze, for an inscription plaque from Amrān shows a variation of this pattern on the upper panel while the lower panel is decorated with a rosette pattern.

Plate 11

A fragment, probably the centre portion, of a frieze carving shows a cherubic-faced winged sphinx facing a decorated bull's head. This appears to have been an antithetical design and serves to emphasize the popularity of the winged sphinx as a motif.

A new fragment of a limestone frieze was recorded in the library of the

Plate 2

Friday Mosque at Mukalla. It shows two identical fish lying parallel and facing the same direction. This suggests the antithetical motif and is probably unique. The fact that these are fish may be due to either an influence of Christianity, in which case the late dating of this material to around AD 300 would be significant; or to a connection with the fishing industry. As it was found in the Ḥaḍramaut near Ḥusn al-ʿUrr the latter possibility is not so valid.

Jewellery is represented on female statues and plaques with necklaces and beads and bangles carved in the stone. However, some statues have holes bored for the attachment of actual jewellery which would have been of metal or semi-precious materials. Some of the male heads have decorative tribal or caste markings carved in the stone and inset with coloured stones.

Several female plaques are votive representations of goddesses, particularly good examples being the plaques of D̲h̲at Ḥamym ʿAt̲h̲tar Yaġul found in the temple areas. The goddess is shown with the right hand raised in an attitude of blessing, while the left hand clutches a wheatsheaf to her bosom. Obviously she symbolizes fertility and the growth of crops, a local type of Demeter, the Greek earth-mother goddess, who is also connected with the sun.

Several of these representations show a matronly figure carved with a Roman stylized wide-necked dress with a necklace, bracelet and beads. The dedicator's name is usually inscribed on the base of the plaque.

An interesting seated statue is the bronze figure of the Lady Baraʾat. She is a compact, draped figure with the form of the body showing slightly through drapery which rests naturally across her knee, falling into a few transverse folds. This recalls a Roman dress style of about the first century AD. She is seated on a stone base consisting of two blocks rebated together, one smaller than the other, and stepped back to allow her feet to rest in the recesses of the lower block. This is one of the outstanding examples of early Arabian craftsmanship, and there is a six-line stoichedon inscription on the lower block of the stone base in the Qatabanian script which is a dedication to D̲h̲at Ḥamym ʿAt̲h̲tar Yaġul. The statue is a good example of the *cire perdue* or 'lost wax' technique, and the original clay core is still in place.

There is sufficient evidence to indicate that the early Arabian artists mastered the technique of casting large-scale statues in bronze. Copper and, of course bronze, gold and silver were put to many different uses by the craftsmen of early Southern Arabia. It is now thought that the gold statues (*dahab*) mentioned in inscriptions may refer to gilded bronze work.

Plate 24

Plate 36

Bronze bases or dowels are frequently left imbedded in the top of inscribed stones, although the statue itself may have been stolen in antiquity.

Plate 39

Copper (or bronze) seems to have been reserved for inscribed plaques, votive offerings and statuettes, usually for temple furniture, although bronze objects were apparently also used for decorative purposes in the wealthier houses.[137]

Plate 38

Bronze figurines were normally made by the 'lost wax' process already referred to. This process involves the use of a clay base onto which a hard wax face was modelled or cut to the finished design. An external mould of clay was then added and during slow firing molten metal was poured in from the top replacing the melted wax which was allowed to escape. This system had been long known in the Greek world and its use may show a link between the craftsmen of Greece or Rome, or even Egypt and those of Southern Arabia. It seems unlikely that figurines and cast objects of this kind were manufactured elsewhere and brought to Southern Arabia. It is much more probable that, in the early stages at least, expatriate craftsmen or their local trainees designed and made the objects in the workshops of the capital towns, to the requirements of a South Arabian client.

At Marib there were found examples of large bronze feet wearing sandals which must have belonged to life-size statues. This is also evident from the size of two bronze heads, one of which, presented to the British Museum, is remarkable for its intricate hairstyle and ringlets. The other head, last photographed at Sanʿa, is noted for its characterization and fine moustache.

Plate 43

Plate 42

Plate 40

In the Sanʿa museum there is a large-scale bronze standing male statue which is unique both for its size and technical accomplishment. The figure is undraped, one arm hangs at ease and the other is upraised. It is unorthodox in character and somewhat archaic in stance, but it succeeds in attaining an attitude of arrested motion, as if in oratory. The statue is not in a good state of preservation and is, in fact, supported by metal bands against the wall.[138]

Several bronze statuettes found at Marib by the American Foundation for the Study of Man excavations also seem, by their archaic stance, to reflect the restriction of the sculptural technique, as if the freedom of movement which could be expressed in bronze had not yet been fully realized. It is impossible not to miss the parallel between these statuettes and the Greek *kouros* type which, at first a rigid standing male figure, developed in movement until attitudes of arrested motion were achieved in stone and bronze.

One statuette of importance which has these characteristics is that of Maʿad Karib, possibly a king, or at least a notable. This man, 37 inches high, is portrayed in bronze, standing in a walking attitude with the left foot forward. He is shown wearing a skirt similar to the modern *lunghi* supported by a belt with a *jambia* and a lion or leopard skin on his back with forepaws across his chest and the tail hanging down behind.[139] The leopard skin was often used to denote high rank, although this is a rare find in Southern Arabia. The stance is stylized and shows a further stage in development from the *kouros* type. This statuette has been dated to about the sixth century BC.

Another male statue, about 17 inches high, shows a further development in the portrayal of movement. He wears a *lunghi* with a rolled top and a straight *jambia*. The legs are missing so the stance remains unknown, but the arms are projecting forward. The right hand is open and raised in a gesture of greeting while the left hand seems to have held a staff.

In the Museum building at Sanʿa there is also another significant bronze work. It was originally a cherub-like figure although only the torso and upper parts of the limbs with the clay core remain, from which it appears that the figure was reclining at ease. The torso shows remarkable modelling of the natural body curves and the work of a craftsman who was master of his material. From the photograph which is the only source for our evidence one can see the head is merely set on the body and therefore its original position can only be surmised. Apart from this the proportions appear to be correct. The face, framed in curls, is heavily stylized with an emphasis on fullness of facial form, and an archaic smile hovers on the lips.

Plate 41

During the excavations by the American Foundation for the Study of Man, two cherub figures were discovered at Timnaʿ[140] by the outer wall of a building near the house known as Yafaš. The figures, made with the 'lost wax' process, are each mounted on 'lions'. They are nude and one holds a pointed lance in the right hand and in the left a chain round the lion's neck. The total height is about 24 inches, and the length of the base is 21 inches. The composition of the metal is: lead 20.36%, copper

I Fine ashlar walling at the main religious sanctuary or temple at Timnaʿ, capital of Qataban. This external wall forms the western side of the hypaethral columned court which leads to the inner sanctum on the raised east level. From pottery and alabaster objects found and the evidence of lateral walls, it is probable there were storage chambers between the court and this wall. The masonry is well cut with tooled faces, laid dry and bonded in courses of reducing height. This straight wall joins the massive irregular blocks of the southern bastioned wall and probably formed part of the alterations when the northern staircase and court were added to the earlier structure.

II The finely cut and evenly coursed ashlar walling of a small building a short distance north of the South Gate of Timnaʿ.

III A carved alabaster dedicatory bull's-head votive plaque, an example of fine craftsmanship, provenance unknown but probably Qatabanian.

IV A statue in alabaster of YaṣDuQ'iL FaR'iM ŠaRḤat king of 'Ausān son of MaʿaD'iL SaLḤaN king of 'Ausān. He is depicted wearing a form of Greek dress, with long hair, or a wig, and a moustache. This is, in all probability, a portrait. The left hand is pierced and may have held a staff of wood or copper (RES 3888).

V YaṢDuQ'iL FaR'iM king of 'Ausān son of MaʿaD'iL. A stylized statue which accentuates features and details including the representation of his finger ring, arm band and feet shown encased in thonged, square-heeled sandals. Depicted with a moustache, his hair or wig style is long and at the back is cut with a serrated edge. The left hand may have held a staff (RES 3885).

I

II

III

V

IV

53.88%, tin 4.35%. The groups are in relief and were formerly attached to a background, and as the figures form an antithetical group there may have been some motif in the centre. The lion-riders are Hellenistic in type with rounded features, curls and chubby faces. The lions seem to be hermaphrodites with the luxuriant mane of the male and the teats of the female. They are thought to belong to the first century BC.

There are several myths associated with mounted figures of this kind in the classical world. The design of the group might be influenced by a solar theology which replaced the lunar religion after the Hellenistic period. This could be the localized interpretation of the motif with the figure representing the Moon controlling the Sun, lions symbolizing the supreme power of the Moon-god 'Ilumquh.

Alabaster and pottery

An impressive quantity of early South Arabian potsherds have been found, particularly on the surface where sand erosion leaves a compact layer. Apart from the endless fragments there are also complete pots usually found by excavation in soft sand. There are vessels in clay, alabaster, limestone and bronze, and examples of work in these materials are found in abundance throughout Southern Arabia. There are no known potters or recognizable stylistic schools, but pottery from specific areas sometimes bears its own individual characteristics of technique and design.

ALABASTER VESSELS

Alabaster containers for unguents, powders and liquids are to be found in all sizes and shapes, varying from slender to squat, with sloping sides. They are all flat-bottomed and have often been provided with lids. Decorations may be carved, consisting of protruding vertical or horizontal pierced lug handles, or small formalized bull's heads which also serve as handles. Lids may have a carved crouching ibex as a centre handle. When the name of the owner is marked on the neck or side of the jar it is often inscribed by a series of small drilled holes forming the characters in the early South Arabian script. Plate 37

Pedestal dishes, bowls and saucers are rarely found on sites, but the small three-legged cosmetic palettes have occurred as far south as Al-Qaraw, Zingibar. There are also small, rectangular, square-sided, boxes decorated with small bulls' heads having circular holes in their top, used as containers for bottles, presumably of glass. The standard of workmanship for items of this type is extremely high and it seems probable they all originate from a central workshop design.

In the Aden museum there are two large alabaster bowls of unknown provenance but possibly found in the Wadi Markha area. They have squat, rounded bellies and both the neck and the rim form an acute angle where they join the body, which is decorated with an incised pattern on the upper surface. They have been worked from a solid block and the thick walls are translucent. The larger bowl has three unique and finely carved handles of ibex with the curved horns forming the actual handle. On the upper portion of this bowl is a small inscription in raised South Arabian lettering. This fact may suggest that the bowl was made during the late Sabaean era, about the third or fourth centuries AD.

An article of temple furniture, fulfilling an important part in religious ceremony, was the libation and sacrificial altar. Many of these have been found and it seems probable that the smaller ones were used in private devotions in the home. They are usually oblong or square slabs with surrounding raised rims, although small circular ones are known. Sacrificial altars are mostly in alabaster or marble but stones ones have been found. All altars have a run-off channel for the liquid, similar to the Gothic gargoyle. Without exception this is in the form of a single bull's-head sometimes highly stylized but always recognizable. The channel is cut along the protruding neck and over the forehead so that the liquid would drip from the actual head.

Horizontally veined alabaster was used in the manufacture of many of the large flat-bottomed jars, suggesting an Egyptian origin, though the finished product is completely South Arabian in concept.

DOMESTIC POTTERY

Pottery used in the home and pottery found in the tombs seem to be very much the same, presumably indicating that the utensils used during life were buried at death. Domestic pottery in Southern Arabia generally was not well fired. It was often decorated with slip, pebble-burnished or merely completed with wet smooth finish.[141]

Plate 27

A design characteristic in Baihān for pottery bowls was a wavy rim. This was formed by pressing alternate fingers round the rim before the clay was cheese-hard. Usually the rim appears to have been finished by hand-wiping as for plain rims, since the use of the wheel here is not certain. The wavy rim is not found in profusion elsewhere, although finds of this type made in Abyan at Al-Qaraw, Zingibar, could perhaps indicate a strong Qatabanian influence, presumably when Qataban controlled the shores of Arabia from the distant capital in Baihān as late as the second century BC.

The pottery from Qataban, Baihān, is usually fairly lightly though evenly fired, and this is no doubt due to the fine clay of the area. The pottery found in the Ḥaḍramaut on the early sites is usually of a red clay, well fired and often with a grey core and a dominant red slip, with ledge rims sometimes impressed with South Arabian characters. Plates 30, 31

In the Ḥaḍramaut and at Marib, the capital of the Kingdom of Saba', the raised dot, sometimes as few as four on a jar, is used as decoration. It is thought to have decorated pottery in Southern Arabia as far back as the sixth to fifth centuries BC. This may also illustrate strong Sabaean influences in the Ḥaḍramaut at an early period, although, to judge from historical and palaeographic evidence, the Sabaeans made incursions and formed settlements far into the Ḥaḍramaut area at a later period, after the third century AD. Plate 32

The pottery at Ṣubr, near Aden, is evenly and well fired, but this type has not been found anywhere else except a small amount near Al-Qurayāt in the Abyan area. At Ṣubr, a micaceous clay had been fired locally and some of the items found here are from extremely large, heavy *ziers* and jars with long, horizontal pierced ledge handles. The nearest examples similar to these large examples have been the finds of jars at Mukeiras which may have been made elsewhere and imported. Generally, the pottery at Ṣubr seems to be unique and to provide evidence of a vast camp site over a very long period. The pottery decoration here consists usually of scratched or indented patterns, the wavy lines, the vertical comb and the interrupted comb, the pie-crust and the herring-bone design. Pottery may also be pebble-burnished internally and externally and frequently there is a slip coat.[142] A date of about the fifth or sixth century BC has been suggested for this ware on the basis of Palestinian analogies. *Figs 11–13*

The unglazed pre-Islamic pottery found in the tombs at Ḥuraiḍah[143] includes pedestal bowls which may be shallow or deep. Some have wide ledge rims which may have impressed or scratched inscriptions. Here also

Plate 28

were goblets with tall stems, a type which has also been found at Al-Qaraw, Zingibar.

Jewellery

Our evidence for early South Arabian jewellery is not extensive and very little of it is excavated material. Most of the best examples result from the handing-on of valuable pieces from one generation to another, together with collections of tribal heirlooms which have become available for sale.

Examples of early South Arabian jewellery are varied and generally of a high standard of craftsmanship. However, some of the surviving material, particularly beads, was found during the excavation of the Moon Temple at Ḥuraiḍah and also at Raibun (Ghaibun) and Sune in the Ḥaḍramaut. Published reports on these beads indicate that they showed a distinct eastern Mediterranean influence, datable between the eighth and seventh century BC.[144] Carnelian, faience, onyx, glass and shells were popular materials for the beads. There are also examples of agate, granite, amethyst and one or two of gold. These materials were wrought into shapes which include bicones, spheroids, discs and segmented beads. At Ḥuraiḍah there were a number of pendants, mostly of shells.

Plate VII

The craftsmanship of the carnelian beads varies, for some pieces are roughly shaped and have a groove where the perforation is made to make it easier to align the hole. This technique was used in pre-dynastic Egypt. Some of the beads also show attempts at intaglio carving.

Green, red, blue, yellow and black glass beads have been found and some of them are made of two forms of glass together, providing an attractive appearance.

Plate VIII

Gold ornaments include nose- and ear-rings, finger-rings, ornamental pieces to enhance necklaces of semi-precious stones and necklaces of gold pendants. The designs are frequently reminiscent of eastern Mediterranean work and the standard of craftsmanship seems nowhere less than that of the jewellery of the Hellenistic world. Occasionally there are fine examples of filigree work, particularly on the flat pendant ornaments and also granulated decoration is used as a sophisticated refinement.

Coins

Plate 44

Through their trading experiences the South Arabians were familiar at an early date with the use of coins, particularly those of Athens.

In the mid-third century BC it became essential for the early South Arabians to strike their own coinage as part of their increasing participation in the system of international finance as well as for internal use. Gold coins are very rare but silver and bronze coins are well attested. Accordingly the numismatic evidence forms an important part of the study of Southern Arabia's history and art.

The coins found are often of silver and the design initially inspired by Attic Greek coins with the head of Athena on the obverse and the Athenian owl on the reverse. The earlier silver coins minted sometime in the third century BC were imitated from the Attic old style coins, although much smaller and on the Persian weight standard. The latest of these had South Arabian monograms and symbols. The later version copied the Attic new style coins except that there was now an Arab male head on the obverse. These were minted in the late second-first centuries BC. The Arab head later changed to an Augustan head and this suggests a date after 24 BC when Aelius Gallus had led his expedition to Southern Arabia.

Another type of small silver coin was minted about the first century AD with an Arab male head on the obverse and a bucranium on the reverse. A later type of this small coin had Arab male heads on both obverse and reverse. The mint of Ḥarib, probably the name of the Royal Palace at Hajar bin-Humaid in Baihān,[145] produced coins of this type in the first to second centuries AD. The mint of Raydān at Ẓafar, capital of the Himyar kingdom of Saba' and Dhu Raydān, produced coins of a similar type about the period between the second and the end of the third centuries AD,[146] when the minting of coins of this type in Southern Arabia appears to cease.

Most of the bronze coins found in Southern Arabia are from the Ḥaḍramaut although the author found some in the Wadi Jirdān. These may be quite late in date and were probably minted late in the third century AD. Some of these coins are of an extremely large size. On the obverse of one is a beardless male head with long ringlets depicting the Moon-god Sīn[147] and on the reverse is a standing eagle with outspread wings and the name Šuqr, a name which in Southern Arabia has been connected with the moon-god. A second type of bronze coin has a radiate male head on the obverse, again with the name of the god Sīn. The radiate head possibly symbolizes brightness, connected with the darting rays of benevolence. On the reverse is a bull and the word Šuqr. Much smaller coins from the same area, particularly al-Barīra in Wadi Jirdān, have also been found bearing merely the legend Sīn with a standing bull, and it is inferred that Šuqr and Sīn were interchangeable. The use of the radiate head-dress may reflect the widespread cult of Mithras, whose worship spread widely from Persia during and after the second century AD.

Early South Arabian silver coins were apparently made with bronze punch dies. Hot malleable metal discs of the correct weight were placed on to the obverse and lower part of the die, set in an anvil, and the impression formed by the reverse of the upper die, set in the lower end of a bronze punch, being struck a sharp blow with a hammer. The impressed metal was then cooled rapidly in water. The concave shape in the silver coins is generally typical of the currency of the later period. Small bronze coins appear to have been minted in the same fashion although large bronze coins, especially those from the Ḥaḍramaut, may have been cast.

The various mints in early Southern Arabia produced coins bearing the names of kings and gods but the relevant inscriptions have so far shed meagre light on the value or the dating of the coinage as there is no definite related evidence.

Finally it seems that, although South Arabian coinage was used as a basis of loans or of interest, as a method of paying fines and as a standard for measuring value,[148] its main role was linked with external trade rather than with internal and domestic transactions.

Lavish expenditure on exotic trade goods was a subject of concern in Rome and Pliny complained that India, China and the Arabian Peninsula were taking good Roman money in payment for mere luxury goods.[149] As hardly any actual Roman currency seems to have been found in Southern Arabia, it appears that the Roman money, acceptable by India, was used by the South Arabians to purchase more goods from the East. This seems to confirm the accepted view that the South Arabians were merely 'middlemen' in this trade network.

However, the Roman currency found in India[150] so far appears to cover a short period and the first coinage seems to have been Augustan. Most of the first-century AD coins of gold and silver were found in Southern India and appear by their discovery in hoards and with cut marks on them, to have been used as bullion rather than as currency. This indicates the period of direct Roman sea trade across the ocean from the Red Sea to India and not through the hands of the South Arabians. It is a surprising fact that no significant finds of Roman coins have been made in Southern Arabia, which one might have expected if the coins had passed through, for if coins from the West were used as bullion why are there no Greek or Southern Arabian coins found in India?

It seems that in Arabia Greek coins were used only as currency where their value would be recognized, in the northern Red Sea and Mediterranean area, and they were necessary for the purchase of goods to bring south on the returning camel caravans. Greek coins reaching Southern Arabia were probably melted down for bullion.

Therefore the South Arabians were the middlemen in the East–West trade by a system of barter. The fact that coins were not minted in Southern Arabia after about AD 300 may be directly attributed to a general reduction in trade and in purchase from the North.

Description of the coins shown on plate 44:

Top row, 1 and 2: ATHENS. AR tetradrachm, old style. *Obv.* Head of Athena wearing crested helmet right. *Rev.* Standing owl right, olive spray and crescent moon behind, all within incuse square. To right AΘE. Weight 16.90. Fifth century BC.

Top row, 3 and 4: SABA'. AR unit. *Obv.* Helmeted head of Athena right. On cheek denomination mark. *Rev.* Standing owl right, behind, crescent moon (olive spray off flan). To right AΘE. All within incuse square. Weight 5.40. Third century BC.

Second row, 1: SABA'. AR unit. *Rev.* Standing owl right, traces of olive spray and crescent moon behind. To right AΘE and monogram (ḥmr). Weight 5.40. Second century BC.

Second row, 2: SABA'. AR unit. *Rev.* Standing owl right. To left monogram (ynf). Above legend in Liḥyānite script (šhr hll). To right crude AΘE and symbols of 'Ilumquh. Weight 5.40. Second century BC.

Second row, 3: QATABAN. AR 1/3 unit? *Obv.* Male Arab head with curly hair. Weight 1.78. First centuries BC–AD.

Second row, 4: QATABAN. AR 1/3 unit? *Rev.* Bearded male Arab head with hair taken up behind. To left part of monogram (š+?). To right symbol. Below mint name (ḥrb). Weight 1.69. First centuries BC–AD.

Third row, 1: ATHENS. AR tetradrachm, new style. *Rev.* Owl facing, on amphora, all within laurel wreath. To left and right magistrates' monograms. On either side of owl AΘE. Weight 16.80. Early second century BC.

Third row, 2 and 3: SABA'. AR unit. *Obv.* Male Arab head, laureate, with hair in ringlets, all within laurel wreath. *Rev.* Owl standing right on amphora within border of stylized handleless amphoras. To left monogram (ynf) and denomination mark. To right barbarous AΘE and symbols of 'Ilumquh. Above legend in Liḥyānite script (šhr hll). Weight 5.50. First century BC.

Third row, 4: SABA'. AV. *Rev.* As above but fillet border and no denomination mark or legend. Weight 5.37. First century BC.

Fourth row: SABA'. AR unit. *Obv.* Laureate Augustan head with moon and crescent above. Behind denomination mark. Weight 5.40. Late first century BC.

Fifth row, 1 and 2: SABA'. AR unit. *Obv.* Male Arab head with hair in ringlets. Symbols to left and right. All within border of dots, interrupted above by moon and crescent. *Rev.* Bucranium with antelope horns, thunderbolt between, within border of stylized amphoras. To left monogram (ḥmr?). To right symbol of 'Ilumquh. Weight 3.00. Late first century AD.

Fifth row, 3 and 4: HIMYAR. AR unit. *Obv.* Arab male head with hair in ringlets, within snake border. *Rev.* Arab male head, similar to above, but smaller. To left monogram (ynf), to right symbol. Above king's name (ʿmdn/byn). Below mint name (rydn). Weight 1.40. Third century AD.

Bottom row, 1 and 2: ḤAḌRAMAUT. AE. *Obv.* Head of moon god within linear border. To left letter (m). To right letters (syn) downwards. *Rev.* Eagle standing right within border. To left letters šqr downwards. To right letters yšh downwards. Third or early fourth century AD.

III

The Sites

The First and Second Governorates

The sites described have been chosen for their importance in history, or because although not well known they are of archaeological interest.

Sites which have been selected are shown on the map and have also been listed under the administrative area or particular governorate of the People's Republic of Southern Yemen, the present name of the area of south-western Arabia.

THE ADEN AREA

This area extends from the most westerly tip of Southern Arabia at the Bab al-Mandab. Little is known of the island of Perim except from medieval times when the Portuguese visited it and erected a cross on the highest part. It was mentioned by Diodorus Siculus in the second half of the first century BC but seemingly it was rarely used, for its lack of fresh water made it vulnerable. The port of Okelis (or Ocelis) mentioned in *The Periplus of the Erythraean Sea*, at an earlier period the harbour of the Gebbanitae (Qataban),[151] was on the mainland a few miles to the north of Perim.

Few signs of early occupation can be seen on the coast although remains of settlements such as the pottery weights and coins found at Bir Naʿamāh[152] may be typical of medieval fishing communities, some of which may be located on the sites of present-day fishing villages along the coast west of Aden. The large Subaiḥi tribe living in this area, who are also herdsmen of sheep and goats, may be identified with the Aṣābiḥ mentioned by Hamdani in the tenth century AD.[153] The small fishing tribe of Aqrabi now located around Bir Aḥmed was mentioned by Ptolemy in the second century AD.

Early sites are found in the Aden area, especially the strandlooper sites near Little Aden, and further inland where they lie within the delta of the Wadi Tiban. Here very early man left traces of habitation north of Laḥej and pre-Islamic and medieval sites are also to be found north of

Aden. There are signs of this whole area having once been watered and fertile; between Laḥej and Aden it was well wooded a century ago, and today fresh water in great abundance still flows below ground level in the delta area of Wadi Tiban where it wastes away into the sea.

Aden

Aden was used before Islam as an entrepôt port, a collecting centre for redistribution of trading commodities. Before the turn of our era, it was an island[154] and had always been secure from attack, for the only real danger was from a powerful fleet.

Plate 46 Both the port and the town were situated within the natural walls of the extinct crater of a volcano. Its harbour facing the open sea was ideally situated for the coastal trading vessels of 2000 years ago as they brought commodities from India and the East, frankincense resin from D̲h̲ufar and particularly frankincense and myrrh from Somaliland across the Gulf. From Aden these goods were transported first to the mainland by small boats and then by camel to the forming-up area for the northbound caravans. These great camel caravans, when the right amount of goods was packed, could then start the long journey to the Mediterranean, passing through the trade kingdoms. Aden was also an important port for vessels from Egypt when they sailed down the Red Sea and along the coast of Arabia, before they dared sail across the ocean direct to India.[155]

The main harbour for centuries remained the beach area which is now called Front Bay. This natural harbour was protected on the north side by the Jabal Ak̲h̲dar and on the south by the Island of Sira. The Bay of Holkat was used as an anchorage during the north-east monsoon. Sira Island gave protection not only from the wind but also through its fortress, for it has always acted as a guardian citadel for the Port anchorage.

In the early times before the universal use of the cannon, mangonals, which were large catapults, were placed on Sira as well as upon Jabal Munzir, the rock outcrop inshore, and were remarked on by Albuquerque when he investigated the defences in 1513. A further protection for the harbour and the port was the massive twelfth-century sea wall with its six gates.[156] Apart from the Saila Gate, which was opened to let the overflow waters out, the most important entrance was the Customs Gate. This was situated at the southern end near the road to Sira Island, and all the merchandise from the trading vessels had to pass through it for the application of local taxation.

The Holkat Bay area was also used by traders for the storage of their wares. This was allowed as there was no access into Aden except through the South Gate, a gate which was strictly controlled and closed at night to stop smuggling. The original wall and gateway here had also been constructed in the twelfth century. It seems that the Holkat Bay area continued as a storage and warehouse area as long as Front Bay and Crater remained the port.

The ancient town is now buried below the modern level. Captain Haines recorded the town buildings he found in 1839 in the Front Bay area. This was the result of a survey before the replanning and rebuilding of the town and the whole of the beach area involved the complete levelling of the area when buildings, many of them already in a ruinous state, were razed to the ground and valleys were filled. Foundations of buildings were discovered in 1963 at about thirteen feet depth together with long sections of masonry walling extending to the present road level. Pottery found at this depth has been assigned to the fourteenth century AD. There are no traces of the sea wall but the medieval walls encircling the town on the landward side remain, as they had been kept in good repair during the nineteenth century.

Remains of small forts or observation posts are still to be seen on the summit of the northern peaks of the old volcano rim. These are thought to have been constructed by the Turks in the sixteenth century, when they also built a ten-feet-wide stone paved road to the northern ridge. Plate 47
The main pass gateway with its three gates was also developed, although these have now been swept away.

The great cisterns which collected surface water from the plateau area *Fig. 6*
are situated in a narrow cleft on the western side of the town. These cisterns are a descending series of collecting tanks filled by rare falls of rain, Plate 48
which is collected by a system of small water channels. No evidence has been found to provide a date for their origin. This method was elsewhere used by the early South Arabians before Islam, but these cisterns have been improved and altered so many times that the original design is lost. There were a great number of wells in Aden and these must have provided much of the water supply for daily needs.

After the introduction of steam vessels, led by the *Hugh Lindsay* in 1834, the port of Aden gradually moved away to the Back Bay on the

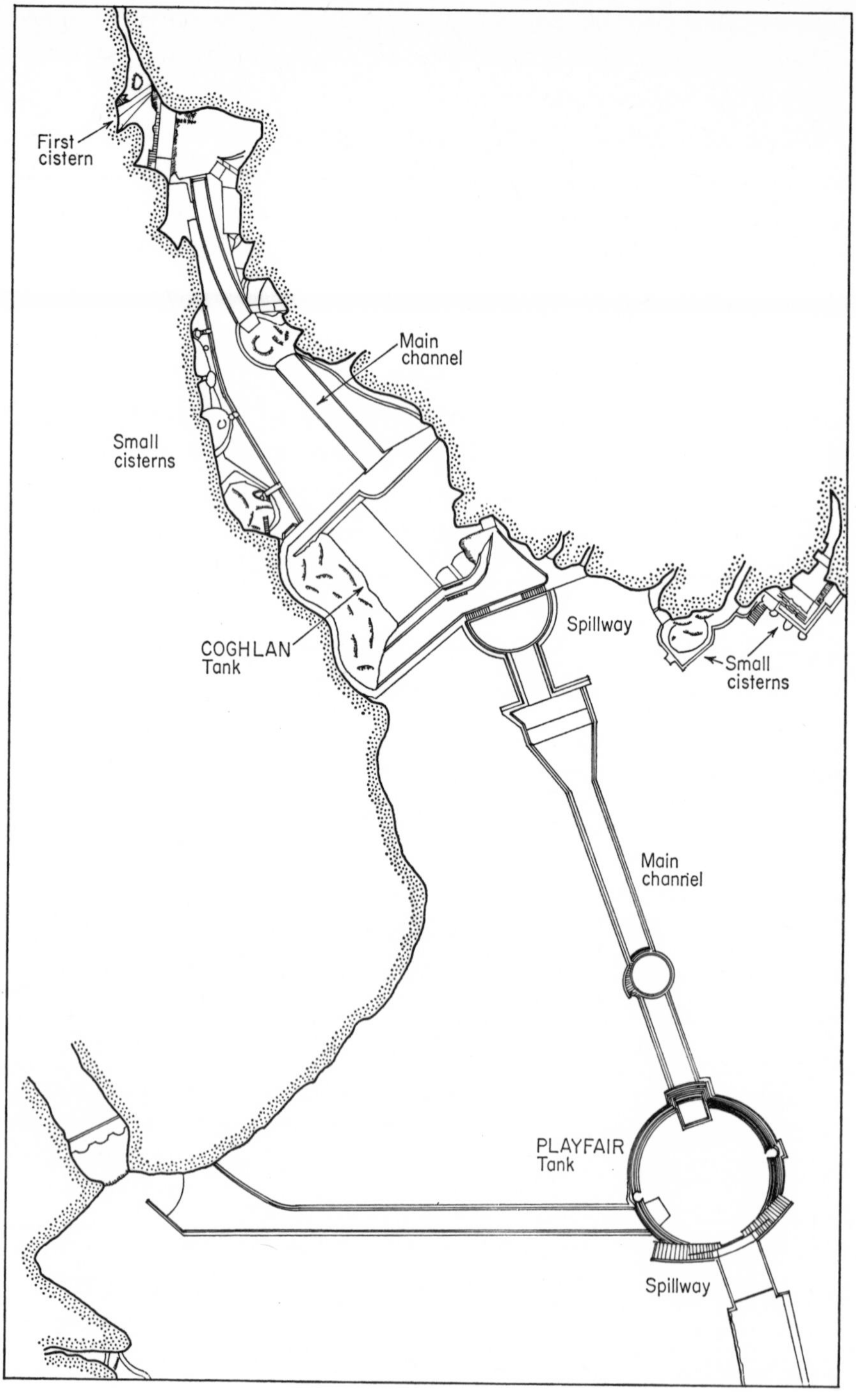

6 The Tanks of Aden, a descending series of cisterns and water catchment system in the Tawīla Valley. From a survey by H. T. Norris and F. W. Penhey

northern side. Here at Steamer Point these early steam packets were fuelled from stocks of coal stored under an early agreement with the ruler of Aden, the Sultan Aḥmed of Laḥej.

The use of the north-western end of Aden for steam vessels of deeper draught than the sailing vessels was to change the pattern of Aden life. This change was also partly due to the gradual silting up of the Front Bay area. The town no longer remained huddled within a natural fortress-area for protection, but began to develop outside.

At the same time the isthmus also silted up, to such an extent that there was easy access by land and the channel or *Khor* which had kept Aden an island was filled, an event probably remembered in the present name of Khormaksar. With the use of a land connection, the northern or Main Pass was developed and widened, for there had previously been no regular or intensive traffic to the barren northern shore.

This reorientation of Aden's commercial community led to an eventual expansion, with buildings and improvements to port facilities at Steamer Point; undoubtedly a great factor in the attraction of traders to use Aden. However, this was not accomplished until two other factors were established; complete security from attack and a steady and not exorbitant system of taxation.

Khor ʿUmaira

HUSN MALISAH

Jabal Malisah and the *husn* with buildings and the wall partly surrounding it on the summit is about 800 feet above sea-level. The site is identified on maps by the word *husn* on the south-east side of Jabal Kharāz (Ḥarīz),[157] the name for the remains of a large volcano which lies some 60–70 miles to the west of Aden. Jabal Kharāz is some 13 miles across and is 2,766 feet high. Husn Malisah is about four and a half miles due north from the police fort at Khor ʿUmairah which in turn is about a mile north of the coastal fishing village of the same name.

To reach the Jabal Malisah one has to pass across the lava fields which spread out from the lower slopes of the western side of Jabal Kharāz. The *husn* or fort is clearly visible from the track leading north to the village of Huwairib some ten miles north of the fort at Khor ʿUmairah. Huwairib is on a bearing of 305° from Husn Malisah. There is no discernible track up the rock but apart from the loose stones and crumbly surface on *Fig. 7* Plate 51

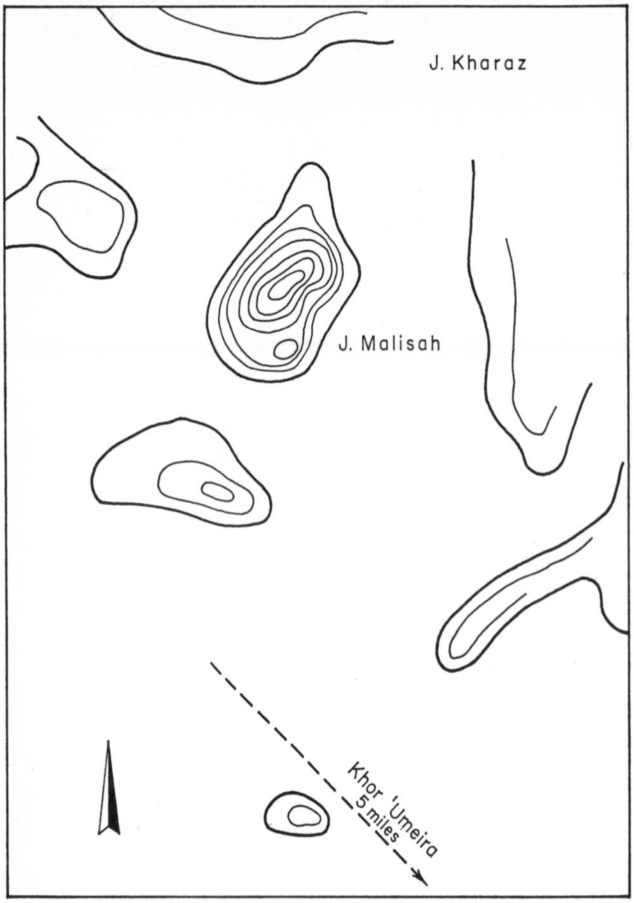

7 *The location of Jabal Malisah, on the west side of Jabal Kharāz, which is surmounted by a group of buildings*

the steep rocks at the top the going is fairly easy on the south face. On the summit where the buildings are situated, the ground falls gradually in a westerly direction from the rock outcrop on which the main *husn* is built. The total length of the built-up area is approximately one hundred yards and the east–west approximate alignment of the site is 240°.

Fig. 8

The buildings are in two forms with square and circular plans. The main building consists of a small group of 'square'-planned rooms. The

Plate 52

greater number of the buildings are of circular construction and the walls are all of uncoursed, random-rubble masonry laid dry with no mortar with an average thickness of fifteen inches. The height of the square-plan walls is about ten to twelve feet, and the average height of the circular single-room dwellings is about five feet. These have door openings, usually facing inwards towards the *husn*, with small window openings. Presumably the roofing consisted of timber branches and matting, although there were no remains. In the same way the timber roofing for the square-plan building has disappeared although in one building, at the eastern side, a long timber lintel remains embedded in the wall.

Pottery discovered on the surface was probably made within the last two hundred years. Stone grinding querns were also found. [158]

The use of this site, either in antiquity or in medieval times, would have been primarily as an observation post overlooking the level ground stretching westwards. A small garrison would have been stationed here for immediate protection of the fishermen goatherds and cultivators of the Ṣubqiḥi tribe in the locality, as well as for the route from Perim to Aden and the route between ʿUmairah and Am-Fadjarah. The only epigraphic evidence discovered in the Ṣubaiḥi region is on a rock east of a *husn* known as Dar ʿAnad near Am-Fadjarah. [159] Here there is a small pre-Islamic graffito mentioning personal and clan names.

Al-Anad

DAR AL-RAIS

This is the ruin-site of masonry which had been originally built on the stone outcrop on the west bank of the Wadi Tiban in the Laḥej area north of Al-Hauta, the capital of the Abadali state.

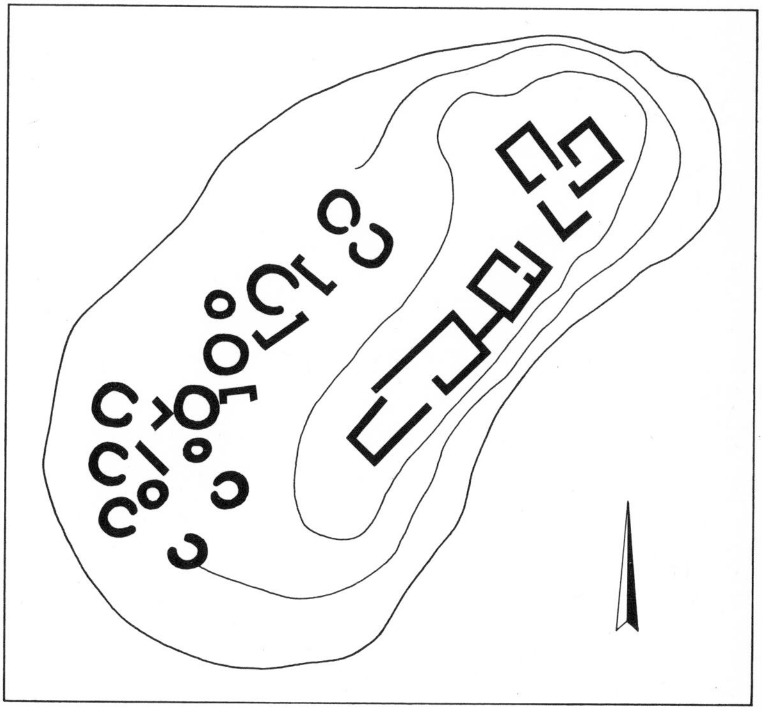

8 A sketch plan of the structures which form the Husn Malisah

VI A group of alabaster statuettes of male and female figures, thought to be votive offerings, with the name of the dedicant usually inscribed upon the base.

VII The date and provenance of this jewellery is not known. It was probably imported during the early years of the Christian Era, and shows characteristics similar to Roman examples of the first to third centuries AD. In the centre a bracelet, 20 cm. in length, of circular gold spacers, with carnelian and onyx beads and two large onyx eye beads in circular gold mounts. The inner necklace, 61 cm. in length, is of carnelian, onyx and gold beads, with two granulated gold lions, circular and lozenge-shaped inlaid gold beads, disc pendants with beads and a central gold pendant. The outer necklace, 68 cm. in length, is of carnelians set in gold caps, granulated gold and onyx beads, with a central gold, melon-shaped, drop pendant with a suspended inlaid gold lion.

VIII Three sheet gold rings with beryl(?) and onyx seals depicting animals. Above, a small gold pendant with domed top connected by corner wires to a cube centre body decorated with granules and a base of four small spheres. In the centre, a gold earring with a flat body of circular motif filigree with four suspended drops. On the right, an earring with circular ring and four granular beads and stop beads on the loop. On the left, two earrings of gold wire with granular beads and a garnet. Below, a gold earring with a thick, crescent, back piece and on a gold wire are threaded two pearls and a gold sphere.

VI

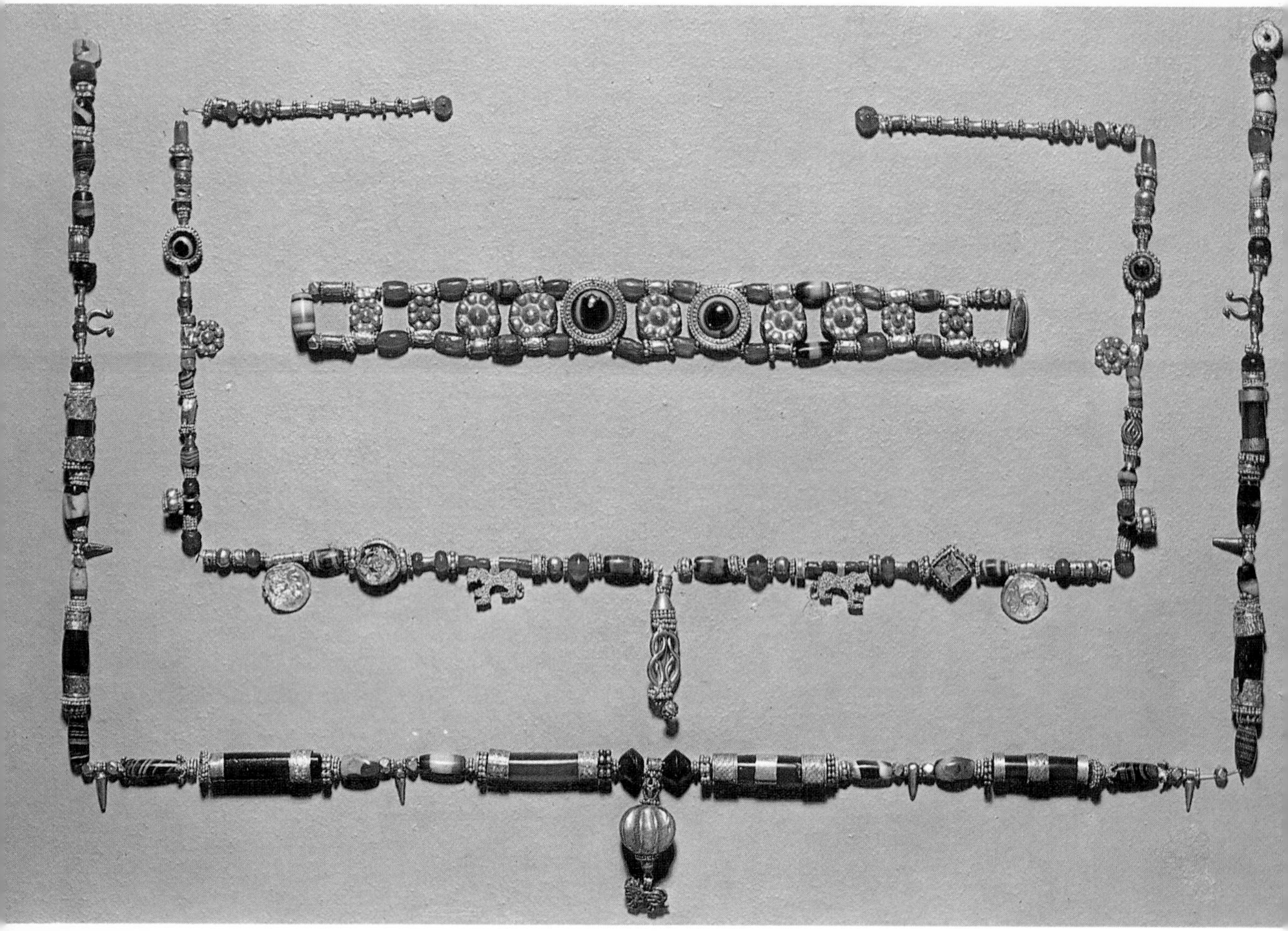

VII, VIII

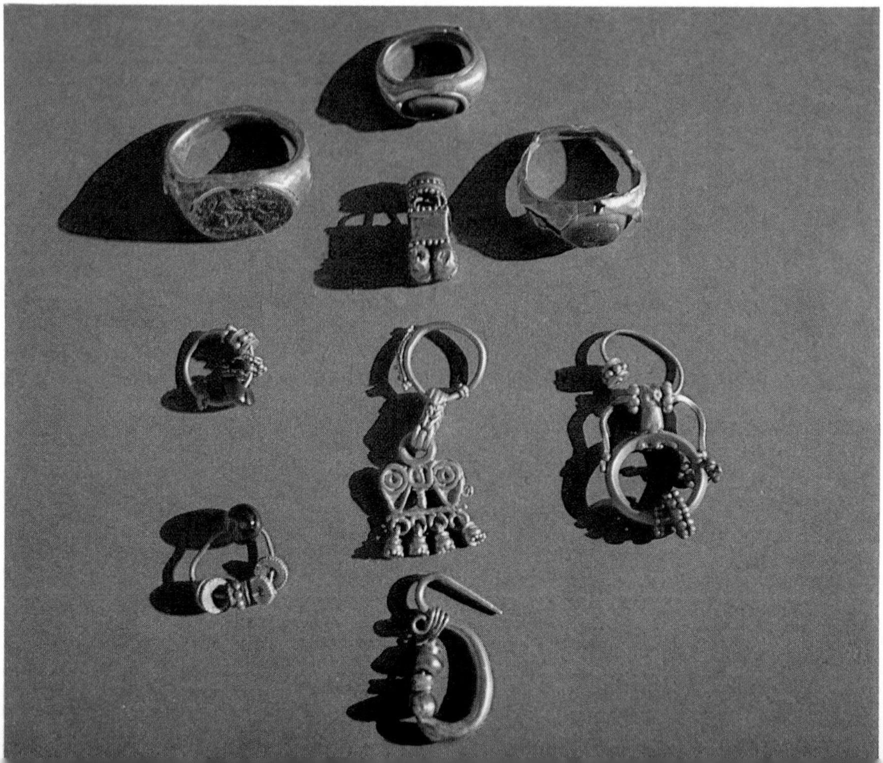

Plate 53

The masonry had been used as a foundation for a mud brick palace known as Dar al-Rais,[160] which is now in its turn disused and in ruins. Its original purpose is not known, but it may have been part of a dam structure. Reference made by al-Hamdani in *Ilklil,* Book VIII, says the dam of Laḥej is the dam called ʿUrāsh.[161] The position of this building and rock outcrop is at a narrow point in the wadi which is here flanked on the east side by a protective alluvial mound, now surmounted by the remains of a Turkish fort known as Al-Anad.

The possibility that an ancient dam stood here[162] is supported by the erection of a modern dam in 1960, approximately a mile downstream; a circumstance which clearly indicated this to be the most suitable point for irrigation purposes.

The stones of the masonry at Dar al-Rais are of a hard blue 'granite' limestone quarried in the stone outcrop nearby and cut in massive blocks squared and bedded, laid dry with fine joints. All sides are tool-worked, and the front face is pecked with an even texture and with marginal drafting averaging one and a half inches to the horizontal edges only. The masonry work and large stones used are unique in this area and may have been designed to withstand the seasonal flood water or *sail* in the watercourse. The largest stones are eleven feet and eleven feet six inches in length by two feet and another stone is nine feet six inches by three feet thick.

The actual dam walling was possibly constructed of earth and faced with stones as at Marib, and may have been continually repaired when the flood waters were due. A small outcrop of stone extending a hundred yards north is at present at the head of an irrigation ditch on the west side making the main structure an island. This may reflect the earlier use of the place, as a sluice control for the normal waters, the main dam diverting through this system.

However, the dating of this masonry has not hitherto been possible because of the lack of associated evidence. The finding of a pecked graffito inscription, although not a formal document, now places the work in the period before Islam, and its identification with the dam called ʿUrāsh may now be possible. Found in 1964, the graffito was on the face of a fallen piece of cut masonry five feet ten inches long. The pecking of the characters and the face-pecking margin drafting or chiselling of the masonry are of the same colour and may be contemporary and executed by the same masons. The characters are all vertically pecked, and two letters 'R' are four inches in height between tips. Epigraphically they may be linked with the latest Sabaean era. However, other characters are of the 'Thamudic' type. This is the first series of early South Arabian characters to be found in the Laḥej area.

The Jabal Tala

The area immediately south of Jabal Tala, west of Wadi 'Abrain, about twelve miles north from the capital town of Laḥej, was inhabited by very early man. Traces of this occupation, which must have extended over a very long period, when the countryside was green and lush, have been found. These consist of quartzite or basalt flakes and hand-axes, the basic tool adopted for daily use and spread over a large area. The dating of the technique of manufacture of these Acheulean hand-axe tools may be broadly estimated at 400,000–200,000 years ago.

Plate 55

This prehistoric site, thought to be the first of its kind in Arabia, is very much earlier than all previous archaeological discoveries in the area. The importance of the discovery lies in what it tells us about the spread of the early people who manufactured these hand-axes, similar to those already abundantly familiar in northern Tanzania. The makers of these tools, of types probably in use for a hundred thousand years or more, may have spread from Africa to Europe and to India, but the route eastwards has not been identified. The hypothesis of a land-bridge across the narrowest part of the Red Sea at Bab al-Mandab may be ruled out by the fact that the rift occurred much earlier than the period of this culture and the waters are deep at this point. It is more likely that this particular hand-axe technique was distributed by the movement of migrants southward on both sides of the Red Sea. Whatever their source, at present it appears that these 'hand-axe' men were the first South Arabians.

Kawd Am-Sailah

Fig. 9 *Fig. 10*

This site is on a prominent mound in the Laḥej plain, close to the Wadi Al-Kabīr and three miles from Shaikh 'Uthmān on the track to al-Waqt. The surface finds on the mound indicate that it was a glass-manufacturing centre; lumps of greenish glass frit and glass fragments have not been found elsewhere in such great quantity. There is also a substantial quantity

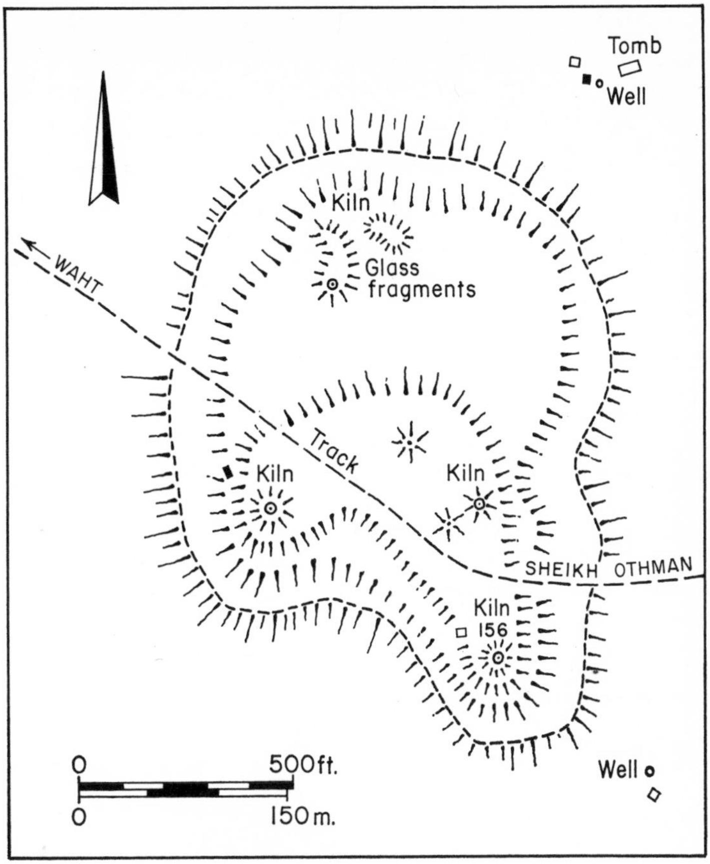

9 A plan of the site of Kawd Am-Sailah showing the positions of kilns found on the surface. The track from Shaikh ʿUthmān to Waqt passes over the mound and the site of a walled structure (Fig. 10) *is indicated on the west side*

of fragments of pottery on the site, glazed and unglazed pieces most of which seem to be of local manufacture. Mis-shapen discards (wasters) were found near to kilns on the mound.

It is probable that most of the glass manufactured here was for export, and that this was one of the places which produced the popular glass bracelets so widespread in the countries fringeing the Indian Ocean, from the Red Sea to the African coast, the Persian Gulf and India, and possibly even as far as China. They were usually triangular in section and varied in decoration from plain green glass to stripes or bands in red, blue, yellow and white with green in various combinations, and sometimes with coloured spots patterned on the outer edge. Their period possibly extended from the fifth or sixth century AD to the sixteenth century. Similar glass bracelets are made in India and are to this day exported to Aden.

This glass manufacturing may have started in Persia, and an early reference to it is found in a Chinese document before the sixth century AD.

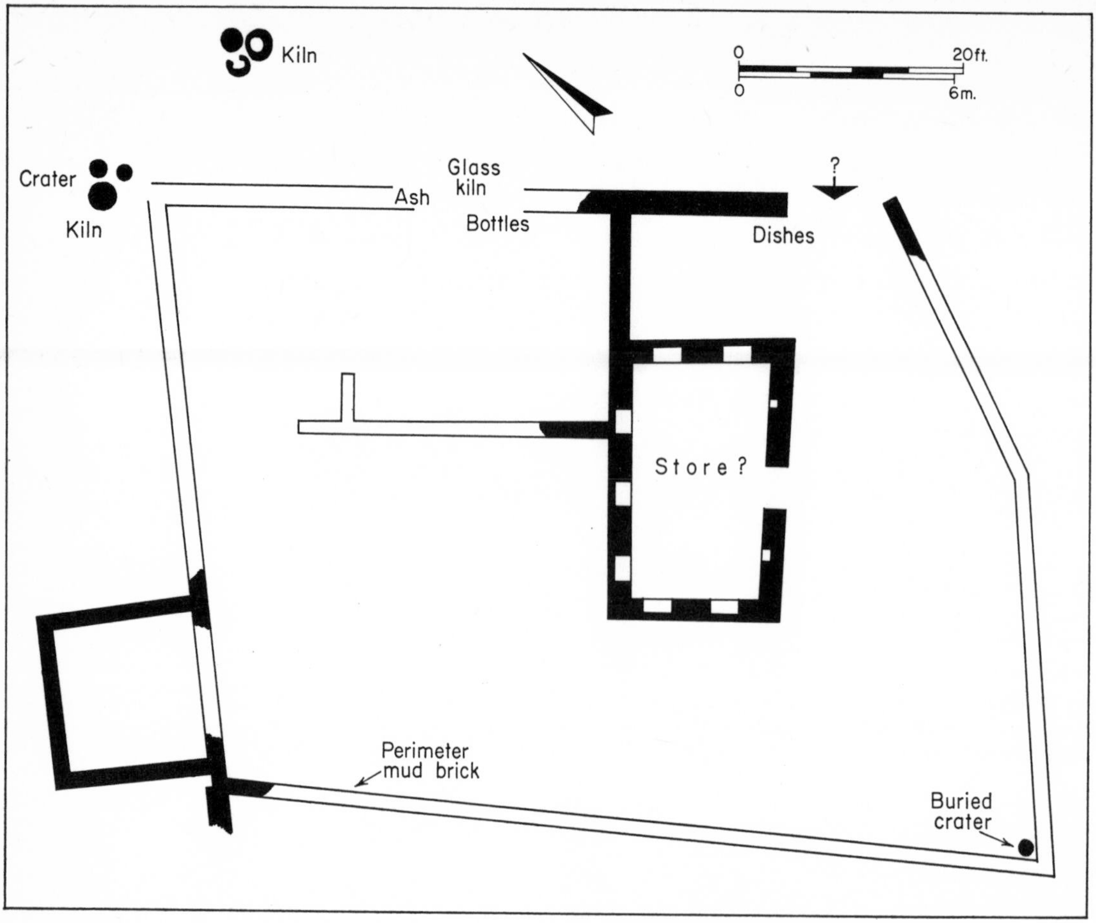

10 Plan of a mud brick walled structure excavated at Kawd Am-Sailah. The central building with wall alcoves was mud plastered and in places decorated with geometric patterns in red ochre. The wall measured 9 ft in height from a rough stone foundation although pottery fragments were found at a depth of only about 4 ft. Small glass bottles and dishes with painted decoration were found against the perimeter wall at a depth of about 3 ft

Here 'glass both transparent and opaque' was made known to the Chinese by the Persians, a term which then included Persia and Southern Arabia.[163]

Recently, considerable traces of glass-making during the Islamic period have been found at the ancient port of Siraf, a hundred miles south-east of Bushire on the Persian/Arabian Gulf.

When the Persians occupied south-west Arabia in the sixth century AD it is likely that they introduced glass manufacture into the country. The very wide distribution indicates that this export must have been a valuable one, and the factories probably closed down only when Southern Arabian trade was paralysed by the arrival of Portuguese fleets in the Indian Ocean in the sixteenth century.

Kawd Am-Sailah, which was possibly once named La<u>kh</u>abah,[164] must have been chosen as a factory because it was so close to the sea, was well watered and surrounded by trees and vegetation, which would have been used for fuel. If this factory was in use for such a long time there must have been some system of re-afforestation to maintain a constant supply of fuel. The area was still comparatively well wooded in 1839 when Captain Haines reported that from Laḥej to Bir Aḥmed and Hiswa was a dense jungle[165] with the caution 'beware of robbers'. The denudation since 1839 is the result of the haphazard felling of trees for the fires of the rapidly growing town of Aden.

Subr

This important site straddles the Aden–Laḥej road about six miles south of al-Ḥauta in Laḥej. It is an open site with no visible remains of buildings on it, and from north-west to south-west it stretches for about a mile before it disappears beneath high sand dunes, although it reappears in places where the dunes expose the original surface. The whole site is completely littered with a layer of red sherds and from a distance the colour of the whole terrain is browny-red.[166] In general the sherds lie on the surface and to a depth of about two feet, although in places they have been found deeper. Plate 54

The thick surface covering of sherds may be the result of erosion of the sand and soil by strong winds. During a small excavation it was noticed that the stratification of the sherds did not follow the lines of the mound but inclined inwards, and at a depth of five feet the pottery fragments remained of the same type as those on the surface. *Figs 11–13*

The site consists of a series of long mounds which have the appearance of *tells* and although superficial examination suggests that the mounds are natural, deep excavation might show otherwise. Superficial scratching of the surface sand on some of these mounds reveals grey soil or mud with pockets of ash. It is possible that mud-brick dwellings made of the local earth, as are the modern buildings in this area, once stood here.[167]

One mound which is larger than the others lies on the western side of the main road, and it is now covered by a modern house. The wells in present-day use are situated close to this mound and nearby some modern mud-brick houses form a small village.

Ṣubr was probably an important depot near the Laḥej oasis where the large camel caravans formed up before their journey northward, after taking over the exotic merchandise which had passed through Aden from the East or from the Horn of Africa.

The presence of so much pottery here must indicate the considerable length of time that this site was used, if only for camping, as also the many sheep and goat bones, the charcoal fires, and large pots that clearly had been used for cooking. The cooking-pot design could account for the great number of potsherds with thin walls and round bottoms, apparently without bases.

When the port of Aden was destroyed and the trade route leading from it disused, Ṣubr must have ceased to be a caravan centre. The date of this event is unknown, but it probably occurred during the wars for supremacy between Himyar, Qataban and Saba'. *The Periplus of the Erythraean Sea* mentions the 'recent' destruction of the port 'not long before our time',[168] but the date of the *Periplus* itself is by no means certain, conjectures varying between the end of the first century AD and the beginning of the third century.

11–13 Pottery from Subr. A selection of the sherds found on this extensive site are shown in the Figs. 11, 12, 13. Generally the clay is well levigated and tempered with local micaceous sand although in a few examples chaff has been used. The vessels are all hand made and have a slip in pink buff and brown; horizontal and vertical pebble burnishing is often used (indicated in the drawing by brush marks) but examples of internal wet smoothing are found usually for necked and hole-mouth vessels. They are all well and evenly fired and only the thickest vessels, usually coil built, are found with a grey core (Fig. 12). *Deep bowls usually have horizontal pierced lug handles with a raised band of indented pie crust decoration* (Fig. 11), *although some are plain. Vertical lug handles are found with interrupted combing from the rim and down the body. Some examples of vertical straight continuous combing are also found* (Fig. 12). *Sherds found are usually rims and handles* (Fig. 11) *and except for an incense burner* (Fig. 13) *no complete section from base to rim has been found in spite of the large quantity of sherds collected. Very few bases to bowls have been found and only a few examples of ring or flat bases have been seen* (Fig. 13). *Two examples of horizontal ledge handles* (Fig. 12) *and few examples of horizontal double pierced lug handles* (Fig. 13) *were found, showing their comparative rarity. Examples of spouts* (Fig. 13) *were also rare and the indented decoration of the central sherd illustrated was the only example found on this extensive site. Except for examples from a site Al-Quraiyat in Abyan, no outside comparisons for any of the ware and forms were found*

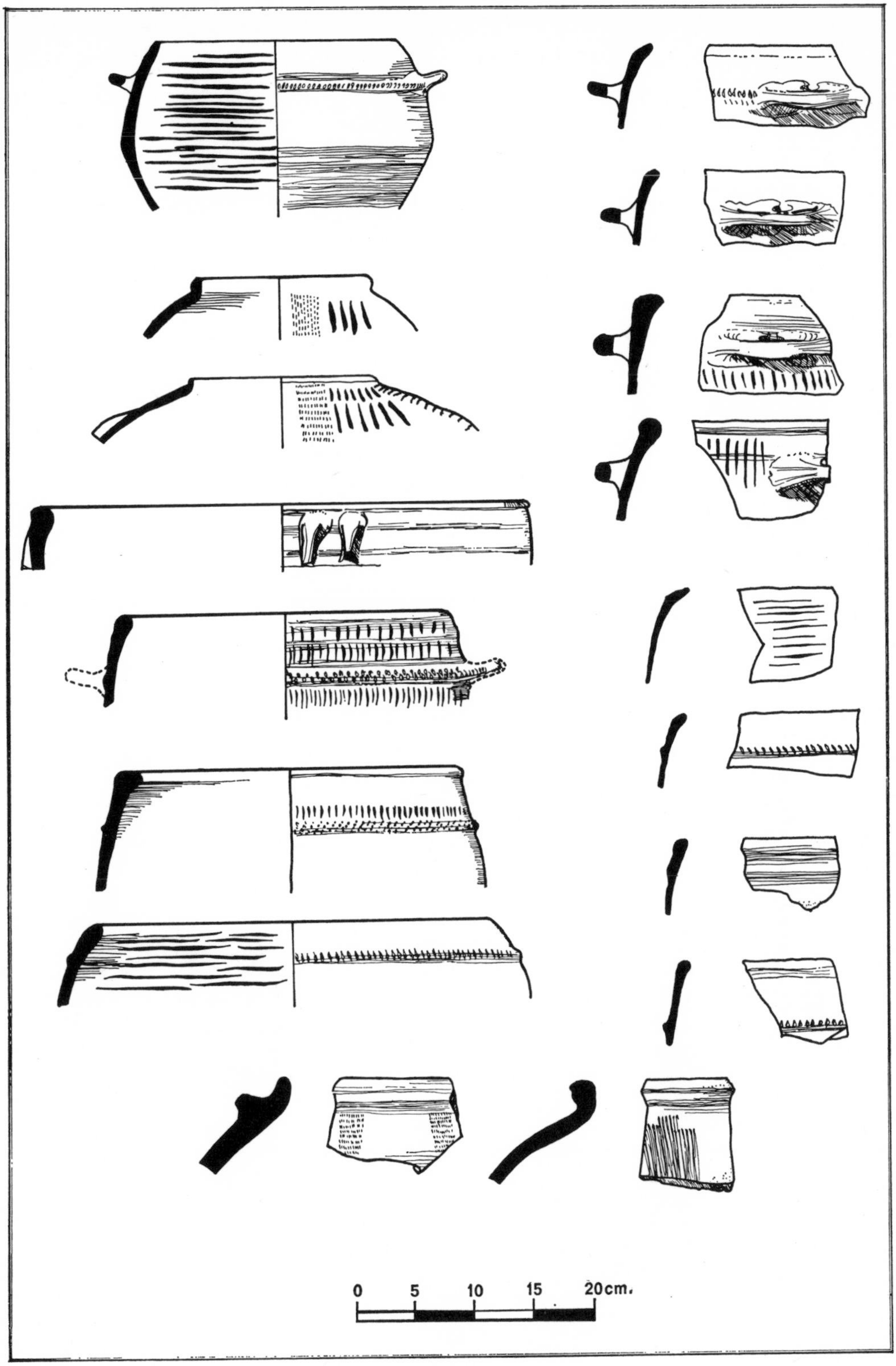
0 5 10 15 20cm.

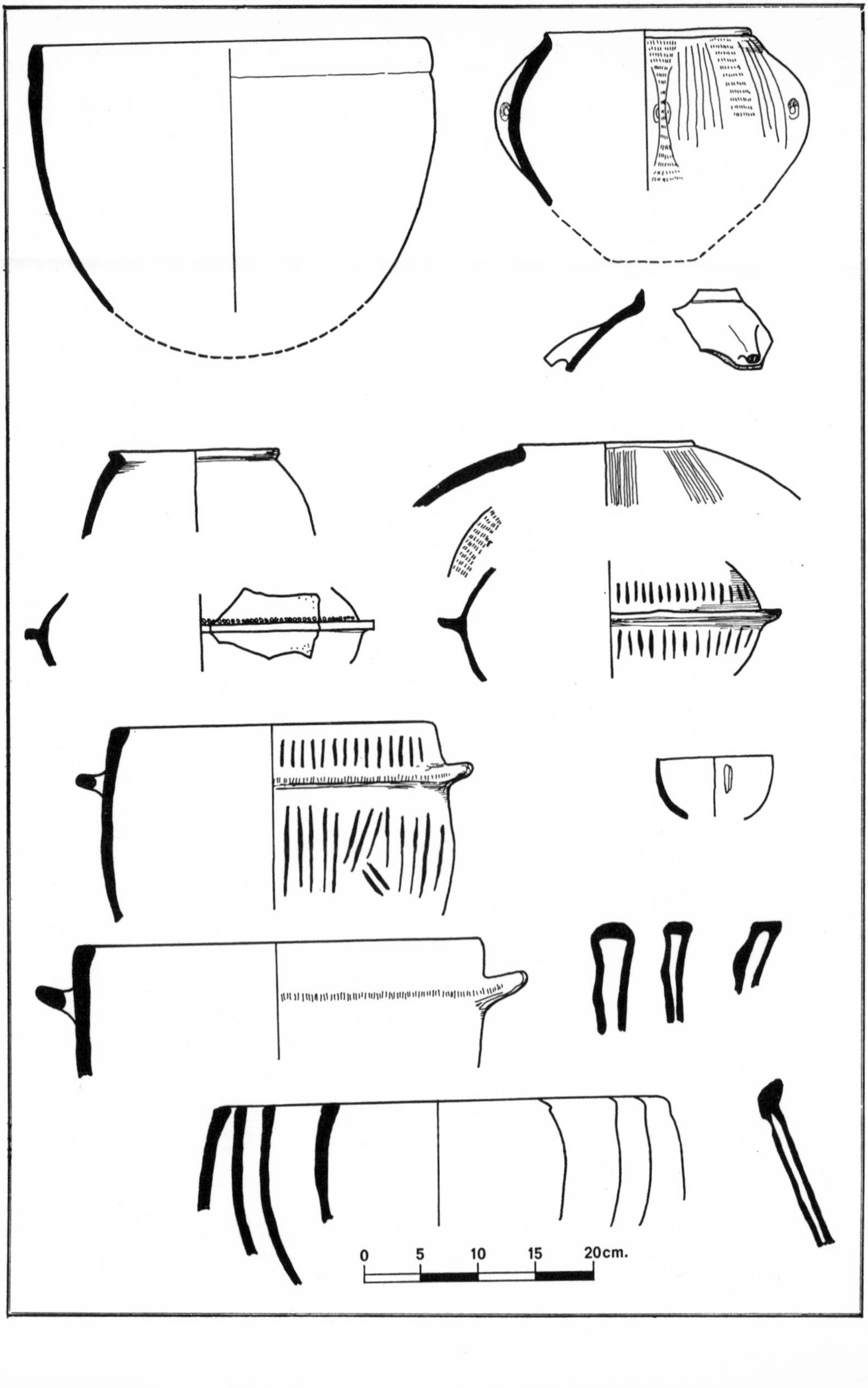
0 5 10 15 20cm.

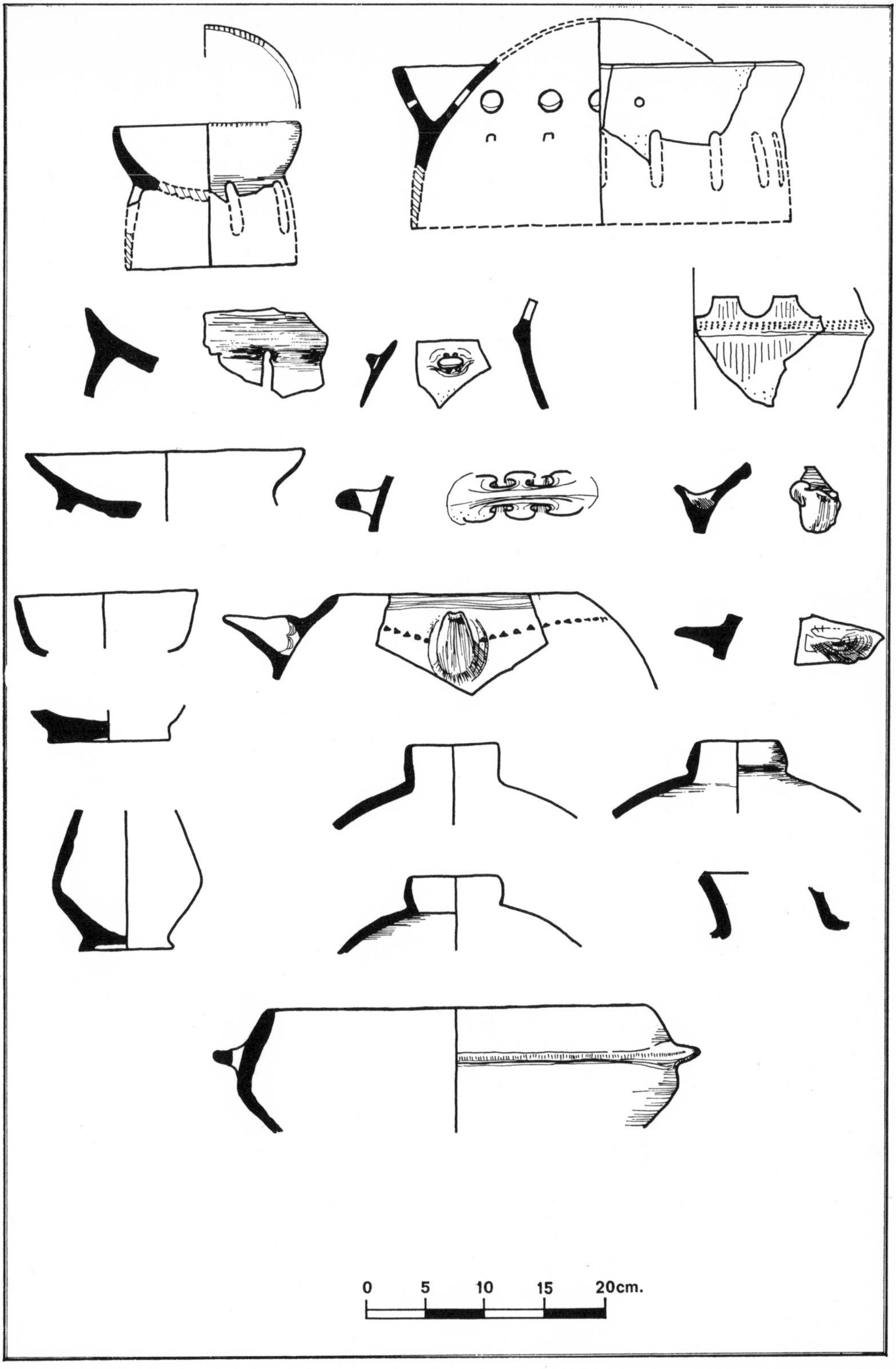
0 5 10 15 20cm.

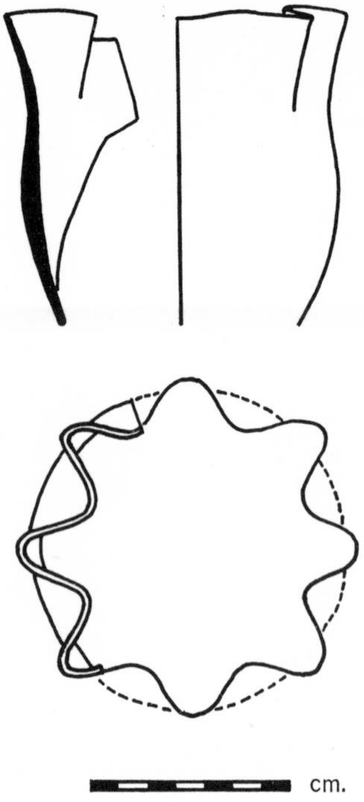

14 This is a fragment of an unglazed bowl with a wavy rim found at Al-Qaraw, the mound at Zingibar. It is very similar to the design of Qatabanian pottery bowls found in the Wadi Baihān and is the only example found outside that area. Whether it was imported or made locally is not known but it suggests a link between the two areas and that the site was in use before Islam

The Third Governorate

THE ABYAN AREA

A distance of about thirty miles along the beach east from Aden is the first sign of the Abyan district in the Fadhli State. This is the small delta area where the Wadi Bana runs into the sea and it marks the turn-off to the high level track leading into Abyan. At the agricultural village of Al-Kud, there is today a cotton ginnery which deals with all the cotton grown in the area.

The Wadi Bana was in ancient times a boundary between the states or kingdoms of Tubanaw (Laḥej) on the west and both Tafiḍ (Abyan) and Dahas (Yafaʿ) east of the Wadi Bana.

The Abyan area (mentioned in CIH 550) is the delta of the Wadi Bana and Wadi Hasan and was the caravan centre for the trade routes from the hinterland. According to Ptolemy's map in the second century AD, Abyan (Bana) was a link in the route between Shabwa and Aden. It is also probable that there was a port here in early times, for Pliny says that white myrrh from a single source was brought to Mesalum Oppidum for sale.[169]

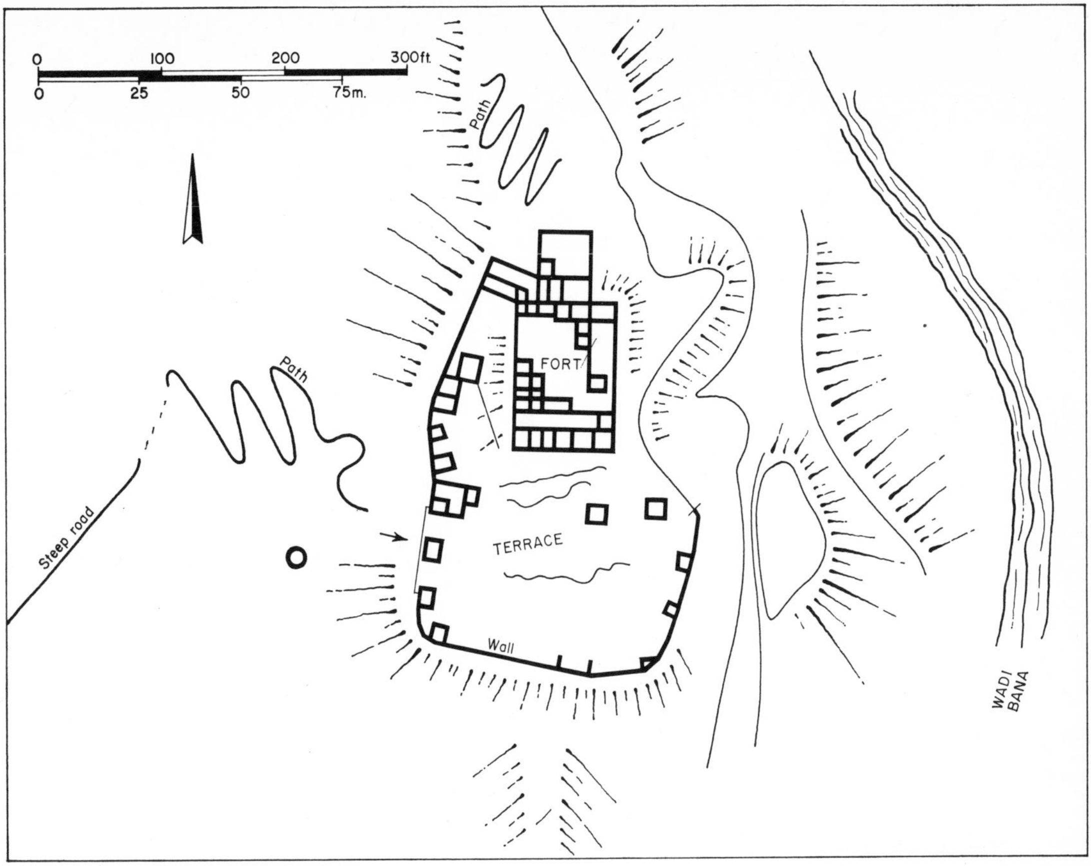

15 A survey drawing of the structure on the summit of Jabal Al-ʿAḥabuš showing the fort and perimeter walls of random rubble masonry. No dateable material has been found on this site. The position, overlooking the territory towards Aden, seems to have been in use as an observation post and fort from early times although, as with other hill forts, this structure was possibly altered when needed as a garrison during tribal disputes

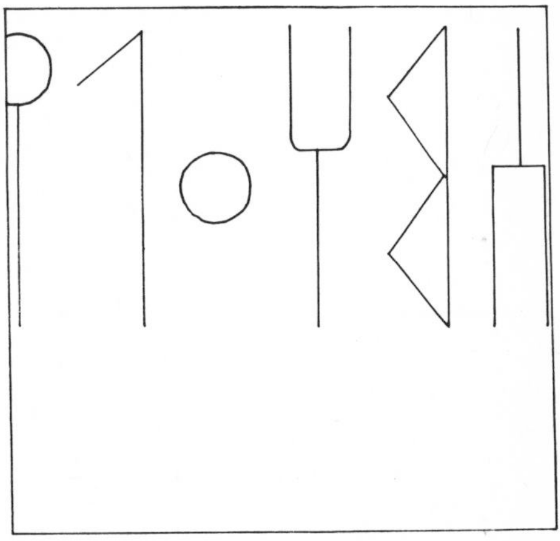

16 A drawing of the earlier inscribed limestone slab which was found built into the wall of a small house north of Jabal Al-ʿAḥabuš

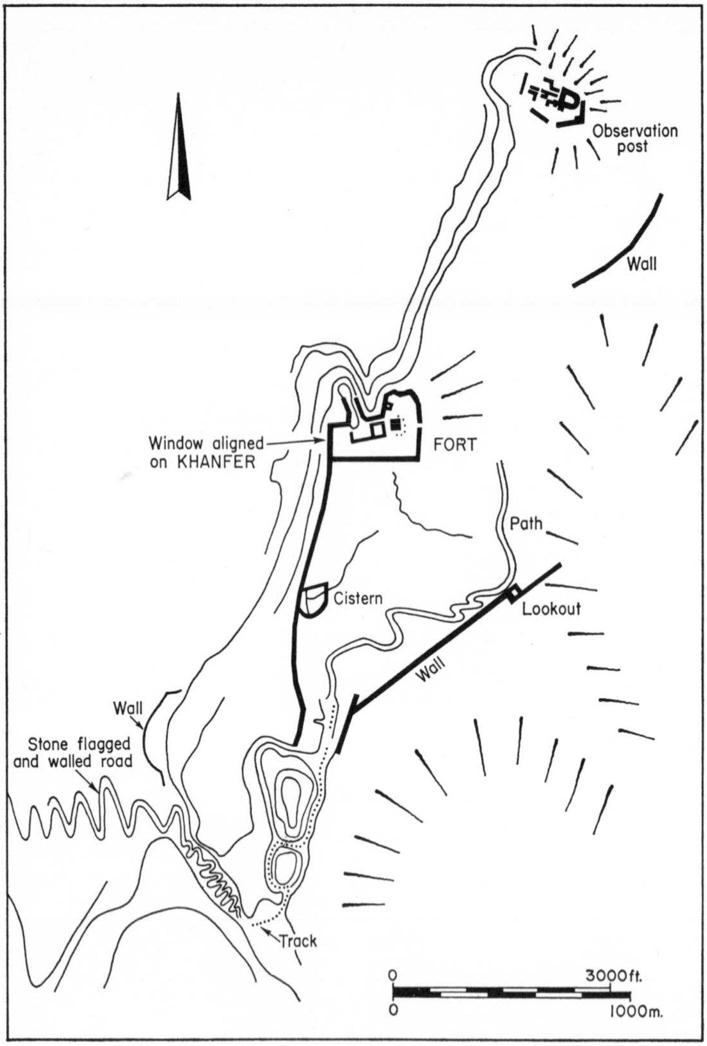

17 On the eastern side of the Abyan Plain the fortifications on the summit of Jabal Sarar dominate the territory eastwards and overlook the area to the south and west. Access along the paved and revetted path leads through a narrow cleft and walls built across the rocks make the site defensible. The actual fort structure has been repaired and altered but the main walls, nearly 6 ft thick, appear to be of medieval construction, although the site may have been in use from the period before Islam when Abyan was an Himyarite trading centre

According to Hamdani this area was Sarw Himyar and Pliny says *Homeritae Mesala oppido, Hamiroei.*[170] When Aden was destroyed, Mesalum was probably the port of Yafaʿ[171] which Ptolemy refers to as the outer land of myrrh. The medieval ruin-town of Al ʿAṣṣallāh between Zingibar and Shuqra indicates the probability of the port being somewhere in the vicinity, near the shelving beaches off the coast of Abyan. The actual coastline here may have been a mile or so further inland in the time of Ptolemy. Abyan was also well known as a port in the tenth century AD.

Plate 61

Zingibar is the modern capital town of the Fadhli State. Immediately north of Zingibar and to the north-east are sites with pottery fragments strewn over the surface. At the mound of Al-Qaraw findings indicate a pre-Islamic settlement. North of Zingibar is the prominent rock outcrop of Khanfer with the town of Gaʿar at its foot, the administrative centre of the lower Yafaʿ State. Just south of here, close to the present fort, *Fig. 14*

18 A sketch plan of the ruined fort and perimeter walling in dry stone random rubble on the summit of Jabal ʾAm-Mʿabeath on the southern side of the Wadi Yeramis. One of the main trade routes from Aden and Abyan passed through this area and forts, of which this is one of the largest, were built on high rock outcrops originally to protect the caravans from attacks as well as to guard tribal boundaries

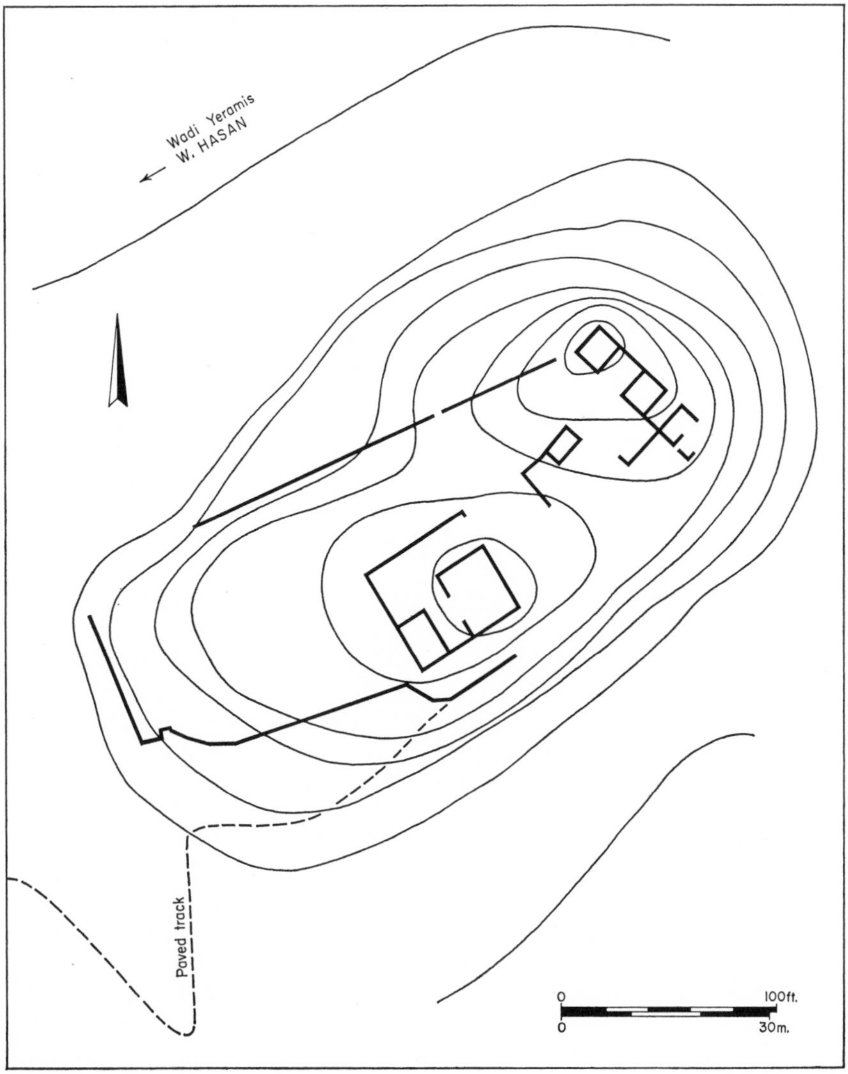

which replaces an earlier fort, is the site of the medieval town, probably once called Abyan.

Fig. 15

About four miles west of Gaʿar is the rock outcrop known as Am-Jabalain. Here there are pottery remains of medieval times. About two miles northward Jabal al-ʾAḥabuš, rising 800 feet above sea level, has a ruin-fort on the summit. At its foot near the bank of the Wadi Bana a formal pre-Islamic inscription was found.

Fig. 17
Plate 58

Some four miles east of Kh̲anfer, rising 1000 feet above sea level, is Jabal Sarar which has buildings, walls and water catchments and cisterns on the summit.

Bordering the wide Wadi Yeramis through which the Wadi Hasan flows on the north side of the Abyan area are ruined forts built on high rock outcrops. The most notable of these are at Jabal ʾAm-Mʿabeath and at Shariah. These forts must have ensured the protection of the trade-routes between the coast and the interior through the Audhilla plateau.

Fig. 18
Plates 59, 60

Abyan Inscriptions

Two recently found formal inscriptions refer to the Kingdom of Sabaʾ which seems to have been active in Abyan, and are most important because they cover a period from about the sixth century BC to about the fourth century AD. They are also especially interesting as they show a long connection with Marib, first as the capital of the traditional dynasty of Sabaʾ and later during the period of Sabaʾ and Dh̲u Raydān.

Fig. 16

The older of the two inscriptions is on a squared, smooth-faced limestone slab which once formed part of a long horizontal single-line inscription. Fortunately the word inscribed consists of the name of Smhʿly or Sumhuʿalay and the proportions of the letters show affinity with similar inscriptions at Marib. Smhʿly was the name of many Sabaean rulers at Marib. The name is mentioned as that of a ruler of Sabaʾ in the inscriptions on the wall of the Temple ʾAwwām. Sumhuʿalay is referred to as being the father of Mukarib Y adiʿ ʾil Dh̲arih in an inscription ascribed to the sixth century BC. There was also a Sumhuʿalay Dh̲arih in about 450 BC (*Jamme* 551) and an early Sumhuʿalay Yanuf in about 540 BC (*Jamme* 557).

Plate 57

The longer inscription has the decorative characters of the later Sabaean period and may be dated to about the fourth century AD. It mentions the name of the Royal Palace Slḥn at Marib and is dominated by a central decorative motif thought to represent the tree of life or ʾIlumquh.

This inscription reads:

2 and it afforded them health
3 and their enemy who (in the direction) of ...
4 and obedience of their souls ...
5 and for their house Salḥin
6 and malicious pleasure of their enemies
7 ... what in the years ...

THE AUDHILLA AREA

The picturesque administrative centre for the Audhali States is at Zara. Here the stone-built medieval and modern buildings blend with the rock outcrops on which they are built on the flat and level plain about 3000 feet above sea level. The market centre of the area is the mud-built town of Lodar, a mile or so eastwards from Zara.

North of the town of Zara and across the level ground there looms the great Khaur, a cliff-face over 3000 feet high, which extends like a dramatic back-drop for the plains which extend east to Dathina.

There are several paths or *aqabas* which wind their way to the top of the Khaur and to the plateau. The Aqaba Talh in the east leads towards the Aulaqi State, but the best known are the two passes of Thira, the modern motor track which is about seven miles long and the ancient partly paved track and also the Aqaba Fid Fada, which links the lower with the upper part of the State. The age of the old Thira Pass is not known, but it must have been in regular use by the inhabitants and by trade caravans for many hundreds of years. Plate 65

On the high plateau the administrative centre is the small town of Mukeiras, a town developed through its closeness to the North Yemen frontier and the consequent trade passing from Al-Baidha in the Yemen.

Mukeiras

The town of Mukeiras, which is the centre for the district of the same name, lies on the 7000-feet-high Audhilla Plateau some 150 miles north-east of Aden. Its position is also north of the ancient Thira Pass which winds up the scarp face of the Khaur from the plains below. It lies astride the ancient trade-route which linked the plain of Datinat (Dathina) and the people of Kaḥad with the people of Aud on the plateau. At one time the whole district was under the great trading-kingdom of ʾAusān, with its ancient capital at Miswara (RES 3945) or at Hajar am-Nab, both of which lie south of Baihān.

Am ʿAdiya, the main city-site in Mukeiras, was close to the southern trade-route to Timnaʿ and Marib, and its prosperity was linked with the caravans passing through with frankincense and myrrh from Somaliland although myrrh was also grown in Yafaʿ. Gold dust, timber and wild life from Africa were added to the exotic perfumes, spices and fine cloths and silks which had been carried on the ships of India.

Along this same route there are many pre-Islamic graffito inscriptions executed on flat rock surfaces, on the edge of the escarpment and at the summit of various passes used today by goat-herds showing how herdsmen long ago passed away their time.

A few miles from the head of the important Thira Pass is the Jabal Ḥakar, noted for an inscription about irrigation development and vineyards. Some four or five miles beyond the modern Mukeiras, and lying east of the old route, is the old settlement upon the Jabal Radaʿ. A short distance further on is a group of burial-cairns, their age confirmed by early South Arabian writings, and from this point one overlooks the plains of the northern Yemen.

Plates 67–69

On the eastern side and south of Am ʿAdiya towards the edge of the escarpment are several of the level, carefully paved areas which appear to have been community threshing yards. Further along the escarpment is a group of stones placed in front of a magnificent boulder, to which may be assigned a religious activity, although this is probably of a remote period.

Plate 77

The Wadi Raḥab is two or three hours' march further north-east passing Marawaha and here is a ruin-site first identified by an inscription brought to Mukeiras by Naib Jabal bin Hussain al-Audhali. The city was called Raḥab and an inscription on a wall also proclaims the fact as well as the royal name of Yadiʿʾab Dhubyan, ruler of Qataban in the fifth century BC, showing the extent of his dominion. North from Marawaha where there are graffito inscriptions is the fertile wadi of Shirjan, an area seemingly untouched by trade for the many inscriptions there all testify to the work carried out on dams and control of flood water for irrigation.

Fig. 19

Fig. 20

Archaeologically this is on many grounds a most interesting area; for the epigraphist and collector of graffiti, a paradise.

67–69 On the north side of the mountain area and Jabal Radaʿ there is a group of stone cairns near the road leading down to Al-Ma<u>dh</u>an. *Above*, a typical cairn in the group and nearby rocks, *below, left*, show modern grafitti drawings as well as rifle shooting prowess; *below, right*, a group of pre-Islamic graffiti

70 An aerial photograph of the extensive site of Am-ʿAdiya in the mountainous region east of Mukeiras. One of the main, paved entrances is seen in the left foreground, leading to the first terrace on the western side (left) of the central high rock around which the city spreads. The plains of the north Yemen are seen at the top left of the photograph

71 A small, walled enclosure, known as Building 'W' on the first terrace at Am-ʿAdiya. Here the finely cut ashlar masonry is of interest for the heavier courses are at the top and the lower three courses reduce proportionally in size and length. Excessive silt inside the structure suggests that the walling above the level seen was of mud brick construction

72, 73 Two inscribed stones from Am-ʿAdiya. *Above*, a finely carved, marble, libation altar stone. The references to the Qatabanian god ʿAMM have been chiselled out in the first and second line and also in the third line where it forms part of a personal name. This indicates its origin before the ascendancy of the Kingdom of Sabaʿ and D̲h̲u Raydān. *Below*, a limestone inscription with two types of inscribed letter and a third type in relief (Ry. 220, Ry. 221)

74, 75 Near the village of Qaraiyat Hussain in the Wadi Shirjān are the remains of a great dam wall. It is paved on the eastern side but the western side, between the centre rock and the west end, has broken away, much of the material probably being utilized in the walls of the village. On the northern face is a small, formal inscription, *below*, two further inscriptions relating to water conservation and irrigation

76 An example of the many graffiti inscriptions found on the smooth rock faces near the *husn*, or fort, on a promontory at the head of the steep *Aqabat* al-Ruqub above the wadi

77 Near the small village of <u>Dh</u>ul Faiyaq, south-west of Am-ʿAdiya, is a large paved area thought to be an ancient threshing floor. On the southern side are the remains of buildings and also several graffiti of the late Sabaean period

78 Part of a long alignment of flat stones, leading from a large, circular collapsed cairn, at <u>Gh</u>anam Al-Kuffār. Evidence from a nearby group (Site 2) suggests that small cairns placed in long rows were also constructed of flat stones

79, 80 The great wall of Qalat was built at the head of the Wadi Mabanaʿ by the Ḥaḍramis as a protection from the Ḥimyar between 24 BC and AD 80. It also controlled the pass into the Wadi Hajar and one of the routes to the capital of Shabwa. The inscription, *below*, is thought to be the oldest one known mentioning Ḥimyar. The dedicator, ŠKMM SLḤN, was in charge of the building of this wall and gate named Qalat for YSKRʾL YHRʿŠ bin ʾABYŠAʿ mkrb of Ḥaḍramaut

81, 82 *Husn* al-Ghurāb rises like an island above the isthmus in the Bay of Bīr ʿAli. The masonry remains of the port of Qanaʾ are on the level ground between the rock and the harbour, dominated by the great fortress rock. This is known as Mawyat (from inscription CIH 621) and has buildings and cisterns on its summit

83–85 The site of Mayfa'at (Naqb Al-Hajar). *Left*, the south section of the perimeter walls and its gate. An inscription *below, left* (RES 2640), on the inner face of the eastern bastion of this gateway describes the construction of the walls. The walls are of one stone thickness and their stability is maintained by a series of bastions. *Below*, the northern gateway has a masonry platform extending out into the wadi and also back into the fort. This may be the gateway referred to in the inscription of Qalat (RES 2687) as the gate YKN for the wall to the left (eastern) side shows signs of extensive repairs after a collapse

86 Al-Ḥauta is the mercantile centre of the Wahidi State. Traditionally goods unloaded at Bal-Haf, on the coast west of Bir ʿAli have always been passed through this entrepôt and it is a tradition that probably goes back to the incense caravans of antiquity. These followed the track from Bir ʿAli through Wadi Amaqīn and Wadi Jirdān to either Shabwa or west to Baihān and Marib

87 The 'Sultan's' Palace at ʿAzzān in the Wadi Mayfaʿah is a good example of the mud brick *husns* of this area. Ground floor rooms are usually store rooms, on the first floor are the reception rooms for male guests and the women's quarters are on the floor above with kitchens adjoining

88 The ruined, mud brick houses of the village of Qarn Bā Jaʿash are built on a group of boulders at the head of the Wadi Amaqīn. They are associated with caves and walled areas under the rock overhang on the slopes of the wadi and the houses were built high above the wadi level as a protection against attack

90 A water channel at the side of the wadi in the Wadi Amaqīn. It is cut through the edge of the conglomerate in order to maintain as straight and even gradient as possible. The water is often collected during the *sail* or flood from a higher level in the wadi and then distributed lower down it

▽

9 The fortress farmstead of Laʿabel do- inates the surrounding area from the high vel jol. The central *husn* is built of flat one slabs prised from the natural rock rface and the other buildings are of mud rick on boulders and rubble foundations. has been suggested that the building orig- ally belonged to the Himyar, which ould place their expansion further west an hitherto thought

91, 92 Painted drawings and graffiti inscriptions in the Thamudic type script on a large boulder in the Wadi Yaṯuf. This wadi is a tributary of the Wadi Jirdan. Presumably the numerous drawings and graffiti found here in dark and light red ochre are the work of shepherds and goatherds

93 In the Wadi Salmūn, on the west side of the Wadi Jirdān, a large boulder resting an another provides a covered resting place in the shade for travellers and goatherds. The rock ceiling of this shelter has been completely covered with drawings and graffiti similar to those in the Wadi Yaṯuf (*above*). Of particular interest here is the camel about to be attacked by a cat-like creature, probably a leopard as they are known to have lived in the mountains roundabout

94–96 Hajar al-Barīra is a masonry walled compound with two entrances near the small town of As-Shaqq in the Wadi Jirdān. It is partly heart-shape in plan but as the eastern edge has been destroyed the overall plan can only be surmised. There is, however, an apparent axis between the north entrance and the heart point. The western bastion of the north entrance is seen, *left*, and *below*, the south entrance from the exterior. Neither entrance shows any signs of gates having been hung in them

97 The main source of employment in the town of ʿAyadh is the mining of salt at Haid al-Milḥ. Present-day practice, following ancient tradition, of spreading the fresh silt over the fields is rapidly making them unusable because, as they rise in height, greater difficulties are encountered in raising the water to irrigate them

98 Al-Binā is a mud brick enclosure site similar to Hajar al-Barīra, and probably the forerunner to ʾAyadh. There is a single entrance on the south-east and on the south side the wall averages 12 ft in height from the native soil. A maximum height of 20 ft was measured and the maximum width of the wall, as seen here, is 13 ft

99, 100 The working of salt at Haid al-Milḥ is quite extensive. *Left*, a view down to the cave floor showing the pick marks on the roof and walls, evidence of several centuries of salt mining. The newly excavated salt is carried in bags out of the great cave, *below*, along a steep and narrow path from the cave floor some 80 ft below. It is then sorted out into small piles, the equivalent of a camel load, ready for transportation to Ataq, some twenty miles away

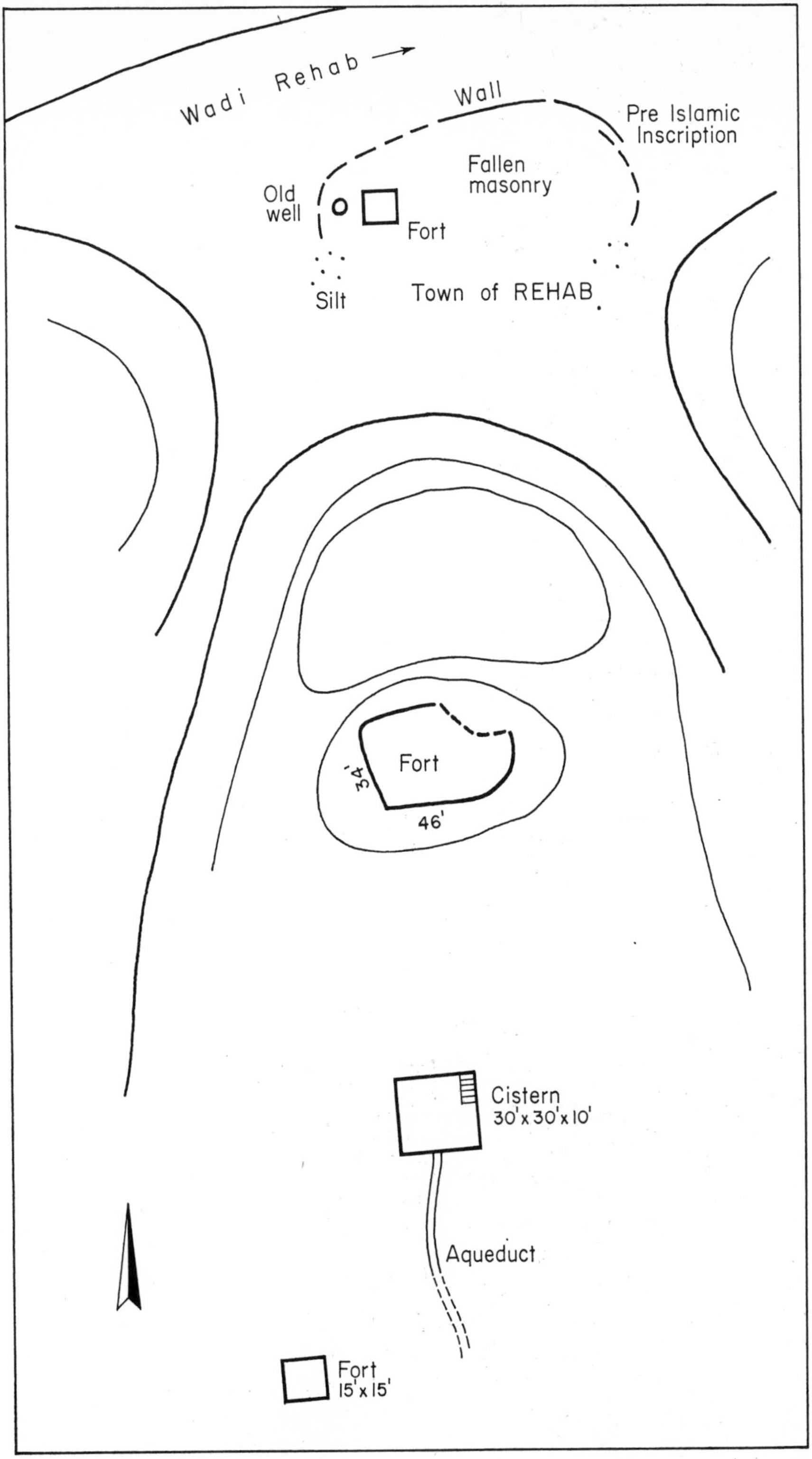

19 *A sketch plan of the site of Raḥab (Rehab) east of Mukeiras*

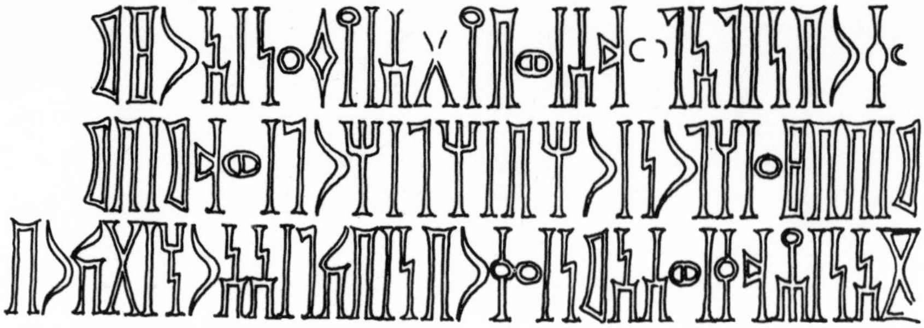

20 The inscribed stone from Raḥab which provided the first information and, from its provenance, the actual location of this Qatabanian city

Jabal Ḥakar

The Jabal Ḥakar lies close to the town of Aryab which is on the ancient trade-route north of the Thira Pass. It is a barren hill about 500 feet high which appears at first to be devoid of interest. However, built into the face of the old Sultan's house at Aryab is an inscription in early South Arabian, with finely cut and well-proportioned letters, which mentions Ḥakar and the construction of vineyards there. This is not altogether surprising as fruits are still grown in the Mukeiras district, but the cutting of an inscription gives a new importance to Jabal Ḥakar. Its eminence also makes it an important point on the trade-route, for from the top it is possible to see Mukeiras. It therefore provides a communication link from the south to the top of the Thira Pass; warnings of caravans up the pass or invasion from the north could then be signalled. It is also visible from as far away as Am ʿAdiya in the mountains to the east.

The whole of the slopes of the hill are strewn with boulders and partly cut blocks of stone. Climbing from the Aryab side is a paved and stepped stairway leading first to a level area which has a small portion of thick masonry walled revetment. From this level another flight of steps leads to the actual top and into a small rectangular building which has been lined with a thick lime plaster, coved at the corners, although little stonework remains above ground level. From this building there are various walls and steps on to a semicircular wall of which portions remain at a lower level. From here are more stone steps and walling leading down to the first terrace level.

At the northern end of this terrace is the water catchment, cut into the rock and guided to a small semicircular plaster-lined tank built in the side of the rock with masonry walling on the outer face. From this tank the overflow continues down to a large rectangular tank cut into the rock with plaster-lined masonry walls and stone steps. Nearby are more ruins and portions of walling and masonry steps and the area appears strewn with the ruins of small buildings; it may have possibly been the original town of Ḥakar, for the inscription was found nearby. Surprisingly there are no traces of terracing for viticulture but erosion and the collapse of retaining walls could account for this on the slopes of the hill. No pottery sherds at all were found.

The remains on the top of Jabal Ḥakar were once a fort, which was probably in use until medieval times. A small Arabic inscription crudely incised on a stone, probably a burial memorial, was found near the lower first) terrace. There are no local legends about the hill. Nevertheless Ḥakar clearly was a place of importance on the trade-route in ancient times; a centre of a wine-growing district with citrus groves and cereal crops.

The earliest visitors to see the Ḥakar inscription appear to have been L. Kirwan and B.J. Hartley who was then Director of Agriculture. The inscription was photographed by them before it was used as building material, and they were instrumental in its preservation. This inscription has been alluded to by A. Jamme,[172] mentioned by Hermann von Wissmann and Maria Höfner[173] and published by A.F.L. Beeston.[174]

Unfortunately there were omissions in the copy of the text published and the inscription is now made to read:

HWFʿM of the clan ʿRLN has completed and planted the
vineyard D̲ʾLN which is in the neighbourhood of the
town of ḤAKAR and his irri
gation system TGYB for himself and his clansmen, the
lords of their houses with the help of their Sun
Goddess and the irrigation deity (Water God)

Jabal Radaʿ

In the mountain range some six miles north of Mukeiras lies a strange ruin-field. A large part of the journey has to be on foot, and the rocks have eroded into a fantasy of shapes. It is an impressive site, and there is an air of entering a religious place. On the approach road are many stones Plate 66 standing about three feet above ground level, with many small pebbles carefully placed on top, a local custom to please the local saint and to keep the devils away.

The entrance leads to a large, level open area covered with fine grass and from this place lead two distinct valleys, one on the north which encloses the ruins, while the other, a narrow cutting, continues to an eminence where there is an Islamic cemetery, with the saint's tomb in the centre. This is the focus of an annual *ziara* for the people of the Mukeiras district.

Across the rocks the stone ruins are strewn over the northern slopes, with portions of walls still standing. The central area is also a ruin-field of scattered, random-sized, uncut masonry and there is an entrance-gate at the eastern end, leading to a wadi, while at the western end the site opens out, with a curved line of boulders obviously erected to form a boundary.

There are two masonry tanks on the northern face of the main rocks against which the town is built. These are semicircular and of roughly coursed masonry lined with plaster, built against the rock, the smooth areas of which form a catchment for the water, for it is clearly possible for the tanks to fill at this altitude.

No pottery of significance was found, and the few fragments available indicate a medieval date.

The interesting feature of the site was the alignment of small dolmen-like stones in two rows down the centre of the site, leading to the eastern end where a large and nearly circular area was bounded by a peristalith of individual stones of about two or three feet in height. On the south-west corner of this area stood a large stone, in which a circular font-like bowl has been cut or worn by weathering. It is likely that the Islamic graveyard was associated with the ruins, when the town was inhabited after the coming of Islam.

Probably before this the place was already inhabited and well known, and the discovery of a small inscription in early South Arabian built reversed into a wall confirms the use of the site before Islam and its subsequent habitation after reconstruction.

At some date, this mountainous place became a religious centre, with a saint's tomb supplanting the earlier religious use associated with the place.

Am ʿAdiya

This is a region of barren rocks and hills where boulders have weathered into shapes which are a characteristic of the landscape interlaced with narrow and fertile wadis often terraced to hold the precious soil. Am ʿAdiya is in the district of Karish which lies about eight miles or so east of Mukeiras.[175]

The site is situated in the saddle of a granite outcrop which rises from a level wadi bed on the west and is bordered by small terraced wadis on each side to the north and south. It is possible to enter the site from all sides, and there are indications of paving-stones on several paths. Apart from stairs in the north wall there appear to be three main entrances, and one at the south-west corner appears to be pre-eminent. It has a broad paved road averaging 12 feet wide which curves in a dog-leg from the wadi bed and up through a cleft in the rock. The slabs at the lower end are large, rough-hewn, blue-black basalt, but where the ground levels out the paving is of smaller blocks of granite. *Fig. 21* Plate 70

About half-way along this road is a large rock which may have rolled from elsewhere; on it is a graffito, part of which mentions Mʿdy – probably the name of the city.

Am ʿAdiya does not seem to have been protected, except by its position in the mountainous country, nor did it need defending, probably relying on its sanctity as a religious centre.

The entrance brings the visitor to the south end of the lower terrace, and close to the fine, well-cut, granite masonry walls of the building known as the House of Lahayʿat, where there is an inscription. The inscription (ʿAdiya 1 = RES 4332) reads: ʻLHYʿT, the son of ṢWBN, has constructed and put in the foundations and completed from bottom to top his house ŠBʿN by ʿMM and ʾNBY and by ḎT ḤMYM ʿṮTR YGL and for his brothers and his children.'

Continuing along the terrace one encounters another building (Building W) with walls constructed up to approximately four feet high, of well-cut masonry with a central entrance. Plate 71

The entrance at the House of Lahayʿat leads to a field of scattered rough-hewn and cut stones with here and there the foundations of buildings visible. This road or path leads to a higher level and continues on a fairly straight alignment between tumbled masonry on the slopes of the rock on the south and the slope of the ground rising on the north, called

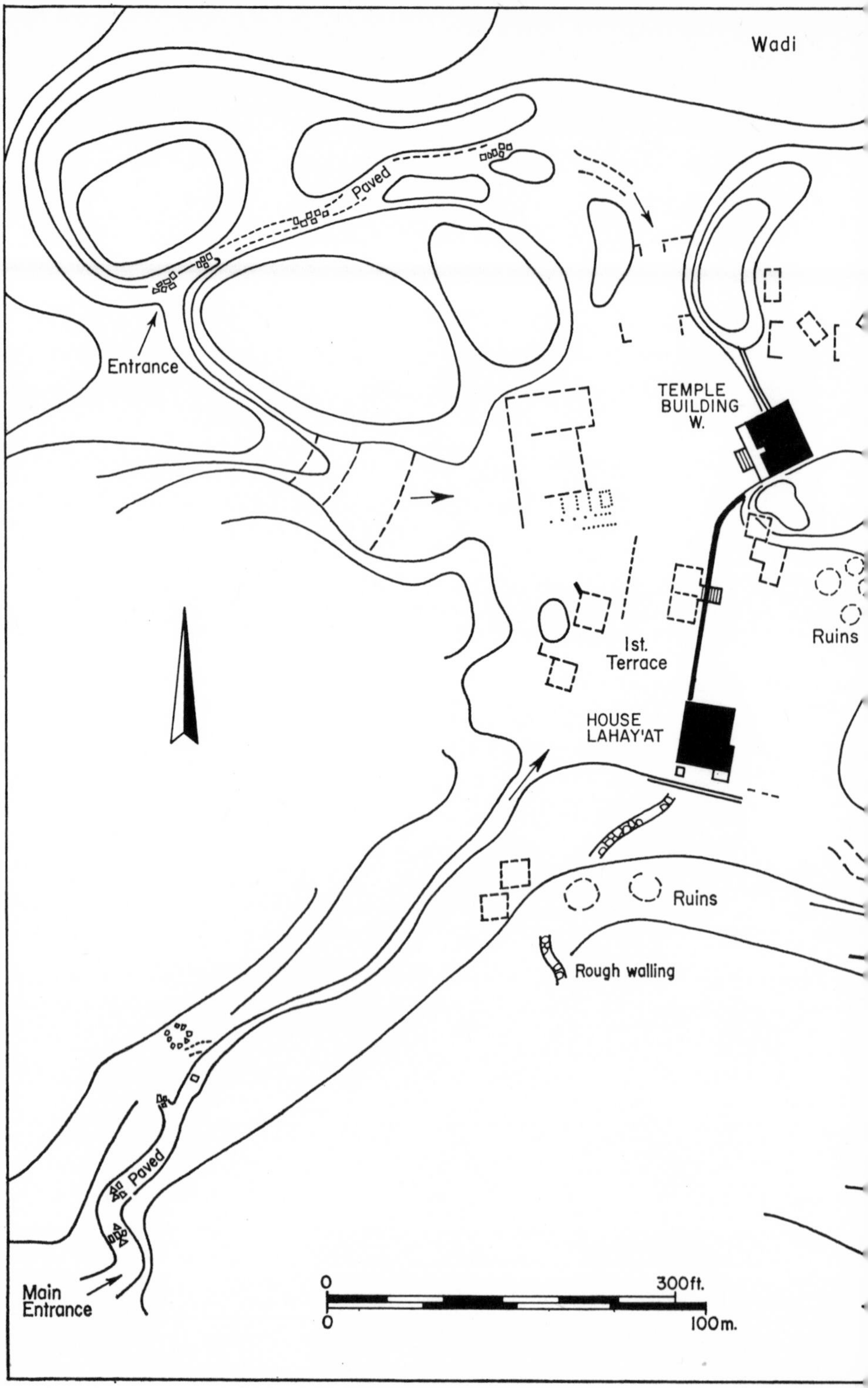
Wadi
Paved
Entrance
TEMPLE
BUILDING
W.
Ruins
1st.
Terrace
HOUSE
LAHAY'AT
Ruins
Rough walling
Paved
Main
Entrance
0
300ft.
0
100m.

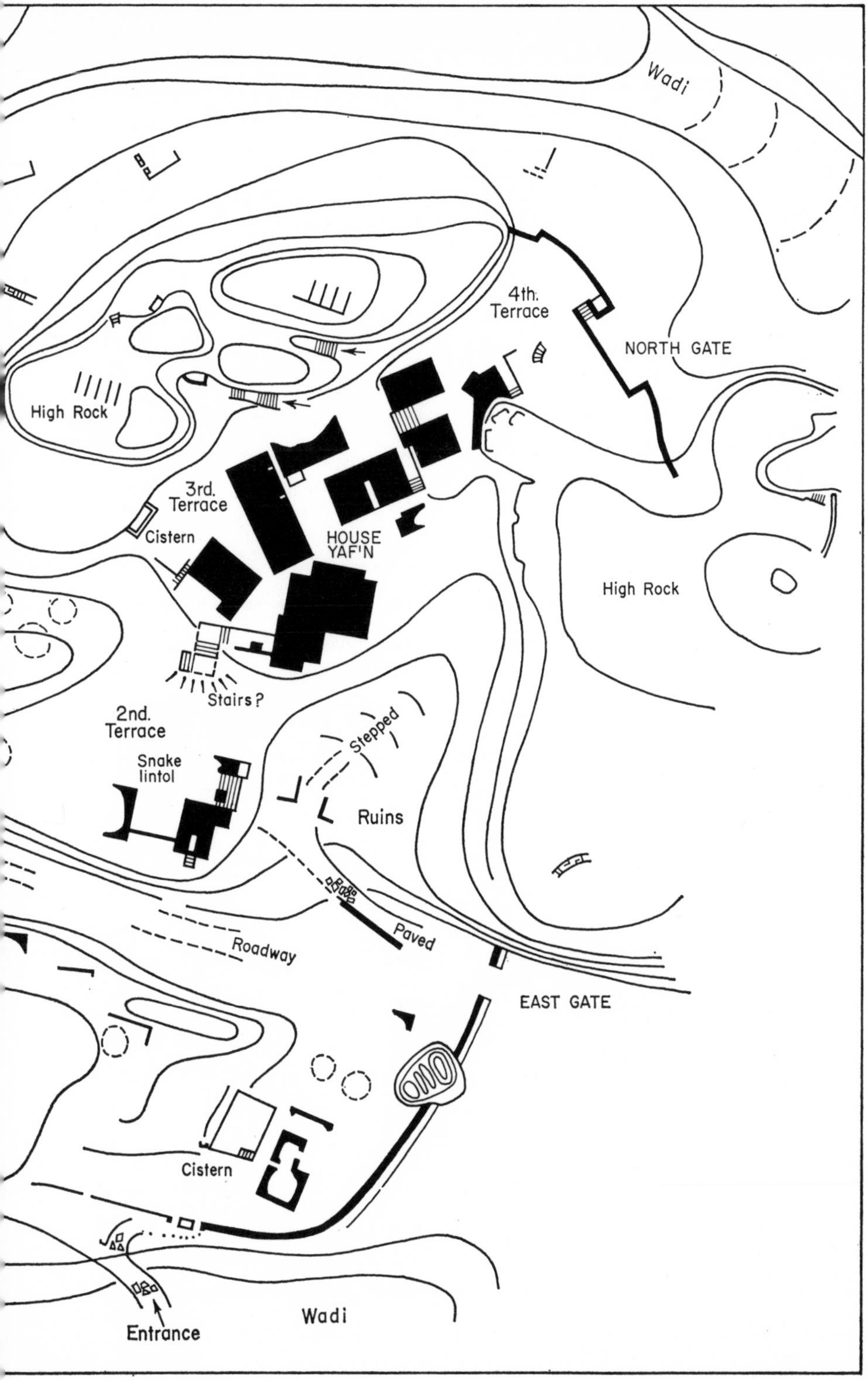

21 *A survey drawing of the site of Am-ʿAdiya east of Mukeiras*

the second terrace. The rock on the south side gradually slopes down to form a water-catchment for a large rectangular-walled and plaster-lined cistern which has steps leading into it and drainage sluices. Nearby is the East Gate and from here a paved road is discernible which connects this level to a building on the second terrace, the House of the Snake from a pair of antithetical snakes carved on a stone lintel, and also continues to a third terrace.

Here is a complex of buildings, most of which are of dressed well-cut masonry. The planning suggests the imposition of a geometric layout upon an earlier set of buildings. The ground level is not always apparent, owing to silting. Of the well-cut masonry lying about, there is clearly not enough cut stone to have constructed high walls. However, the large amounts of roughly cut stone, suitable for random rubble walling above the lower ashlar, could have been laid in a mud mortar and plastered.

The House Yafʿan is a large rectangular building of well-cut masonry walling. This building has two large stones built into the east wall, one with Waddʾab and the other with Yafʿan in letters some fifteen inches high. This is a well-known 'magical' formula for invoking the protection of the gods for the building and people associated with it. Literally it is Wadd, the name given to the moon-god, the father of Yafʿan.

The north wall of the site is well constructed though damaged and rebuilt, and has a stepped gateway to the north wadi. Beyond are remains of well-built stone walls for small and probably domestic buildings.

From the top terrace the remains of a wide flight of stairs lead through a cutting up to the top of the central (west) rock. Here on the summit are the remains of a large building of well-cut masonry.

Surprisingly, the survey showed a lack of potsherds, such as are usually strewn over the sites. The few sherds found were portions of *zeirs* or bowls and a jar, and the base of a pot. They were all of hard, well-fired mioaceous clay, probably imported from another district. Colours are grey core with surfaces of pink-brown slip. Rims appear to have been wheel-finished, with decoration incised below the rim and horizontally burnished internally. The ware is heavy and coarse.

It is, of course, not definitely known if Am ʿAdiya was a religious centre but it is of interest that locally it is still known as a place where idols were worshipped and it is significant that the site is nowhere used today as a place of habitation. On the other hand, this area was the scene of intertribal warfare and for a long time was disputed territory, a fact which itself did not encourage settlement there.

The Wadi Shirjān

The Wadi Shirjān[176] lies about ten miles beyond the Jabal ʿAdiya, east of Mukeiras. After travelling along a winding track into the Wadi Nʿabata and up the steep side of the northern ridge of Jabal Jurundish, it is pleasant to look down upon the attractive green valley of the wadi and to see the Qariyat al-Hussain Muhammad, a village surrounded by level fields of crops, huddled opposite on the lower slopes of Jabal Salima. The track then descends the south-west face of Jabal Jurundish and dips down to the northern end of the valley where the flood channel sweeps from the south in a wide curve and passes through the cultivation in front of the village which is situated in the centre of the valley. Past the village, the *Fig. 22*

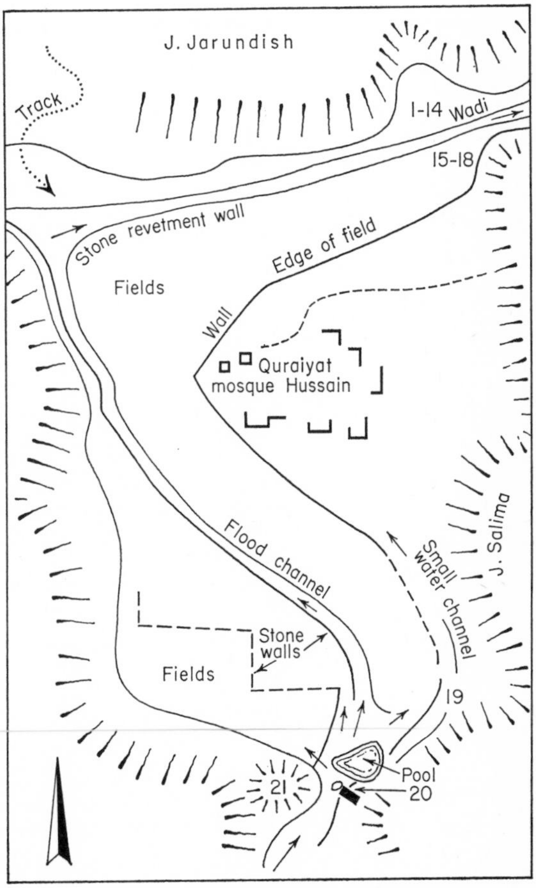

22 Sketch map of the Wadi Shirjān showing the location of the village of Quraiyat al-Hussain Muhammed and the positions of the groups of inscriptions and the remaining portion of the dam. The numbers refer to the texts which have been recorded, some of which describe the construction of irrigation works

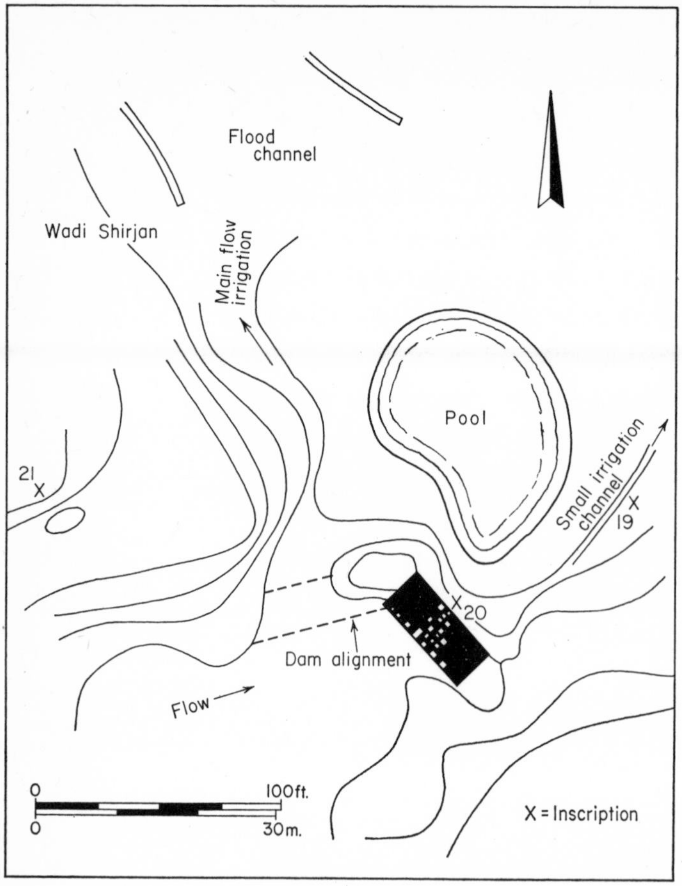

23 Sketch plan of the stone faced and paved dam wall of the Wadi Shirjān. Cement found on the centre rock and on the west rock provides evidence of the position of the missing section of the wall

wadi narrows at its most southerly point and it is here that the remains *Fig. 23* of an ancient stone dam are to be found. The dam was built between two rocky outcrops, its walls abutting on a small rock in the centre of the channel to form a 'V'. The old masonry walling with a paved surface on the eastern side still stands but no trace remains of the west wall which probably contained a sluice gate, thus weakening the structure which would have been under great pressure from the flood-waters. A large pool at the foot of the dam is evidence of the force of water passing through during the *sail* period. Beyond the pool, the main flood channel Plate 74 flows down the west side of the valley and an irrigation channel leads to the village on the east.

No less than twenty-one inscriptions have so far been discovered in the Wadi Shirjān and these fall roughly into two groups; north of the village and in the vicinity of the dam in the south. According to these inscriptions, the Wadi Shirjān was known by that name in ancient times. The exaggerated characteristics of the letters are typical of the late Sabaean period which extended as late as the sixth to seventh centuries AD. Of particular interest are the large well-designed monograms of the second group which appear to be variations on the same name, that of 'Iltubba 'Al-šar, son of Marthad'iln 'Ašwa', who built the dam. The inscriptions contain information about building works connected with the conservation of water and irrigation and they describe the families concerned with the construction and mention names of neighbouring tribes. *Fig. 24*

Two articles have already been published about the inscriptions in the Wadi Shirjān. The first, in 1951, by Professor A. Jamme[177] refers to four inscriptions executed in the ornate fashion of the late Sabaean era which he found on Jabal Maghaniymah, the hill rising behind the dam. The second, by Mahmud 'Ali Ghūl,[178] mentions further inscriptions which have been recorded, of which one relates to building-work carried out and reads: Plate 75

1 HWF'M 'WLṬ NḤLN, with his [two] sons H
2 L'W and ḤṬBM, [the servants] of the qayl, directed the dressing of the rock [or stones]

24 A drawing of the inscription No. 21, which overlooks the dam in the Wadi Shirjān. The names of the dam builders are repeated in the ornate monograms

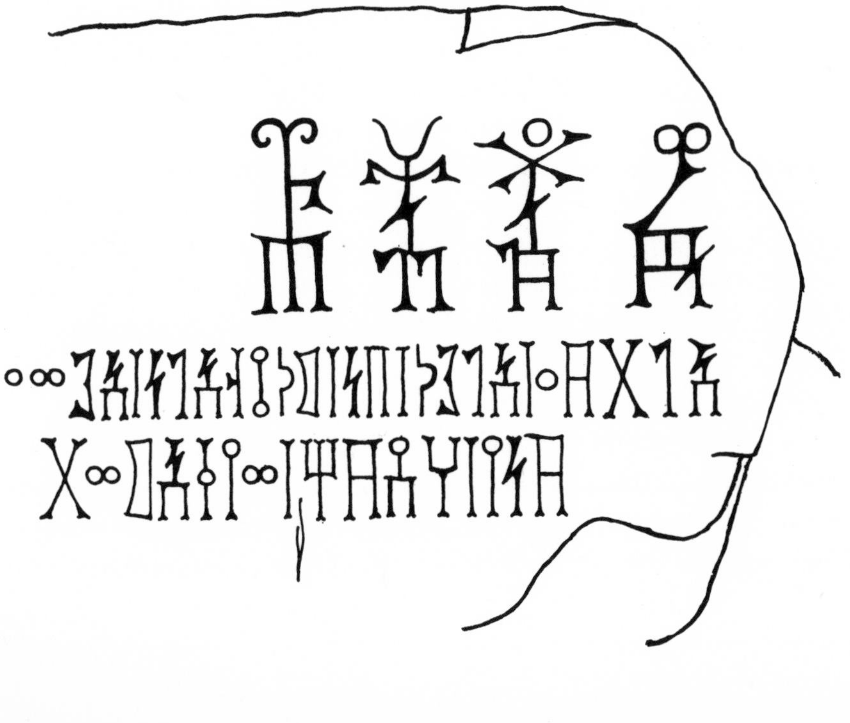

3 and the building and the plastering and [the construction of] the stepped interior facing and supervised
4 his [contingent of] helpers in [the work on] this water-reservoir BN' in accord-
5 ance with what ordered him his lords Ba-
6 nu Haṣbaḥ and he completed the work.

THE NORTHERN INSCRIPTIONS

The flood channel, which runs down the west side of the valley, turns east after passing through the fields in front of the Qariyat al-Hussain Muhammad and flows past the foot of Jabal Jurundish. Here, the level ground cultivated by the villagers is higher than the floor of the water course by about five or six feet and it is protected by rubble-retaining walls. Thirteen inscriptions are located on the slopes of Jabal Jurundish at this point (Nos 1–13), and immediately facing them, on the vertical rock face forming the *sail* passage or *nuqb*, are five more inscriptions (Nos 14–18) although the last three of these are badly defaced. It is probable that more inscriptions will emerge on this side of the channel if a thorough examination can be made. One name recurs in this group of inscriptions, that of Hwf ʿm whose family was probably closely connected with the irrigation schemes.

It is possible that some form of water control once existed at this spot, where the channel is sufficiently narrow to dam, and this argument is supported by the discovery of a small piece of cement clinging to the rock face of the north bank. Probably the bed of the flood channel was once at a lower level than it is today and the ground formerly irrigated has since silted up, but it is difficult to see the necessity for a flood gate here when the impetus of the water flowing from the south dam would have been lost and the water prevented from flowing on to more distant fields. Furthermore, the inscriptions carved in the vertical rock face of the south bank would have been partially submerged.

THE SOUTHERN INSCRIPTIONS

A spring rising on the slopes of Jabal Maghaniymah and seasonally reinforced by rain water is the source of the water supply into Wadi Shirjān. The watercourse enters the valley through a narrow defile at the southern end where the dam was constructed in ancient times. Only three inscriptions have been found in this group so far: one (No. 20) is built into the outer face of the dam wall itself, the second (No. 21), which contains four monograms, is on the west rock outcrop facing the dam and overlooking the whole area and the third (No. 19), containing three monograms, is carved into the granite rock face of Jabal Salima, north-east of the dam, but the final lines of this inscription disappear beneath the waters of the irrigation channel leading into the village.

Ghanam al-Kuffār, in the Wadi Aḥwar

Aḥwar is the capital of the Lower Aulaqi state, and its impressive mud-brick houses spread over a wide area at the broadening of the Wadi. It is situated some miles inland, for the coastal area is dangerous and unusable for trade craft because of rock and lava outcrops. Entry by road from Shuqrā is over a vast lava field exuded from geologically recent volcanos.

Many places are marked on the maps with the three or four dots indicating sites of ruins. Ghanam al-Kuffār[179] was such a site and, apart from an approximate knowledge of its location, no description has been previously available. This site is immediately south of the junction of the Wadi al-Jaḥr with its lava field and the Wadi Kaiqah, where it widens out south and eastwards and is renamed Wadi Aḥwar. There are two sites a mile apart about twenty miles along the track to al-Mahfidh. They consist of alignments of flat stones or slabs set in varying directions,

25 *The stone alignments and cairns of Ghanam al-Kuffār. The northern group, site 1*

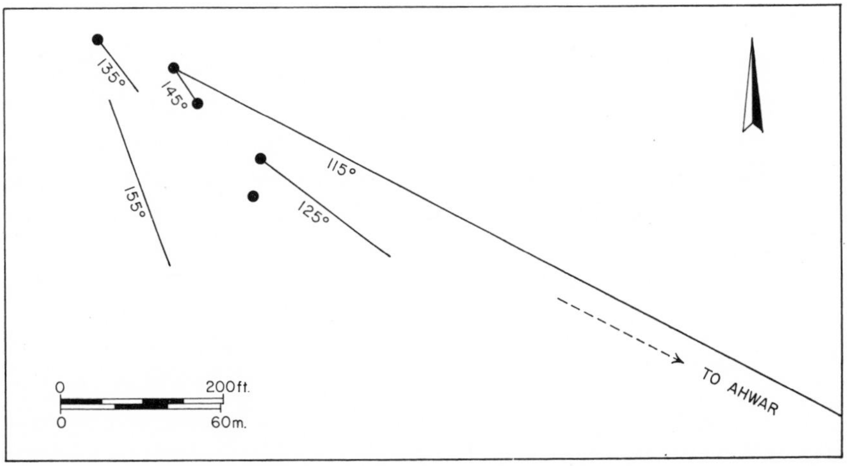

usually leading from cairns and circular areas strewn with flat limestone slabs.

Fig. 25

Site No. 1 (Northern). The flat stones appear to be merely laid on the surface of the ground, which here is a raised table of pebble conglomerate above the level of the main Wadi. The alignments of stone leading from the circular areas are unmistakable, and these are generally about six feet wide, although the longest line of about 935 feet is about 10 feet wide. The light mounds which form the circles of stones may have been some form of burial cairns. The various alignments are on bearings which vary between 115° to 155°, each with a difference of about 5 degrees.

Plate 78

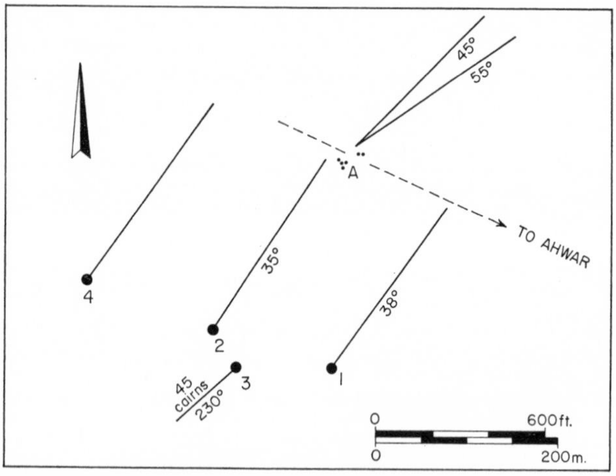

26 The southern group, site 2, Ghanam al-Kuffār

Fig. 26

Site No. 2 (Southern). Here also there is a system of cairns with stone alignments although not in the same radiating pattern.

Fig. 27

No. 1 cairn has a peristalith of six vertical slabs *in situ*, originally nine, on the perimeter. This cairn, placed on a slight mound, is 6 feet 7 inches in diameter and the tallest vertical slab is 4 feet 4 inches high. On the interior surface of one slab is a pecked graffito of a camel and a rider with an Himyaritic 'W' character, probably a tribal *wasm* over the hind-quarters of the camel.

The alignment of stones from this cairn is on a bearing of 38°. Nearly parallel is a cairn (no. 2) of a different construction; it consists of a circle

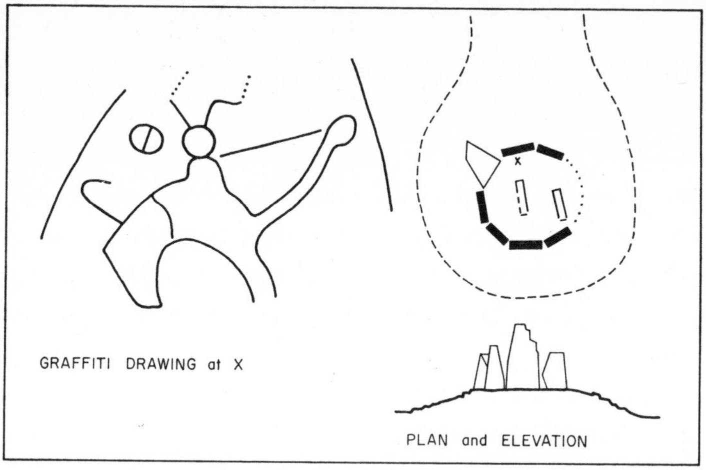

27 Plan and elevation of the cairn of vertical slabs with the graffiti drawing inscribed on the inner face of an in situ *slab at site 2, Ghanam al-Kuffār*

12 feet in diameter and about two feet high of five courses of horizontal stone slabs. The alignment of stones on a bearing of 35° consists of small 18–24 inch high piles of stones.

Lying face-downwards between Cairns 1 and 2 a limestone slab 13 inches long was found. It bears a pecked graffito inscription of three lines; this inscription, now in the Aden Museum, indicates that the site was pre-Islamic. *Fig. 28*

Cairn 3 is similar to cairn 2 but it is ten feet in diameter and approximately two feet high with slabs of masonry laid dry. The total length of

28 The inscribed stone found on site 2, Ghanam al-Kuffār

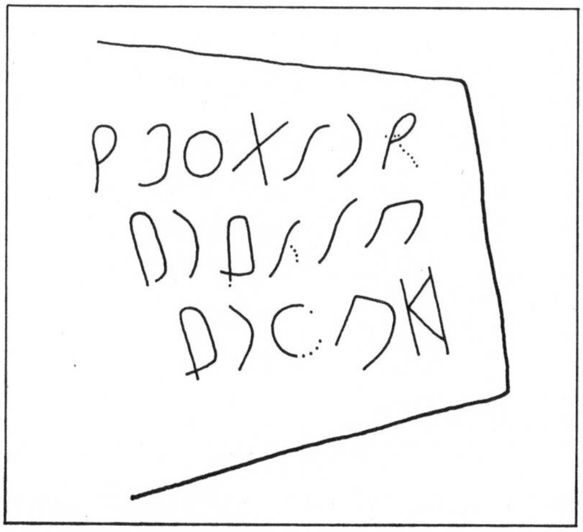

the alignment is about 300 feet and along it there are forty-five piles of stones which consist of a central vertical stone two to three feet high surrounded by other small stones. The appearance and construction of this cairn and the stones on its alignment probably show the original pattern of the other cairns.

Circular cairns with alignments of smaller cairns or groups of stones are to be found in other parts of Southern Arabia. They are seen on the hills in the Wadi ʿIrma and on the ridges of hills and rock outcrops around Al-ʿAbr. These cairns are usually placed so that they are clearly visible against the skyline to any traveller in the wadi, but at Gh̲anam al-Kuffār they are not built in this manner.

The geometric layout of the alignments of the small cairns is unusual, and one is led to believe that the angles of the lines of stones may be of astronomical significance, as has sometimes been ascribed to megalithic structures of Europe.

Gh̲anam al-Kuffār means 'Goats of the Unbelievers'. 'Unbelievers' once referred to all who were not followers of Islam and the graves here could be of Christian Abyssinians, or they may be of early Southern Arabians before Islam.

The Fourth Governorate

THE WĀḤIDI AREA OF WADI MAIFAʿAH

The Wadi Maifaʿah flows south-east from the mountains towards the sea and changes from a narrow pebbled wadi walled by high rock to a broad, level, sandy mouth as it reaches the coast.

The main trade route in ancient times from the port of Qana' on the coast passed along this great wadi towards Mayfaʿat, the ancient capital of Lower Ḥaḍramaut, situated about half-way along the wadi near the town of ʿAzzān. Plate 87

Plate 79 The wall and gate of Qalat is on a precipitous ledge; guarding a pass in the mountains north of Qana', it was built to control trade through Ḥaḍramaut when the port was captured by the Himyar.

The Wall of Qalat

This ancient wall and gateway to the Ḥaḍramaut lies north of the small fishing village of Jilʿah, which is close to Bal Haf, the main port for the

Wahidi State. Von Wrede in 1843 referred to it as Obne and early visitors knew the site as Libna; but Al-Mabna' is the correct name.

The site was visited by the Austrian South Arabian Expedition and later in 1938 by the Ingrams on their visit to Sidara. It was subsequently examined by the present writer in 1965.

My guide, Shaikh Muhammed Al-Qurra, whose tribal name Shaikh ba Suwait is reflected in the name of the mountain clan Shaikhain, in the location of the Wadi Al-Mabna', led along a dry wadi and through mountain flood-beds strewn with large boulders. A great portion of the journey at the summit has to be achieved on foot, and it is understandable why so few have visited this lonely place high in the mountains. The site is a remarkable one, for not only is there a massive wall and gateway, but alternative lines of approach were carefully walled off, leaving only one possible way of entry. The purpose of the wall is clearly described in the text of the inscription on the south-east bastion. This was to protect the Hajr district of Ḥaḍramaut against the Himyar in the south, for it seems that at the time of its construction the Himyar were in occupation of the port of Qana' which they had captured from Ḥaḍramaut. The Himyar probably controlled the whole coastal region during the late first century BC to the late first century AD. This is according to the palaeography of an inscription (known as RES 2687) which is probably the earliest one to mention the expanding Kingdom of Himyar. It is interesting to note that Von Wrede, the first to record the text, also inscribed his name on the corner of the inscription. The text says that: Plate 80

ŠKMm SLḤN son of RḌWN led for his master YSKR'L YHRʿŠ son of 'BYSʿ, mkrb of ḤḌRMT, when there commanded him his two masters HYSʿ'L ʿLHN son of BN'L and DWSm MSBḌ son of ẒRB:

to build the pass QLT and the passes which separate the two hills from the sea, in front with rough stone and hewn stone, and also to construct the wall of QLT and the pass, when they defended themselves against ḤMYRm. And he followed HYSʿ'L and DWSm their and relatives amongst the fathers of ḤḌRMT. And he seized MYFʿT and the narrows in battle, and built and levelled the passes of the narrows, and built the wall and the two towers YḎ'N and YḎT'N and the gate YKN with squared stones, and a barrier and a refuge ... and the gateways from the ground to the top with sun-dried bricks: in the (year) of YŠRḤ'L ḏʿḎḎm, the second, in three months and with 200 men in massive construction.

It is significant that the inscription records the military position and reconstruction of the defences at Mayfaʿat.

The wall of Qalat is constructed of long, well-cut limestone blocks with hammer-dressed face, laid dry and well bonded. A feature is the use of long (average thirty inches) horizontal quoins alternating with courses of headers in the main gateway. Its total length is approximately 540 feet extending from the ridge of the wadi cliff to the rising mountainside and it averages fifteen feet in height. The entrance is approximately in the centre, and although there is a reveal or recess within the entrance there are no indications of supports or hangers for gates.

Qanaʾ

Fig. 29
Plates 81, 82

Dominating the sandy shore at Bir ʿAli rises the black volcanic rock of Husn al-Ghurāb. The white sands shimmering at its foot serve to emphasize the black lava, which now spreads across the ground between the rock and the sea.

Husn al-Ghurāb means the Fortress of the Crows, but its ancient name was ʿUrr Mawiyat, the fortress and lookout guarding the port and trading city of Qanaʾ. Between Dhufar, with its port of Moscha, and Aden, Qanaʾ provided the only good natural harbour. It was well positioned and suitable as the outlet for the Kingdom of Ḥaḍramaut and of Shabwa, the overruling capital city. Qanaʾ was the port which fed the most important caravan route leading to the north because the incense from the frankincense trees of Dhufar and the Qara mountains was the very best, and the fact that it came also through Shabwa increased its value.

The port of Qanaʾ was probably first mentioned in *Ezekiel* (xxvii, 23), referring to the time of about 600 BC. 'The merchants of Sheba and Raʾma have traded with thee [Tyre]: they occupied thy fairs with chief of all spices, and with all precious stones and gold. Haran, and Kanne and Eden, the merchants of Sheba ...' (Masoretic version). Probably Kanne and Eden are Qanaʾ and Aden. It seems that they were the main ports on the Indian Ocean, trading with Somaliland, East Africa and India. In *Ezekiel*, they are the southernmost places mentioned. As long as the 'incense road' from Sabaʾ and also from the states of Ḥaḍramaut, Qataban and Maʿin to the Mediterranean was of importance, Qanaʾ must have been the main port of transfer from the sea to the mainland of precious goods. This was up to the second century BC and may have been a geo-

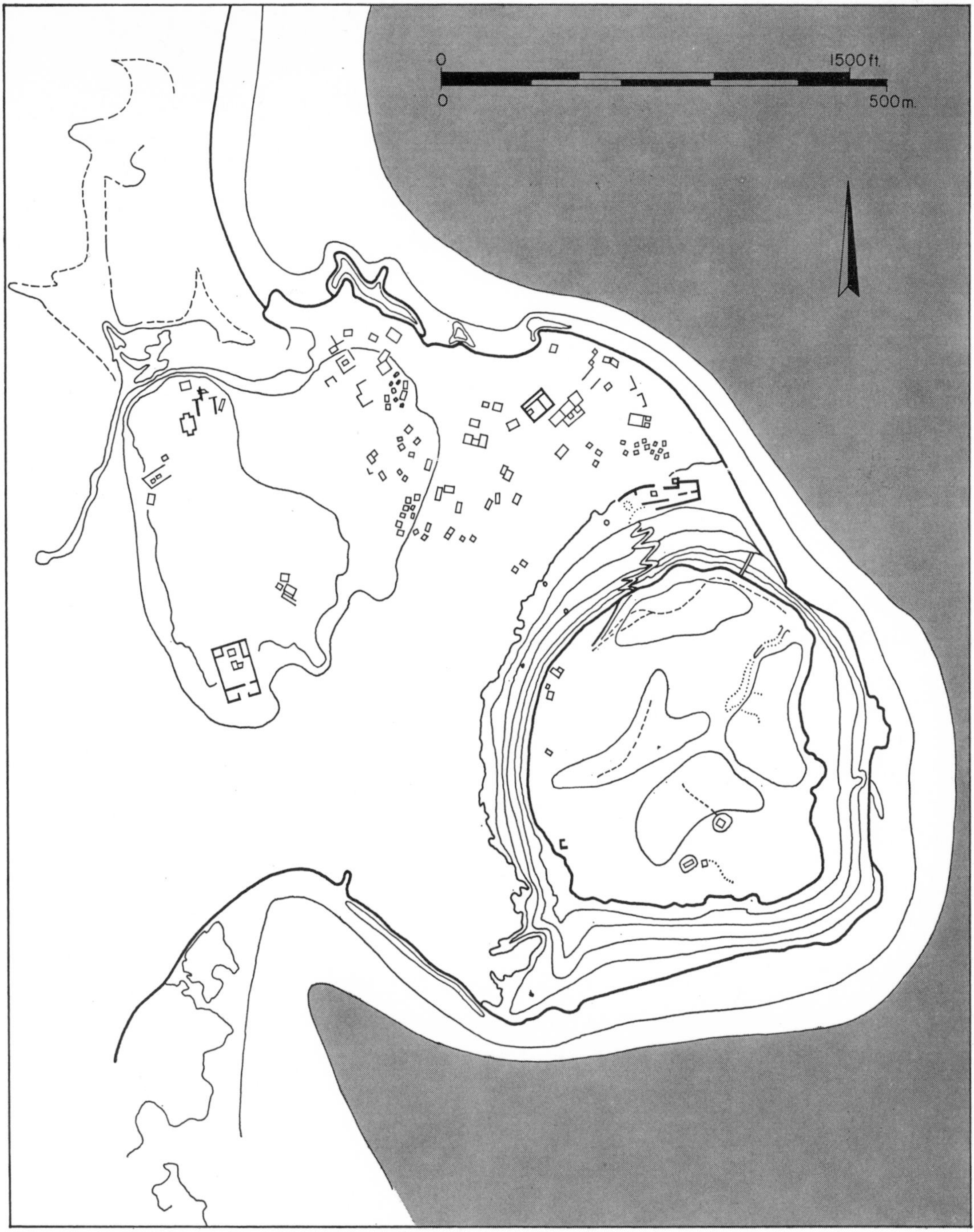

29 Sketch map of the site of Qana', ancient port of the Ḥaḍramaut. The paved path which is shown on the north side, ascends the rock of Husn *al-Ghurāb, the 'Urr Mawiyat mentioned in the inscription on a rock face. There are remains of stone buildings on the lower slopes of* Husn *al-Ghurāb, and also there are further structures of the fortress on the north-west side of the plateau*

graphical necessity after the destruction of Aden. The frankincense of D̲h̲ufar (Ẓafar) probably also travelled overland through Wadi Ḥaḍramaut as well as by sea.

When Egypt was a Roman province the direct trade to India was vigorous, but it touched only at one place, Okelis, the harbour at Bab al-Mandab, which had poor water. Aden at this time was destroyed and not used as a port. However, according to *The Periplus of the Erythraean Sea* Qanaʾ was the main port of the Ḥaḍramaut and it had considerable trade with Oman, Persia and India.

There are two inscriptions on the rock face at the top of the path climbing Husn al-G̲h̲urāb. The smaller one, known as CIH 728, says that the defender of Qanaʾ has written an inscription on ʿUrr Mawiyat. This inscription is placed so as to face and overlook Qanaʾ. The long ten-line inscription (CIH 621) describes the repairs to the fortifications and water cisterns by a group of men from the tribes of the Ḥaḍramaut by Sumyafaʿ ʾAšwaʿ, who was probably a relative of the King with the same name. This was in connection with the wars during which Abyssinia attacked the Kingdom of Sabaʾ and Himyar to avenge the persecution of Christians in AD 525 or 531:

> SMYFʿ ʾŠWʿ and his sons ŠRḤBʾL YKML and MʿDKRB YʿQR, sons of LḤYʿT YRH̲M, they of KLʿN, and D̲YZʾN and GDNm and MT̲LN and ŠRQN and ḤBm and YTʿN and YSRM and YRŚ and MKRBm and ʿQBT and BSʾYN and YLGB and GYMN and YŚBR and LBḤm and GDWYN and KŚRN and RH̲YT and GRDN and QBLN and SRGY and the banu MLḤm and their tribes, and ḤẒT and ʾLHN and SLFN and ḌYFTN and RYḤm and RKBN and MṬLFN and SʾKLN and ŚKRD, and the kabirs and leaders of SYBN d̲NṢF:
>
> inscribed this inscription on the rock MWYT when they restored it [in respect of] its walls and its gate and its cisterns and its access-roads, when they strengthened themselves in it, when they returned from the land of ḤBŠT and the ʾḤBŠN sent the expedition in the land of ḤMYRm, when they slew the king of ḤMYRm and his chiefs the ḤMYR and ʾRḤBN:
>
> its date d̲ḤGTN of 640 years.

The inscriptions known as *Ryckmans* 533, CIH 334 and *Jamme* 632 tell us that from Marib and Ẓafar the troops of Šaʿrm ʾAutar, King of Sabaʾ and D̲h̲u Raydān,[180] attacked Shabwa and Qanaʾ but this was some two to three hundred years before Sumyafaʿ ʾAšwaʿ cut the inscriptions on the rock face. This attack was to make the King of Ḥaḍramaut ʾIlʿazz a vassal of Saba' in <u>Dh</u>u Raydān.[181] Much booty was collected including four statues and a bronze bull which was dedicated to the temple in Marib. The active history of Husn al-<u>Gh</u>urāb ('Urr Mawiyat) seems to have ended by the seventh century, but Qana' by the end of the third century AD was already slowly collapsing and no longer an active trade port.

The rock of Husn al-<u>Gh</u>urāb was capped with buildings, a watch-tower, and plastered masonry cisterns or water-catchment tanks. The citadel was connected to the port below by a narrow, zigzag, stone-revetted path with a protective ramp. Where it changed direction the path was stepped in fine-cut masonry, and towards the top was only sufficiently wide for one person at a time, thus making it easily defensible. Its entrance at the bottom was protected by a tower and gateway.

In 1834, Lieutenant Wellsted from the survey vessel *Palinurus* under Captain S.B. Haines, I.N., visited this site and recorded it in *Travels in Arabia*, London, 1838. He noted that there was a trace of the main harbour on the north and also a silted second harbour on the south-west.

Qana' seems to have contained several distinct building areas. Rubble on the eastern side appears to be the remains of small dwellings, and just to the north of the fortress gateway were many circular structures. In the central area the buildings were of squared masonry, plastered internally with about one inch thickness of lime plaster. It is probable that the houses were constructed of stone for the first few courses, with wood and matting or mud brick above, although the thickness of the walling would have supported a second storey in masonry.

Towards the north-west of the site there is a rise in the ground on which large buildings and further ruins extend inland near the present-day sea inlet.

When Lieutenant Wellsted visited Husn al-<u>Gh</u>urāb the fortress gateway was marked by two towers standing by themselves but little now remains of them, although it is possible to discern their foundations and the steps leading to the paved space before them. This entrance, with its two bastions, was probably similar to the entrance at ancient Mayfa'at and it has a gently sloping walled ramp on the right in the same fashion.

There are few signs of Qana' having been a walled town, especially on the land side, although there appear to be the remains of a wall beyond the fortress gateway extending seawards in a northerly direction, and the eastern shore appears to have had a masonry wall and rock protection.

An interesting walled enclosure aligned on 148° is to be seen on the south-west of the main building area. The paved court within this possible temple precinct surrounds a structure which was either an altar or inner sanctum. There are several small rooms in the eastern portion of the enclosure.

The site of this ancient port deserves detailed investigation for, although much of the foundations of walls are built directly upon exposed rock outcrop, there are many buildings now covered by blown sand which have footings at a greater depth. These require excavation as well as the smaller, probably domestic structures which cluster on the lower slopes of the great rock near the entrance to the paved road to the summit.

Mayfaʿat

Fig. 30 Plate 83 Mayfaʿat, or Naqb al-Hajar as it is known today, is the most spectacular walled city in Southern Arabia. It is built in a high commanding position on the easternmost tip of a long ridge of pebble conglomerate which extends into the centre of the main wadi. The distinguishing feature is the continuous high walling surrounding the city, constructed of pecked, hammer-dressed limestone blocks. It dominates the whole area, and in the past no camel caravan loaded with spices and luxuries from Qanaʾ could have passed unnoticed. It is thought that Mayfaʿat was the capital city for the Lower Ḥaḍramaut, and from the size and strength of its walls and the extent of its once cultivated fields this seems possible.

Mayfaʿat is strategically placed to protect and prevent entry to the north and to control the direction of the caravans. From here the caravans could go north either along the Wadi Limatah and the Wadi Habban to Timnaʿ, capital of Qataban, or north to the Wadi Amaqīn and over the mountains to Wadi Jirdān and Hajar al-Barīra. From there the caravans could go direct to Shabwa, on the main route continuing through Al-ʿAbr and across the desert to Najrān of Maʿin.

The site of Mayfaʿat, which measures approximately 500 by 1000 feet, slopes towards the centre, for it is placed on two mounds with a small intersecting valley. On the north side of this valley leading to the flood Plate 85 channel of the great wadi is the northern entrance, or so at first it seems, with great masonry bastions flanking a masonry platform nearly 43 feet wide which is today some 20 feet above the wadi. There are no steps or signs of a masonry ramp, but probably the level of the wadi floor is much

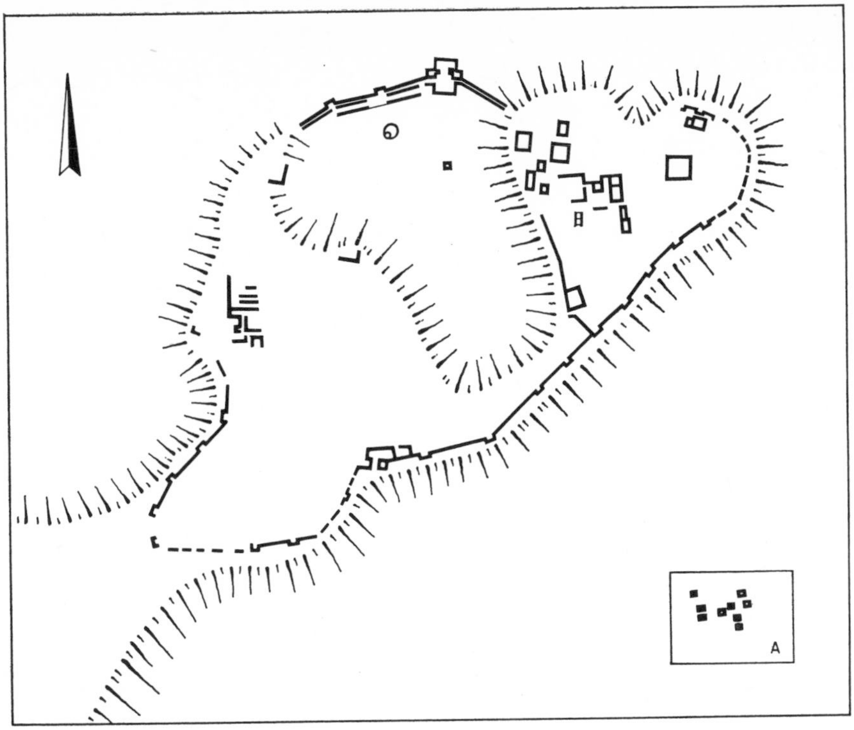

30 A plan of Mayfaʿat. The walled city, thought to have been the capital of lower Ḥaḍramaut, lies on the north-western route from Qanaʾ to either Baihān or to Shabwa. The positions of the two massive gateways are shown and their different designs may indicate that they were not contemporary. It is likely that the northern walling and gateway are the result of the rebuilding work recorded in RES *2687 at Qalat, whereas the southern gate and the other perimeter walling are the original work as recorded in the earlier inscriptions* RES *2640 on the southern gate and* RES *3869 which is in the Museum of Bombay. The portions of the site not walled would only be scaled with difficulty and the north-east section is undercut. The main well lies to the west of the northern gate. Beyond the south of the site are eroded fields and irrigation ditches. The small stone buildings of what appears to be a burial area are drawn at inset A although their actual position is further east*

lower today. The space between the high gate bastions is nearly 29 feet, narrowed by two contemporary walls of 5 feet, not, one might have thought, a practicable defence in case of attack. On each side walls with ramparts and towers extend across the small valley between the mounds.

The main well is close to the North Gate and it appears to have been re-used at a later date, for the rope-worn lining stones have been refitted. Part of the well structure consists of a high, stone-faced tower probably used for lifting the water to a higher level for a conduit. It is possible that the site was re-used by local tribesmen during the time of the founding of the mud-brick fortresses and *husns* that now line the Wadi Maifaʿah.

Directly south from the northern gate across the site's narrow axis is the southern wall and the most impressive feature of the city, the South Gate. These great bastions, although without any indication of hangings for gates, flank what is obviously the main entrance. The pathway leads up a steep slope of rock and proceeds through the outer portal where an inner wall diverts all visitors to the right hand. Possibly at this point the gate entrance would have been defended by enfilade fire.

The bastions, built upon the rock conglomerate, are erected on the slope so that the west bastion foundations are about six feet higher than the other. The towers rise about 31 feet and 36 feet, and their south faces are 10 feet 9 inches and 16 feet wide respectively. There are three inscriptions built into the town walls: one at the top centre of the third bastion west of the South Gate; one in the left (west) wall immediately inside the South Gate, and the most important, the long inscribed stone on the inner face of the east bastion of the South Gate. The first two inscriptions are well weathered but they repeat information contained in the long inscription.

Plate 84

The text (RES 2640) is as follows:

> HBSL son of ŠGB was in charge of the buildings of the wall of MYFʿT and its gate in stone and wood and wicker work and the building of the houses which he placed against its wall, from bottom to top. In addition, his son ṢDQYDʿ heightened the wall.

Most of the perimeter masonry is *in situ*, and the exterior view is a most impressive display of strength. However, the inside view is not so convincing, for the walls are generally of one stone thickness only. The strength of the wall relies on the weight and size of the hammer-dressed and cut stones, which are on average a yard long, and the construction of supporting bastions at regular intervals. From the debris and infill remaining it does not seem possible that these perimeter walls were ever of thicker construction or strengthened by internal masonry. Walls so constructed at a height above the sloping external ground would have been a suitable deterrent against attack, and no battering-ram could have been used effectively. The puzzle of the ever open gateways remains. In places, particularly on the western and highest level, the walling has all but disappeared and only foundations are left.

Inside and near the South Gate is the western prominence of the site; both here and towards the north there seem to be the remains of some of the earlier buildings. Their construction resembles early wall-construction at Shabwa, built of large pebbles laid in courses on the inside with a facing of fine ashlar.

In the centre of the site and at the low level near the well are the remains of a small square building, the facing ashlar of which is of finely chiselled work. On the eastern slope above the northern gate lies a small square building, thought by Lieutenant Wellsted in 1834 to have been a temple. Without excavation this identification will remain uncertain, but the fine limestone facing he saw is now missing, leaving only the protruding bonding stones, which had been part of the original ashlar face.

Immediately above this building are the remains of a wall with well-cut and bedded ashlar, pecked in the centre panel and marginally drafted or chiselled. Again, close to this are the remains of a building most of which appears complete, although filled with rubble. Here the white, smooth-faced limestone slabs are still extant with fine joints, well bonded and laid dry. It is easy to see how Wellsted thought from this type of workmanship that the stone on the other building was marble.

On the crest of the east mound it is apparent that at some time the inhabitants had utilized earlier material for new buildings, with large amounts of mortar to fill the interstices. The random-stone wall bisecting part of the site is also of a much later period. In the centre portion of the east mound is a large raised masonry platform floor, with walls 40 feet 8 inches by 35 feet 6 inches, which has a bearing of 280°. This was probably the site of the main guard- or custom-house, commanding a view of the whole wadi to the north-west.

A *naqb*, or watercourse cutting, probably reflected in the present-day name of the site Naqb al-Hajar, excavated across the arm of the conglomerate is a major engineering feat. This is a conduit of some 25–40 feet deep by 25–30 feet wide and about 560 feet long, fashioned to collect water from the wadi on the north side and by the use of masonry sluices irrigate the fields on the south-west side of the city. On the wadi side, a well-constructed channel followed the contours of the hills as a catchment system as well as seasonally constructed earth dams which collected the *sail* or flood-water from the main flood channel for the *naqb*. Due to scour against the conglomerate the ground level of the wadi gradually lowered while the seasonal floods also brought fresh silt which had to be cleared regularly to prevent the field levels rising until they were too high and impossible to irrigate. There is evidence that this eventually occurred and that at a later stage a secondary cutting was made to lower the floor gradient of the *naqb* in an effort to fill the pool area on the south side when the sluices were unusable to irrigate the high fields naturally, but this must have been a short-lived project.

On the ancient silt at a short distance south-east from the site, placed 265° to the south gate, lies a group of rectangular structures of cut masonry the walls of which average now only some two to three feet in height. This appears to be the necropolis and a small excavation into the side of one eroded building produced human skeletal remains from within a little chamber of small stones and mortar which seems to indicate a secondary burial.

The area of the silt close to the site is strewn with human (and animal) bone fragments. Whether they are burials contemporary with the necropolis is not known, but fragments of glazed and unglazed ware found outside the southern wall seem to confirm later habitation of the site. No significant pottery was found on the surface inside the walls.

However, material from the confines of the city include fragments of marble friezes of ibex heads; small limestone tablets with names in early South Arabian; portions of cornice with bird-beak drip from Wellsted's 'temple'; and several pieces of pecked and marginally drafted ashlar and decorative panels.

The date of this ancient walled city is at present indeterminate and its use as a centre for the organizing of camel caravans may have long preceded the use of the site as a walled city. The walls were clearly built for defence purposes and from the inscription at Qalat we can assume that they were intended after repair as a defence against the Himyar when they captured Qana'. This would be between the first centuries BC and AD, so the date of their original construction may have been several centuries earlier and this seems to be confirmed from the palaeographic evidence of the long inscription on the South Gate.

THE WADI JIRDĀN AREA

The Wadi Jirdān area, though rich in archaeological material and ancient sites, has been seldom visited. At the entrance of the wadi is the modern

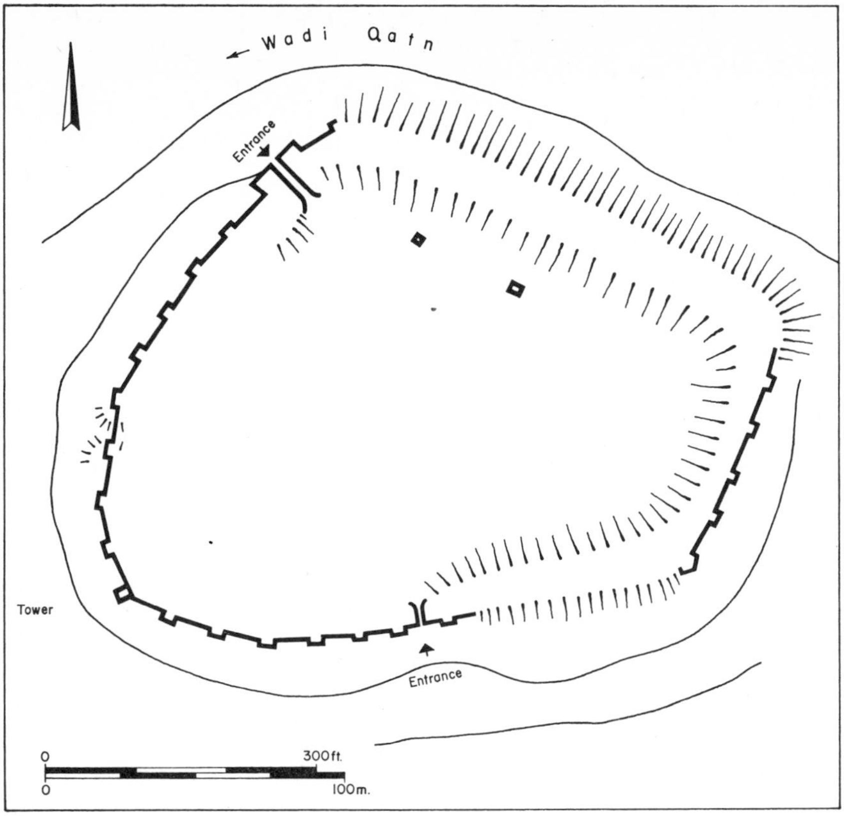

31 A plan of the walled site of Al-Barīra in the Wadi Jirdān

town of ʿAyadh. East of this is a pre-Islamic 'fortified' place called Al-Binā similar to the Al-Barīra design. Al-Barīra itself lies between the flood beds of Wadi Jirdān and Wadi Riša (Qatn). Plate 97

In front of the mouth of the Wadi Jirdān, there is a level moraine or raised heap of old flood debris, and sand valleys have formed. The village of Ṣaʿda lies on the edge of this and a canal or *naqb* has been built in the east which leads water into this little valley. It is a pre-Islamic work and there are several dams, ancient irrigation works which still operate today.

Al-Barīra

Al-Barīra[182] lies south-east of Al-Binā and some ten miles from ʿAyadh. It is approximately four miles east of Ṣaʿda and a mile and a half west of al-Shiqq.

This site consists of a stone-walled area with a heart- or oval-shaped circumference but it would seem that the northern portion of the plan is *Fig. 31* missing from the wadi edge, and was probably washed away in the floods. Silted agricultural fields lie on the south-east, south and south-west sides. The walls are constructed of limestone blocks laid dry, with no mortar, in horizontal courses and of random sizes roughly cut and faced. Smaller stones in the interstices maintain the course-lines for the larger stones, which grade downwards from such sizes as four feet by eighteen inches and two feet square. In some places near the North Gate the wall still retains a maximum height of eleven feet and consists of six courses of masonry, while at the South Gate the wall is at its lowest level of merely one or two courses.

Throughout its length the walling was furnished with bastions averaging sixteen to eighteen feet in length with projections of about six feet. The distance between bastions averages thirty-six feet, and there were twenty still visible, the others having collapsed or been buried under debris.

Plate 94

The North Gateway is the most important feature of the site. The entrance is flanked by two large bastions 27 feet long and 16 feet 5 inches deep, and the western bastion is 11 feet high at the outer corner. This entrance, with flanking walls along a length of about 60 feet, is aligned on 140° and narrows from ten feet to a width of seven feet at the inner mouth. Flanking the external bastions, though seen only on the west side, is a support wall 46 feet long and about ten feet high with a ledge set-back from the ground.

Plates 95, 96

The South Gateway is the entrance with flanking walls 24 feet 6 inches in length, aligned on 335°, which widen at the inner end, and their average height is about three feet. Neither gateway show signs of having been fitted with doors.

We have seen that Mayfa'at (Naqb al-Hajar) also bears no sign of having had doors hung in its gateway, although there is a protective wall built at right angles to the entrance.[183] The straight entrances here at Al-Barīra may indicate the easy access necessary for a camel caravan staging post.

The seventh bastion, westwards of the South Gateway, is of a larger size than the others. It is 13 feet wide but 17 feet long and it is probable that this was a watch-tower.

East of the Gate and on a bearing of 75° over a length of wall which lies under debris stands a corner bastion with its outer faces angled. The east side of the corner bastion is 18 feet long at an angle of 10° and consists of one great stone. It is 315° and 656 feet from this corner bastion to the North Gate.

The plan, checked with air photographs, shows the North Gate facing the road to Shabwa and suggests a symmetrical layout. Presumably there would also have been a partner to the South Gate in the opposite wall. No signs were seen, however, of masonry or other remains in the wadi as a result of the inroads of flood-waters, but it is probable that much of the material was used in the building of the nearby town.

The interior of the site is level silt with low mounds on the northern sides covered with a thin layer of pottery fragments. There is also a slight slope down inside from the walls and wall alignments. The general level of this area is about ten feet above the entrance at the North Gate. A certain amount of digging has been carried out by treasure seekers, and by so doing a small portion of walling, part of a building, exposed.

Large numbers of potsherds lie strewn over the surface of this area, especially on the slopes near the walls. The pottery found here may be compared with that discovered at Al-Binā and Raibūn, Ḥuraiḍah in Wadi ʿAmd, and Mushgha in Wadi ʿIdm and is dated about the fifth century BC or even earlier; a dating supported by comparison with material found in Baihān.

Two stones from this site both bear inscriptions and the letters, extremely well cut and proportioned, are typical of the early period, probably between the fifth and third centuries BC.

On an alignment of 261° from Al-Barīra, across the old cultivation area is the large rock outcrop situated on the edge of the flood channel of Wadi Jirdān. There is a large water cistern at its foot and it is surmounted by a fort known locally as the Husn Barīra. From its position, it was probably always used as an observation post for the benefit of the people of the wadi.

The old agricultural fields of Al-Barīra end on the northern side with a boundary of rough stone walling – about 300–400 yards long, with a remaining height, in places, of 9–12 feet. There is a return wall at the north-west corner. Its purpose appears to be twofold: to contain and protect the fields from *sail* washout, and to divert flood water from the watercourse of the Wadi Qatn (which becomes the Wadi Riša as it flows north) into the main channel of Wadi Jirdān. *Fig. 32*

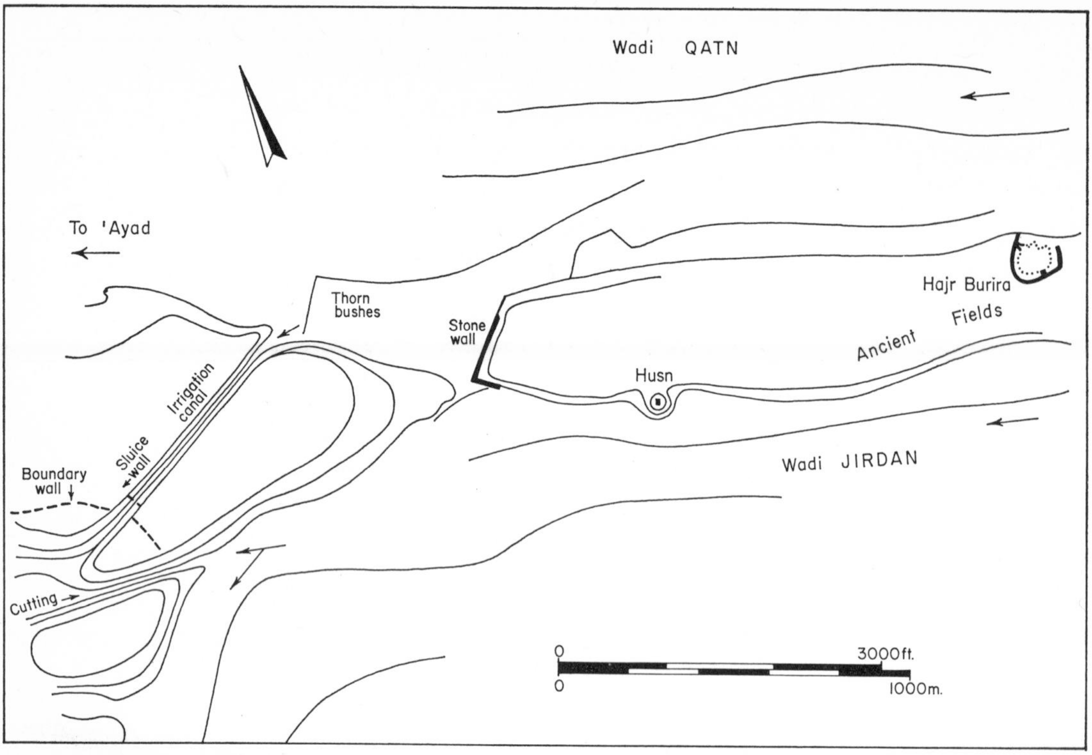

32 A sketch map of the ancient field system of Al-Barīra and the two canals which convey flood water to the fields of Saʿda within the scree hill

There are two irrigation channels or cuttings leading into the central flat agricultural area of the little valley of Ṣaʿda within the surrounding scree hills. The main canal is designed to allow the waters of the wadi to flow unhindered out and onto the fields of Al-Binā. Overflow waters from Wadi Jirdān passed along the south of the scree hill and, in a re-entrant, the signs of ancient fields once irrigated in this way indicate the possibility of another ancient town, or that Ṣaʿda nearby has ancient foundations. The canal channel system diverting the wadi flood may have been excavated after the silting up of this land.

It is considered that these canals are pre-Islamic and they were sizeable feats of workmanship. The main cutting or *naqb*, which is on a general alignment of 180°, is about 90 feet deep and about 120 feet wide at the top and, on the inner mouth, about 90 feet wide and some 50–60 feet deep.

The second canal, which enters the valley through the scree hill from the north-west, is designed to collect the waters of the Wadi Qatn. It is absolutely straight and in section is 70 feet across the tops of the banks, with equal sloping sides of about 45° angles, extending 34 feet to the bottom. Its total length from the mouth to where it joins the valley is 650 feet but at 550 feet from the mouth there are a few large stones built into the sides of the scree banks, which probably indicate the site of the sluice gates. The inner mouth of this canal debouches about 30 feet above the lower level of the valley and the floor of the main cutting. Surrounding the whole valley and edging the inner lip of the scree hills were remains of rough stone walling, in some places as much as three feet wide, probably indicating boundary lines.

What link there was between Al-Barīra and Al-Binā is not certain, for here are two walled areas built in materials easily obtainable from the vicinity of each site, and both of nearly the same area and circular form. It has been suggested that these were forts flanking a town of Hajar Jirdān, but local inhabitants know of no other sites or remains of masonry walls. The people in the district who possess and work the salt hill of Jabal al-Milh nowadays live in the district of the mouth of Wadi Jirdān, in ʿAyadh, Ṣaʿda and as far as Al-Barīra; a continuation of labour which probably extends back to those earlier days when the salt trade and incense caravans were of the utmost importance. It is likely that the Hajar Jirdān suggested in inscriptions is in fact the site of Al-Barīra. Plates 99, 100

Beitwan Mugraf Saʿad

There is a small *husn* or fort on a prominent hill south-west from Ṣaʿda on the north side of the track from Husn al-Barīra to Ataq.

Graffiti inscriptions, mostly of names, are cut into the outer surface of the roughly laid stone walls of the fort. Westward from this building is a level area and the topmost treads of a flight of steps cut in the stone at the south-west corner. On a flat rock surface nearby is a further series of graffiti inscriptions and also a shallow recess with the perimeter shape and size of a human foot close to a hollowed-out circular bowl which is about five inches in diameter and two and a half inches deep.

There are in addition many names on the south side of the small fort cut or pecked into the rock, which has in places weathered badly.

This seems to have been an Ḥaḍrami observation post, with a field of view commanding the widening mouth of the wadi and the terrain between Al-Barīra and Al-Binā.

Al-Bināʾ

Fig. 33

Al-Binā is located in the Wadi Jirdān north of the Barīra and south-east of the town ʿAyadh. It is a walled area, roughly circular in shape and surrounded almost completely by agricultural fields and irrigation ditches, now all silted up.

Plate 98

The walls are constructed of mud bricks which are each about 15 inches long, and on the south-west face it is possible to see that the wall is about 13 feet thick. Here it seems to have been repaired on three separate occasions as three lateral faces are exposed where the wall has eroded and fallen away. The total height of the existing wall above the wadi bed is 20 feet, and it appears to have been built directly on to a pebble conglomerate, but G. Lankester Harding noticed that there had been two distinct periods of building. He found that the lowest level consisted of two to six inches of deposit of fine grey dust, fragments of wood, straw, charcoal and a few non-descript sherds. Above this was a layer of mud brick varying in thickness but not exceeding eleven and a half inches, and above this again a four-inch-thick layer of blackish debris, on top of which the lower courses of the present enclosure wall are built.[184] From the entrance on the south it is 644 feet on a bearing of 300° to the centre of the opposite wall, on the long dimensions and it is 550 feet wide. There appears to have been only the one entrance, located on the southern end which was originally protected by a mud-wall barrier, now collapsed, fronting the opening.

There are three buildings or constructions visible: Building A is 300 feet from the entrance on a bearing of 270°. It may have been a tank or small cistern 13 feet by 20 feet for it is constructed of burnt brick and four coats of fine lime plaster have been applied to the inside face. Building B is situated 100 feet from Building A. It appears to have consisted of several rooms and the wall-bases extend a short distance along the edge of the wall. One room measures nine by twenty-two feet, and the walls have stone bases, roughly cut and laid in courses with a packing of pebbles beneath the floor, which is finished with lime mortar. The level of this floor is about 20 feet above the wadi bed. Remains of stone walling or footings of walls are visible also on the northern side about 443 feet away.

The central area within the site of Al-Binā is level and strewn with potsherds where the ground gradually slopes up to the wall alignment, much of which has now collapsed with sloping outer edges. This is also

101, 102 Hajar Am-Nab is raised above the *sail* bed in the Wadi Merkha. It is surrounded by a pattern of eroded fields and the silted up irrigation system, *above*. A typical building on the site, *right*, is constructed of roughly coursed, random size masonry. It is typical of the area and is probably evidence of later building on an old site

103 The Jabal Raydān dominates the Wadi Baihān and the modern town of Baihān al-Qasab. Laid out on the ground to dry in the sun are mud bricks for new buildings

104 On the southern side of the summit of Jabal Raydān are a series of buildings in roughly coursed, random masonry laid dry. Above the buildings are several small, plaster-lined cisterns for storing water

105, 106 The site of Timnaʿ, the ancient capital of Qataban, covers about 52 acres, *right*, and was originally built on a bed of silt about 50 ft above the wadi level. Recent discoveries include a gateway at the south-east corner and some houses (upper left of site in photograph). *Above*, is an oblique view of the main temple, with much of its basic plan still visible

107, 108 The main temple at Timnaʿ. *Above*, the forecourt of the temple looking west towards the steps and stylobate of the temple proper (*see also* Plate 105). *Right,* part of the south side of the massive masonry walling of the main temple. The pecked decoration is the religious symbol Wadʾb with the moon crescent and orb of Venus together with a human hand with outspread fingers

109–111 Hajar bin Humaid is a *tell* site that covers some four acres about 70 ft above the wadi level. Pottery was found in excavations in 1951 down to a depth of 23 ft, below which there was bed silt formed from earlier irrigation and fieldwork. In the photograph, *above*, the masonry at the top left is re-used old material. On a stone built into this wall, and reversed, was found pecked the three ostriches *right*. This wall was probably built in the early centuries AD. On the surface of the *tell* is the inscription, *right*, of NABAT YUHAN'M bin ŠAHR HILAL. It also mentions the royal palace of ḤRB but its exact original location is unknown

112, 113 The *Aqabat* Najd Marqad is a walled and paved road over the rock outcrop at the edge of the sand sea between the Wadi Baihān and the Wadi Ḥarib. The walls are about 30 ft apart in the middle of the pass and 55 and 67 ft at the ends. Only two sections of the paving now remain although it was once paved throughout with irregularly shaped blocks. Najd Marqad served as a camel caravan and taxation check point

114 The ancient Qatabanian town of Ḥaribat in the Wadi Ḥarib nearly opposite the entrance to the *Aqabat* Mablaqa. The site, about 14 ft above the wadi level, is about 880 × 600 ft and many of the buildings are exposed with well cut, coursed, ashlar masonry

115 A typical frankincense bush being tapped near Hanun, north of Salalah and the Jabal Qara, in Dhufar

116 A general view of Shabwa from the western approach. The village of Maiwan is on the left and in the centre are the buildings of Mathna with Hajar behind them. The 'temple' is at the right of the centre

117, 118 Two details of architectural features of the temple at Shabwa. *Left, above,* the right hand podium which flanked the temple steps. The grooves and recess suggest that some feature, perhaps a statue, was once placed at the top. *Left, below,* the four column bases of the temple building (the right hand podium is beyond). The grooves around the base and the centre dowel holes seem to indicate that the columns were formed of circular stone drums, not of monoliths as found elsewhere in the area

119, 120 The main boulder on the south side of Jabal ʿUqla has a masonry structure on top referred to in the inscription as ʾANWADUM. There are two plastered cisterns and part of the lower one is built across an inscription of ʾIlʿazz Yalit, king of Ḥaḍramaut. It records, *below*, a ceremony performed by him (RES 3909) and the other inscriptions are those of supporters, some of whom were probably the recipients of titles

121 A general view of the Wadi Aqābih from the *jabal*. The inscriptions are in the section passing across the middle distance. Al-ʿAbr lies about ten miles south-west

122 In the Wadi Aqābih looking south-west across the centre section

123, 124 Incised and pecked graffiti inscriptions on the rock at the southern end of the Wadi Aqābih. A common motif here is a series of right hand palms with fingers outstretched with a small inscription all contained within a perimeter line. *Below*, faint graffiti accompanying the pecked outline of a camel

125, 126 Pecked drawings of figures riding apparently full-tilt at each other, *above*, and *below*, several figures riding the same horse, two of whom seem to be holding their rifles aloft

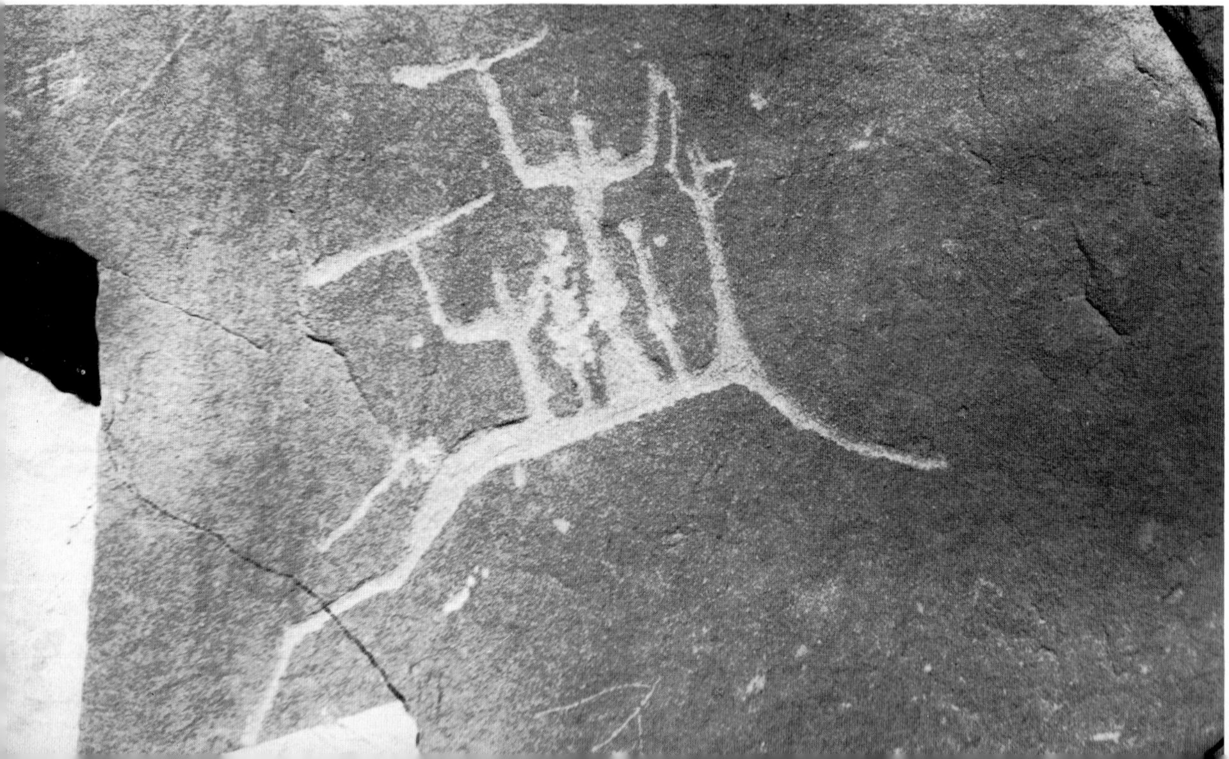

127, 128 The cairns on the ridge of Jabal Aqābih are visible for miles from the northern plain. Those seen here, *right*, form part of the 'tail' of 33 cairns extending south-eastward from the main cairn which is 15 ft in diameter. *Below*, pecked graffiti are not uncommon on any flat surface of rock in the wadi

129 The extensive site of Mushgha is situated in the Wadi ʿIdm on the west bank of the wadi flood bed. Much erosion has taken place and the channel has eaten into the east side of the site. Here the wadi bed is seen beyond the exposed masonry in the foreground

130 Husn al-ʿUrr is a large fort situated upon an isolated rock in the main wadi west of Tarim. Once the fort was decorated with finely carved door joints, lintels and capitals. The best limestone pecked and drafted masonry has been reused but there seems no doubt that this was a building of significance beyond that of a normal *husn* or fort to protect the valley

131 In the middle of Sūk on the island of Socotra is a small church with a level plaster floor set on a small mound. There are nine pillar bases constructed of limestone and coral blocks and apparently two plaster floor levels. These may be part of the Portuguese alterations to the earlier, Arab building

132 The northern, plastered, entrance and walls of the church at Sūk. This rectangular structure is built directly upon the second plaster floor and against the plastered north wall

133 Column bases of limestone and coral in the northern entrance to the church at Sūk. The bases are of different designs, the columns being probably of blocks plastered externally and supporting a roof of palm frond matting on palm trunks

134 A burial, one of several, found walled up on the lower slopes of Jabal Hawāri, east of Sūk. The pelvis, apparently male, had been inverted from the skull and this, together with fragments of a second skull, suggests an ossuary burial. No associated material was found to assist identification and it may be surmised from the position of the Portuguese fort higher up the remains may be of members of the garrison

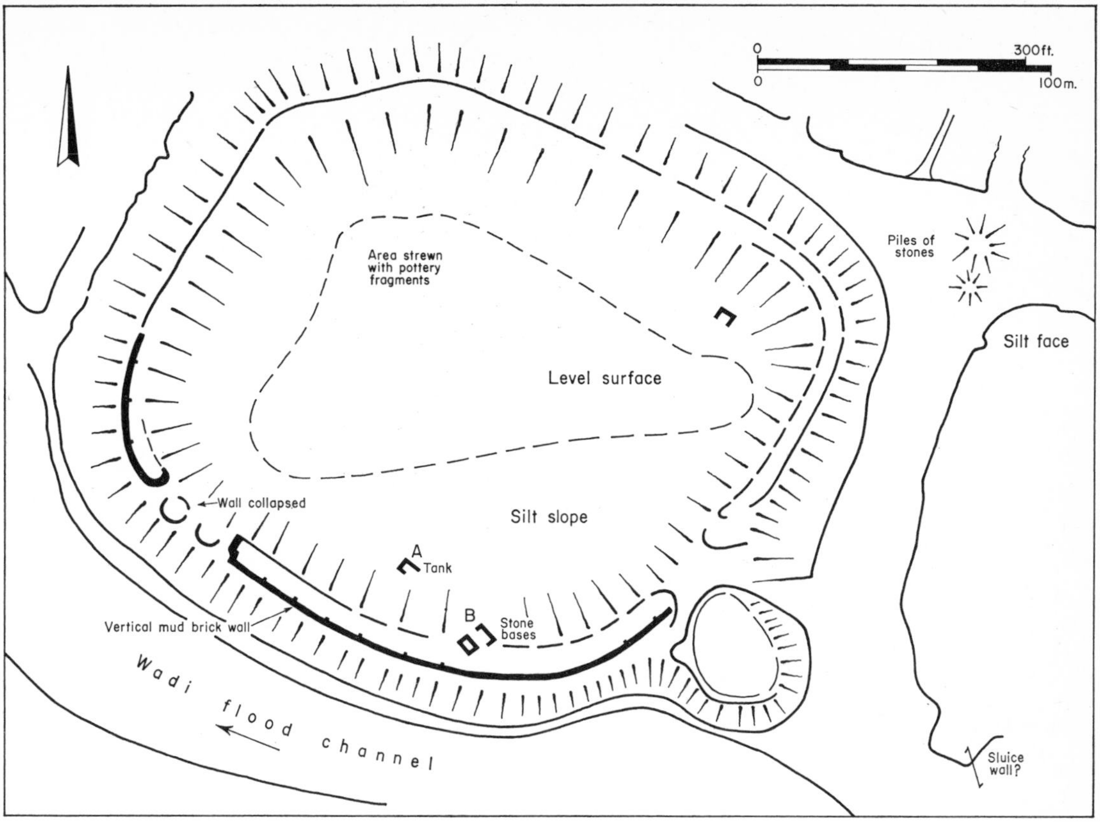

33 A plan of Al-Binā. It was walled with mud bricks and seems to have been a fortified settlement situated close to the wadi flood bed for the irrigation of the surrounding fields. The piles of stones shown on the plan may be the remains of the sluice gates controlling the flow of the water through irrigation channels

covered with fragments of pottery exposed by erosion. It is probable that the walls were once much higher, judging by the interior silting, and that the relative level of the interior was accordingly lower.

The site is bordered on three sides by irrigation channels and a main wadi flows along the northern side where the *sail* is collected through three channels and sluices which diverted the water. The piles of stones in the wide channel at the east corner may be the remains of sluice gates. The main sluice gate to this portion and also the main collecting-channel and off-take wall is clearly shown by aerial photography. The northern end of the agricultural area is fed by a straight wide channel which branches on each side along its whole length. *Fig. 34*

It seems likely that Al-Binā was a fortified village and most of its houses and buildings were constructed of unburnt mud bricks. It prob-

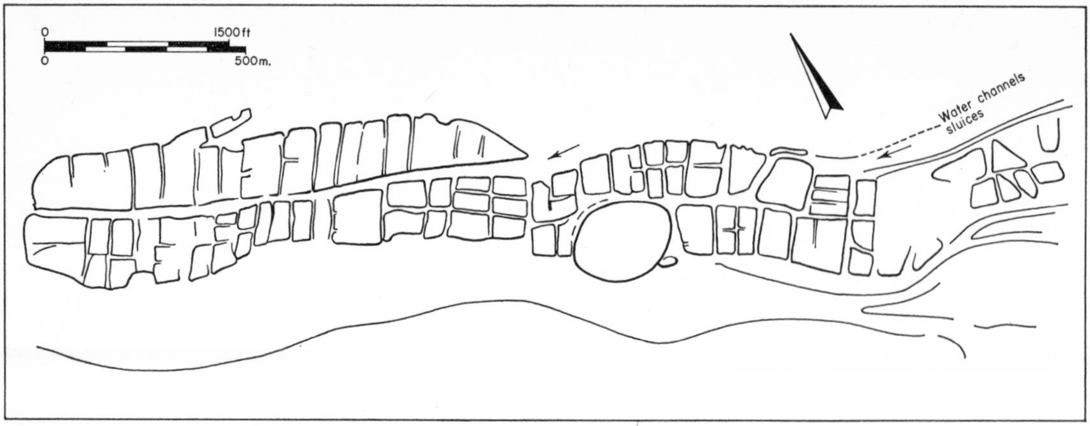

34 A sketch map, based on a photograph taken by the Royal Air Force, which shows clearly the remains of the field and irrigation canal system at Al-Binā

ably guarded the nearby salt mines until its land became silted and it was replaced by the neighbouring town of ʿAyadh, when fortifications were no longer necessary.

Potsherds found so far on the site are very similar to those discovered at Al-Barīra and, by comparison with material found at sites in the Ḥaḍramaut, these appear to date from about the fifth century BC.

A piece of marginally drafted and pecked white limestone ashlar masonry was found at Al-Binā at the south-east side of the site. Discovered lying on the surface this may not be significant, but it is unlikely that it was deposited there after the period of Al-Binā's occupation. If this stone is accepted as belonging to the site it shows a high standard of workmanship usually associated with places of importance.

Wadi Markha

The Wadi Markha is thought to have been the centre of the Kingdom of ʾAusān.

There is a wide level area towards the mouth of the wadi which flows north-eastwards at the southern side of the Jabal Nisyin. Here are still visible the remains of irrigation works and large silted areas of the geometrically planned ancient fields.[185]

There are four town sites which can be identified from the air, and probably more could be found by extensive ground survey. The most notable site is the one known as Hajar am-Nab, a level area above the general ground level close to the present main channel of the wadi. There

Plates 101, 102

are remains of masonry buildings there and artifacts in alabaster including statuettes and bronze figurines of the pre-Islamic period have been collected locally.

THE BAIHĀN AREA

This important valley is a broad sandy silt bounded by steep rock walls which extend north-east, sloping south to north where it flows into the sand desert.

Baihān al-Qasab, once capital of the Amirate of Baihān, is situated at the southern end of the Wadi Baihān. The whole of this wadi was an important centre of the Kingdom of Qataban, one of the five important city states that grew up along the trade routes. Timnaʿ, the ancient capital, was on the site of the mound known locally as Hajar Koḥlān at the northern end of the wadi. Plate 103

There are several tells or habitation mounds in the wadi and also vast areas of ancient fields irrigated through sluice gates from a canal fifteen miles or so long which held the seasonal flood-waters from the mountains.

To facilitate control of the camel caravans, there were two passes, the *Aqaba* Najd Marqad, close to the sand sea and the *Aqaba* Mablaqa. The pass of Najd Marqad lies between the mouths of the Wadi Baihān and the Wadi Ḥarib and it was within the area of Qataban in ancient times. It is a paved roadway with walls on both sides. It probably served as a customs post for levying taxes on merchants and their camel caravans which passed from the desert route travelling westwards direct to Marib. The Mablaqah pass leads westwards across the long narrow paved road over the mountains to Hajr Henu Az-Zureir in the Wadi Ḥarib and through Marib about 50 miles away on the long journey to Gaza and the Mediterranean in the north. It is between 12 and 15 feet wide, stepped at the steepest parts and formed on terraces with hair-pin bends. Its total length is about three miles and the top length of about 1000 feet is cut through the rock about 1000 feet above the wadi. Whether by chance or design, there is a small reservoir at each end of the pass for the refreshment of travellers and camels. Plates 112, 113

Hajar Henu Az-Zureir is the modern name for the site of another important Qatabanian city named Haribat. It was strategically placed at the western side of the Mablaqa Pass, as Hajar bin-Humaid was placed on the east side.

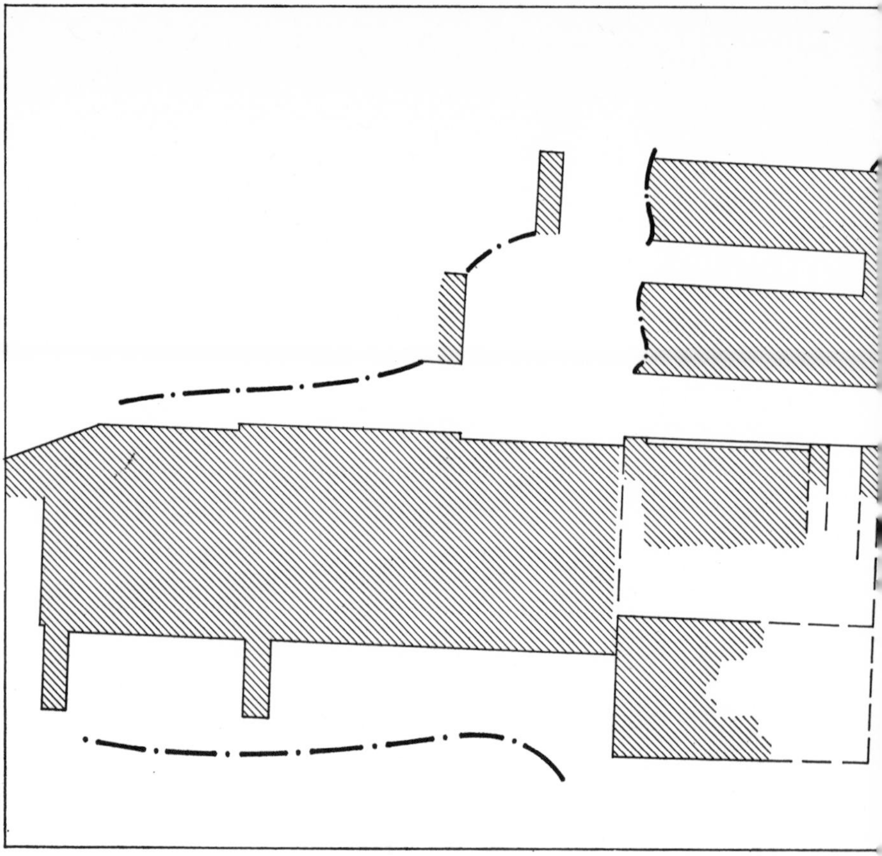

Plates 109, 111

The oldest site of the Wadi Baihān is probably the stratified mound known as Hajar bin-Humaid about nine miles south of Timnaʿ. Here excavations have shown a series of habitations dating from about 1000 BC, the most ancient of which is built on the silt of a still earlier irrigation system. The mound of Hajar bin-Humaid stands opposite the division of the Wadi Mablaqa, and was once a town of some importance because, from an inscription, it is probable that the mint of the palace Ḥarib was here.

South of Baihān al-Qasab and south-east of the modern village of al-Harejah are some ruins very near a village called Maryamah. Here can still be seen masonry walls of houses which are buried under irrigation silt at the confluence of the two great wadis as well as buildings constructed on the ridge of a rock outcrop. This area with its remains of irrigation works is important and requires further research.

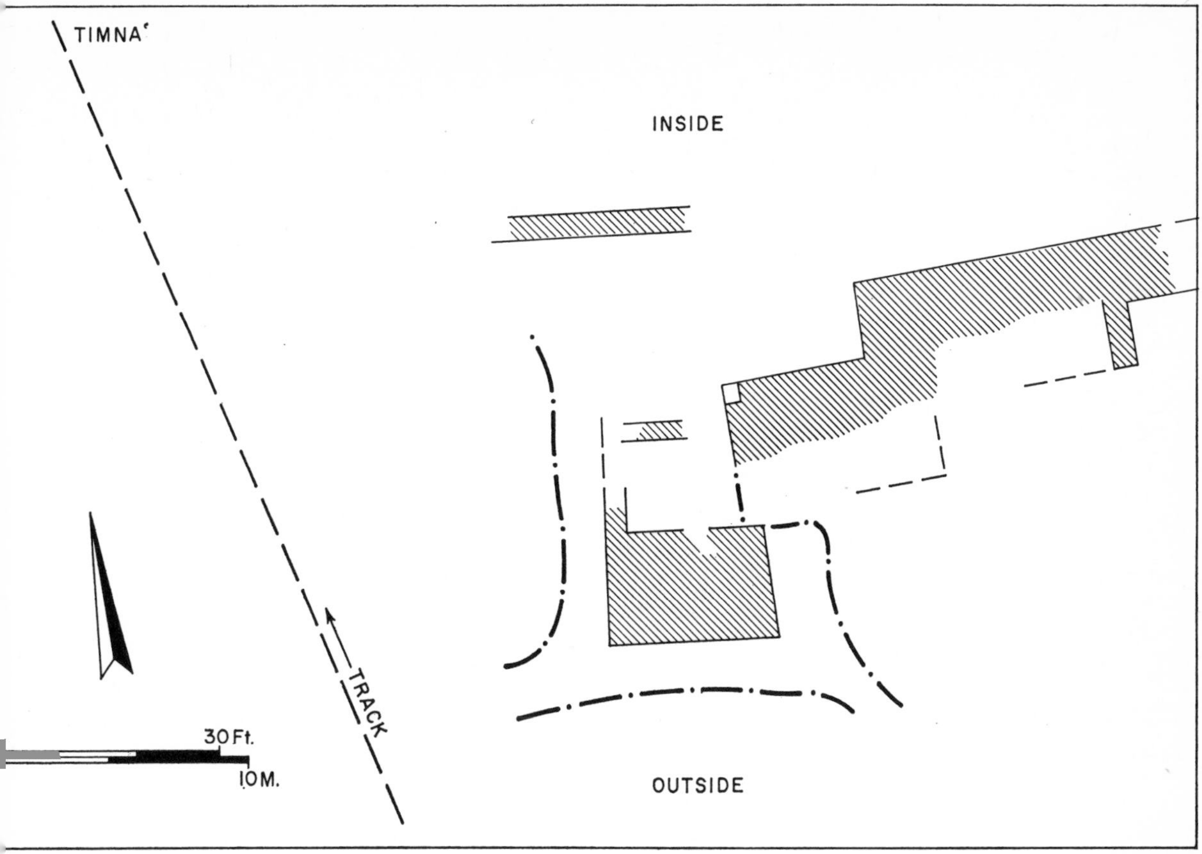

35 A survey drawing of part of the recently exposed south-east entrance gateway and walling of Timnaʿ in the Wadi Baihān. The heavy dot and dash lines show the extent of excavation

Timnaʿ

Timnaʿ, the Thomna of Pliny the Elder,[186] was the capital city of the ancient Kingdom of Qataban. It has been identified by the inscription on the wall of the south gateway. The city was probably finally destroyed in the first century AD during wars with Ḥaḍramaut. The material found on the site, including the discovery of potsherds of *terra sigillata* within some houses,[187] provides a possible *terminus post quem non* for the habitation of Timnaʿ. Plate 106

However, the destruction of the capital did not mean that the kingdom ceased to exist, and it seems that another site, that of Hajar bin-Humaid, became the capital, a development which seems to confirm the continued activity of the inhabitants of Wadi Baihān.

At Hajar Koḥlān the ruin-site is of about 52 acres, measuring approximately 670 yards at its longest dimension by 350 yards at its narrowest point. Its height above the main wadi bed is 26 yards near the south gate and it appears to have been built on the natural cliff at the north gate of the wadi. It was a walled city with several gates. In parts the main wall incorporated the outside walls of houses, and there are masonry remains of houses outside the walls on the southern side.

Fig. 35 There appear to have been four gates, one on the south-west known as the South Gate, others on the south-east, the north-west and the east.

The South Gate, set between two flanking bastions and, about ten feet above the paved floor, is most important epigraphically because inscribed on its massive stones are the laws of the city.[188] It is of archaic masonry construction of large roughly laid stones, one of which is about eight feet by two feet and appears to be of an earlier period, probably contemporary with the lower walls of the main temple. The left bastion of the gate seems to have once formed the foundations of a small guard house, and a high level platform for the guard is still *in situ*.

Unlike many of the gateways found in Southern Arabia there were two vertical grooves in the masonry[189] for wooden frames to take hung gates, and it seems from cut grooves that a horizontal beam was also placed across the opening as a gate bar.

The other gateways on the east and north-west are still unexplored, but the gateway bastions on the south-east have now come to light by the excavations of local contractors in search of building material. Here the walling is more sophisticated with well-cut, hammer-dressed, coursed rectangular blocks and bonded masonry, very similar to the walling found in later domestic construction in the city.

Plate 106
Fig. 36

Near the centre of the city and oriented on an approximately east–west axis is the main temple which covers an area of about 160 feet by 12 feet, generally known as the temple of ʿAṯar.[190] The lower walls of this large building are of massive blocks of undressed granite, roughly coursed with deep reveals and bastions on the east, north and south sides which

Plates 107, 108

suggest a Mesopotamian influence. On the higher level the masonry work in well-cut limestone is more refined and appears to show additions and improvements. Its construction was probably in four phases, the massive masonry of the lowest portions of the temple proper being the earliest of this building although there are the remains of an even earlier structure

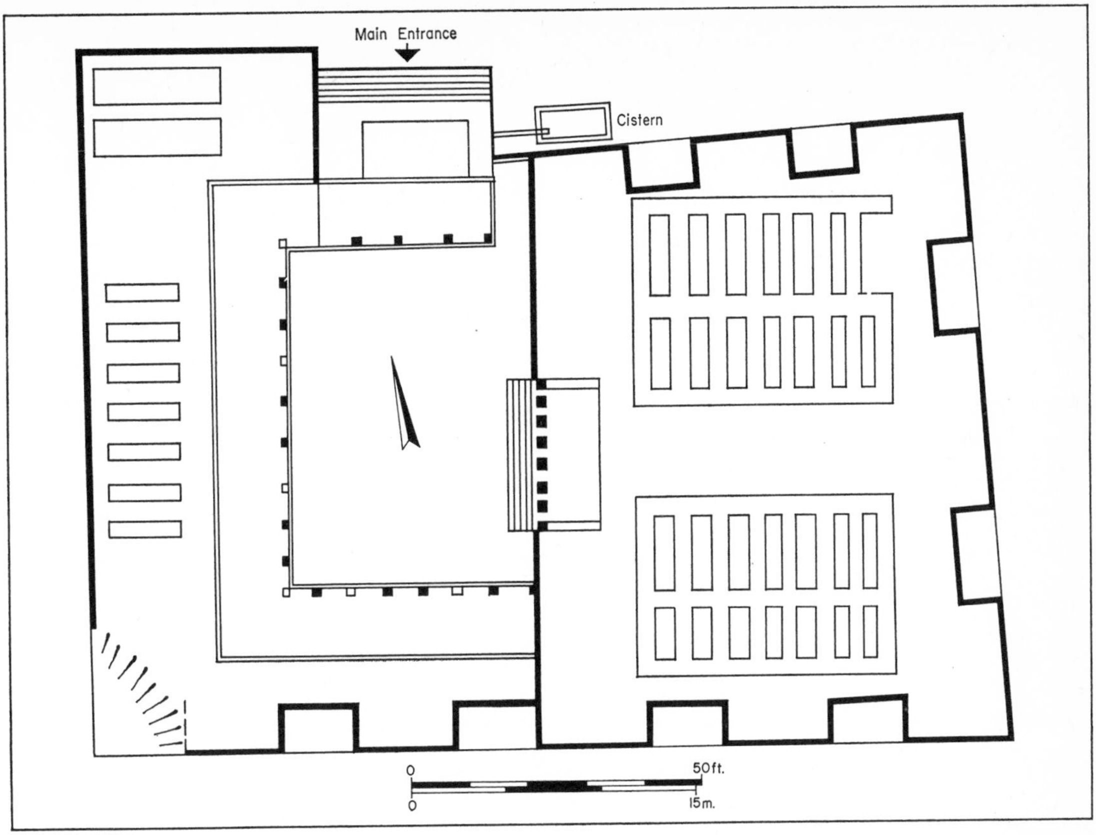

36 A plan of the temple or religious sanctuary at Timnaʿ, the principal structure exposed by the American Foundation Expedition. It is unfortunate that much of the superstructure has now disappeared, although sufficient remains to show the different construction phases, the earliest work visible being the base walling with the large bastions

below this level. The second period consisted of extensions during the third century BC; the court and steps were probably added during the time of the Kings in the first century BC. From examples found on the site the walls of the temple were faced internally with deep red and cream coloured polished marble slabs one and a half to two and a half inches thick.

Principally the design consists of a wide, stepped entrance on the north which leads to a columned forecourt or atrium paved with pink limestone slabs, and some of the bases of square columns still remain. A small staircase of limestone built into one of the reveals of the early masonry walling leading to the forecourt was demolished in about 1955. The five steps of limestone, about 25 feet wide, and the portico of the inner temple building are on the eastern side of the forecourt. On the surface within this

higher portion of the temple are the remains of many low walls which once formed separate rooms placed on both sides of the central axis. The use these were put to if they were not burial chambers is not yet known. The temple store rooms were on the western side of the court, and the west wall of the temple, in fine ashlar or well-cut masonry, shows that
Plate I this section was one of the later improvements.

The obelisk of King Šahr Hilal which had for years protruded from the sands of Timnaʿ was cleared by the American Foundation Expedition. The notable inscriptions (RES 4337 A and B) on this monolith refer to the laws of the city relating to commerce, marketing of goods, and taxes imposed.

Two well-constructed buildings excavated by the American Foundation Expedition were known as the house Yafaʿan and the house Yafash. They are situated on the west side; the house Yafaʿan is the closest to the South Gate. The house Yafash is important because of the six inscriptions associated with it. These texts found during the excavation show not only a development in the script but also provide information on the succession of a group of Kings of Qataban. Fronting the centre of the wall of this house, near the South Gate, the antithetical group of bronze lion riders was found.[191]

Nearby and also facing the South Gate are the remains of an important
Plate II building where the standard of ashlar masonry is far superior to that of Yafash. This consists of the south-west corner of the building in fine-cut, smooth-faced, ashlar-properly coursed and bonded and laid dry with fine cut joints. On the south side of this building are the remains of a cut-stone stairway, and there may have been another on the east side.

Further northwards and lying about a hundred yards west of the main temple further discoveries in 1967 included a complex of buildings with masonry walling very similar to that of the house Yafash. There are the
Fig. 37 remains of two buildings, each with a house and workshop, close together and divided by a narrow street. Formal inscriptions found built in the walls of each provided the names Šabʿan and ʿAthʿan (Aʿṯaʿn).

The design of the buildings known as Yafash,[192] excavated by the American Foundation,[193] is described in the inscriptions found built into the outer walls. The house seems to consist of a series of ground floor rooms and workshop with an external staircase leading to upper store rooms, presumably for incense and an open verandah. This description

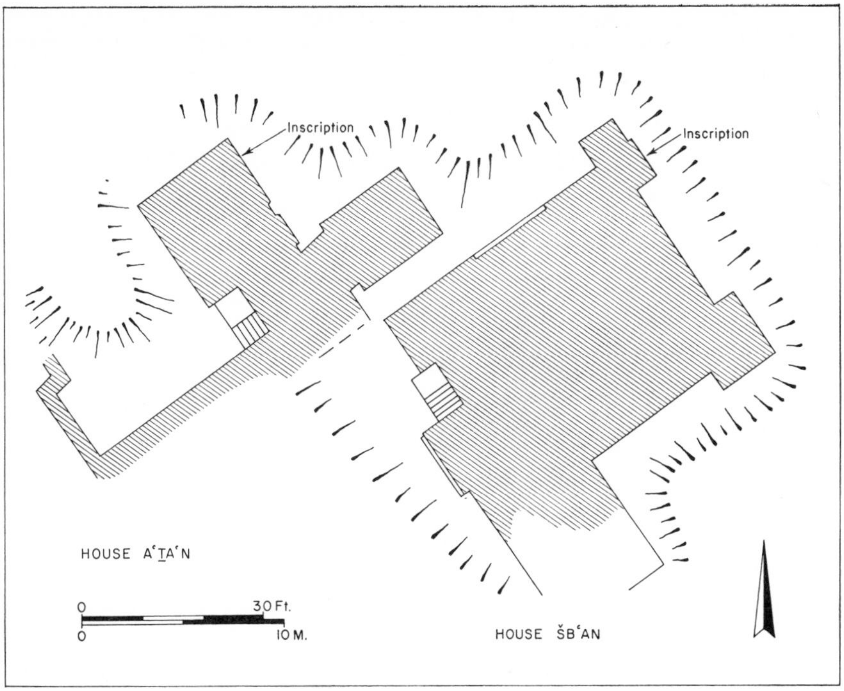

37 Plans of the external walls of the domestic structures Šabʿan and ʿAṯaʿan which were excavated in 1967. The inscriptions found on the walls described the buildings with the workshops and the external staircases, which are shown on the plans

is confirmed in the inscription found built in the wall of the house Šabʿan.

The masonry for these buildings seems to be a similar type of hammer-dressed cut stone laid in even courses, but some of the lower courses in house Šabʿan had an external facing of thin, vertically placed, fine-cut smooth face limestone blocks.

As well as the Hellenistic bronze lions with their cherubic riders other finds included two bronze circular incense burners, with high backs on a raised base, and with a free-standing ibex forming the handle, from near the temple. Many small bronzes came to light, including South Arabian letters which had been plugged direct into a stone face and the hooved feet for wooden furniture legs.

A discovery of great importance found in the House Hadath by the American Foundation was the bronze statue of a seated lady modelled in the dress of the late Hellenistic period.[193]

Recently discoveries were made by local inhabitants in the houses ʿAthʿan and Šabʿan. At the house ʿAthʿan a large bronze bath three feet in diameter and 20 inches deep was found. It has a round moulded rim and there are two pairs of vertical lug handles on opposite sides and stumps of four feet beneath the belly. There is an inscription in raised lettering beneath the whole length of the rim and also beneath the handles and some slight evidence of decoration on the belly. It was placed in the small museum store at Baiḥān al-Qasab.

A further find here was a fragmentary but well-modelled, free-standing deer, a remarkably naturalistic figure with arched neck portrayed in the act of listening. It was probably about 21 inches high.

Works in alabaster, marble and limestone are usually votive pieces presented by a dedicant to the temple although they are also used as memorials to the dead. From Timnaʿ they include the carving of stelae, which extend in design from plain slabs of alabaster, plaques with a bull's head in honour of the lunar deity, to formalized male or female heads representing the dedicant. Sometimes these have bases of the same material, but often the base is limestone, into which the stela is inset with a lime mortar.

Libation altars with bull-head spouts, friezes of ibex heads and architectural designs in rectilinear patterns have also been found on the surface and during excavations for building material at Timnaʿ.

INSCRIPTIONS

The inscriptions found at Timnaʿ, particularly at the South Gate, are still *in situ* as fortunately the stones are too massive to be moved and used elsewhere, but they have suffered much modern damage.

A group of these inscriptions which promulgate the laws of the city was recorded by E. Glaser. Some were published by N. Rhodokanakis in 1924 and the inscription dealing with homicide was published by A.K. Irvine in 1967.[194] Known as RES 3878, the text is a decree by King YDʿB ḎBYN, son of ŠHR, made about 200 BC dealing with the penalty for murder. Briefly, if a Qatabanian or a member of one of the associated tribes killed one of his fellows he was placed under a ban and outlawed. If the ban was ignored then the king authorized that he must die if he remained in Qatabanian territory and whoever killed the murderer need have no fear of the law or reprisal.

The inscription RES 3879 is a tax law decreed by ŠHR YGL, son of YDʿʾB, probably YDʿʾB ḎBYN's father. It deals with the tax laws of the country which were imposed not only on the relatives of the king, both male and female, but on all people born in Timnaʿ and the surrounding countryside as well as the male and female slaves.

The inscriptions known as RES 4337A and 4337B found on the obelisk of King ŠHR HLL in the centre of Timnaʿ deal with the trading regulations, in an endeavour to centralize all trade within the ŠMR market-place and to limit any trading in the BRM or close neighbourhood. These inscriptions were recorded by E. Glaser and published by M. Höfner in 1935 and by A.F.L. Beeston in 1959.[195] The following is an extract from the latter publication:

Thus decreed and ordained and enacted ŠHR HLL son of YDʿʾB, king of Qataban, and the Qatabanians in TMNʿ and BRM and the region (?) of the two alluvial-valleys of ḤWKM, and the 'Children of ʿm', and the controller of the 'Children of ʿm':

1. That whoever is a trader of TMNʿ or BRM in any form of merchandise must pay the market-tax within TMNʿ and have a trading-stall in ŠMR.
2. And one who travels to Qataban with merchandise and bales [?] and goods shall have a trading-stall and conduct his business and sell in ŠMR, no matter what tribe he belongs to.
3. And when such a one establishes a trading-stall, thereafter he may either trade (on his own account) or enter into partnership with any [other] stall-holder or merchant, without the intervention of the overseer of ŠMR.
4. And when the overseer of ŠMR announces that he desires Qatabanians to make (trading) journeys among the tribes while he himself trades in TMNʿ and has a trading-stall for his merchandise in ŠMR, then Qatabanians may trade on their own account with the tribes.
5. And when they inform the overseer of ŠMR that any foreigner has attempted to visit any part of Qataban with merchandise for Qataban, or (that) someone has consistently cheated a fellow-trader, he shall be fined fifty gold pieces ...
6. ... they shall not reckon a 'seeds-privilege' on any merchandise which is traded and purchased by Qatabanians, or by those in respect of

whom the overseer of ŠMR has assessed a trading-tax of N gold pieces, over and above what the Qatabanians pay in the market of ŠMR, in Qatabanian coinage.

7. Any Qatabanian, Minaean, or (other) inhabitant of TMNʿ who leases his house or his *(m)ẖtn* to a stall-holder, shall pay the market-tax in TMNʿ to the king of Qataban, either out of that which is included in his (the stall-holder's) possessions and stock-in-trade or, insofar as it exceeds such stock-in-trade, by means of his own personal effects.

8. No business of any sort may be conducted by any person who pays the TMNʿ market-tax with the intention of doing business with a foreign tribe instead of with Qataban and Sfln; [this is] in order that the Qatabanians may have their just rights according to the ordinance which the king of Qataban ordained for them and that ...

9. If anyone deals wholesale in merchandise with which he trades in ŠMR, it must be retailed in Qataban through middlemen.

10. If any person attempts to sell any merchandise in ŠMR at night, let people hold aloof until day dawns.

11. The king has supervisory authority in respect of every transaction and every commodity which passes in his territory.

12. Let every king give support to this decree.

On the east side of the main temple at Timnaʿ is a pecked design with the central motif of the crescent moon and orb of Venus with the formulae of Wadʾb. Although on the inner face of a recess of the massive foundation masonry this work may be contemporary with the superstructure.

Translation of one of the inscriptions found during the excavations by the American Foundation of the Study of Man in 1951 of the House of Yafash has also been included. It was published by A. Jamme[196] in 1958 and is of interest because of its description of a house design.

Jamme 118

Hawfiʿamm, son of Ṯawnab, has bought and taken into possession and acquired and secured title to and constructed and restored his House Yafash and its workshops and its incense sanctuary and its arcades, east from this house, and their two upper rooms and their roof-terraces and their parapets [?], from [the] foundation to [the] top, all together, according to the law of ʾAnbay and of ʾIl Taʿalay. By ʿAṯtar and by ʿAmm and by ʾAnbay and by D̲ât-Ṣantim and by D̲ât-Ẓahrân and by his lord Yadiʿ ʾab Ġaylân, son of Fariʿkarib, king of Qataban.

The Cemetery of Timnaʿ at Haid bin-Aqil

This cemetery[197] is approximately a mile north of Timnaʿ, and the remains are to be found on the west side of a large rocky outcrop, where there is a series of Qatabanian structures of stonework and mud bricks. In the lowest building at the foot of the rock, thought to be a mortuary temple, there is a deep shaft which extended some 60 feet down, and many objects including an inscription were found there. The area of the rock surface contained tomb structures with a series of crypts or chambers, each one about six feet long and about eighteen inches wide. These were formed in groups of about eight or ten and were divided by stone slabs into upper and lower chambers.

The Timnaʿ tombs have been well plundered in the past but they yielded material which includes a fine gold necklace,[198] sculpture, both free-standing and carved in relief, inscribed tablets and carved friezes, stelae, bronze objects, incense burners, beads and pottery, some of which was complete. This will serve to confirm the periods from the earliest occupation in Baiḥān to the time of the destruction of Timnaʿ, especially when the sequence of pottery and artifacts discovered during the excavation of the mound of Hajar bin-Humaid[199] about ten miles south of Timnaʿ, is made known.

Hajar Henu Az-Zureīr (Ḥaribat)

These important remains of the Qatabanian city of Ḥaribat are still little known. The city lies north of Jabal Qarn ʿUbaid, and its strategic position commands the western end of the great Mablaqa Pass. The site is a completely level, roughly rectangular area measuring about 884 feet east to west by about 600 feet north to south, and raised some fifteen feet above the wadi level. The lower courses of ashlar-faced buildings laid out in an apparently orderly town plan suggest that these were all buildings of importance. It was entirely surrounded by a wall, though this has completely collapsed and only piles of rubble remain. At the south-west corner there is a magnificent structure consisting of two side wings of fine ashlar with central recessed entrance and paved court and steps leading west from the city level.

Plate 114

An inscription, *Ryckmans* 391, is on the north face near the north-west corner, with a tablet Wad'b on the west face of the same corner. There is a stone similar to the lintel at Am ʻAdiya depicting two snakes with heads meeting at the centre on the south wall, but the finest carving consists of two standing long-horn bulls with the Wad'b formulae (RES 3643). Nigel St John Groom, Political Officer in Baihān in 1948, was the first to record these inscriptions. Archaeologists are indebted to him for his work and interest in discovering and surveying places of antiquity in the Baihān area and in ensuring, with C.H. Inge that these inscriptions were delivered to G. Ryckmans for translation.[200]

The great advantage of this site archaeologically is that it is free of blown sand. The buildings are quite visible without excavation, and some walls of fine masonry are about ten feet in height. It is perhaps significant that the orientation of the main building at the south-west corner and the other buildings generally are aligned directly north-south.

The Fourth and Fifth Governorates

THE WADI ḤAḌRAMAUT

The great valley of the Wadi Ḥaḍramaut extends from the desert sand of the Ramlat Sabatain and the ancient city of Shabwa in the west towards the junction at G͟hurāf and the mouth of the Wadi ʻIdm and Tarīm in the east. Although the Wadi extends further eastwards, coursing southwards to the sea and changing its name to Wadi Masailah in the process, the former portion is the more important, fertile and prosperous, with the cities of Shibām, Saiwūn and Tarīm. The valley is enclosed by steep cliffs with their characteristic flat tops known as the jōl. Access by road to Mukalla is either down the Wadi Duan or Wadi ʻIdm.

It seems possible that at some early period the flood waters flowed from the west depositing silts on the eastern end, gradually levelling up the wadi ground levels. Man manufactured his artifacts in this area on the level jōl and on lower shoulders of the cliffs during the Neolithic period. Other signs of early occupation of the fertile wadi extend to the much later period of the eighth to fifth centuries BC – evidenced by sites such
Plate 129
as Mashg͟ha in the Wadi ʻIdm and at Ḥuraiḍah in the Wadi ʻAmd. Graffiti inscriptions are to be found on boulders along the sides of the main Wadi, usually written or pecked in 'Thamudic'-type characters, not

as formal documents but merely giving names of persons, many of them of Sabaean origin.

Prehistoric material in the Ḥaḍramaut

Dr G. Caton-Thompson found flint implements in the area of the Wadi Ḥaḍramaut during her expedition in 1937, and published three groups of palaeolithic implements found between Wadi ʿAmd and Tarīm.[201]

The area around Fort Habarut located some 180 miles east of Tarīm near the Dhufar border has produced neolithic artifacts lying on the sand surface. A date of between 3500 and 3000 BC for similar material from Rub ʿal-Khali has been suggested.[202]

G. Lankester Harding published flint implements which he found at Makainan east of Tarīm in 1959–60 as well as a selection of those found at Habarut and on the edge of the Rub ʿal-Khali north west of Al-ʿAbr. He suggests that there is an apparent affinity with artifacts found in Egypt and the possibility of a connection between the two areas during the Neolithic period,[203] although it must be added that this period in Southern Arabia has not yet been dated.

A sustained and scientific search for early material was carried out by G. Cole when with the Smithsonian Expedition of 1961–2 under the leadership of G. W. Van Beek. Certain aspects of this work have been broached in the Smithsonian Institution Report for 1963.

Near the outcrop of Qarn Qaimah located west from Hainin and north-east of the headland of Khor Malik, a hand-axe, probably Acheulian, was found. However, it had a reddish weathered surface unlike the local grey limestone, and the scarcity of specimens cannot be taken as evidence of an Acheulian occupation here. Similar specimens are well known on the Somaliland coast.

On the flat summit of Jabal Jibb south-west of Ghurfah is a thick concentration of reddish brown artifacts of good quality chert spread over a large area of the upper plateau. This was a workshop area in use much later than the main plateau area, which was used probably during Upper Pleistocene times. There are indications that much later the waste material and flakes here were re-used. According to Cole and Van Beek in the preliminary report, the earliest widespread industry is based on a Levallois technique. This continued for a very long period and was followed by a Desert Neolithic industry, to which it is possible to assign the megalithic structures and circles of standing stones found elsewhere. This level of culture probably continued here until the late second millennium BC.[204]

Shabwa

Plate 116

The most famous of the ancient cities of Arabia, Shabwa, capital of the Ḥaḍramaut, was well known to the geographers and historians at the beginning of our era. It was linked with the luxury trade of the East and with stories of its magnificent temples and public buildings; its name stirred the imagination of the early travellers.

However, in fact, little is known of Shabwa today. It is difficult to get to, and visitors are not welcomed by the inhabitants of the ruins. (The author was probably not the first to be discouraged from picking up a pottery fragment by the clearly recognizable sound over the still air of a rifle bolt ramming home a cartridge into the breach!)

Shabwa is situated about ten miles east of ʿUqla and it lies in the valley of the Wadi ʿAtf – a continuation of Wadi ʿIrma – which north of Shabwa divides into the Wadi Maʿshar and Wadi Mihbadh.

Fig. 38

The site is contained at the southern end of a valley between low hills and is bounded to the south by a large mound which diverted the waters of the wadi to prevent flooding of the open area. This long mound, which is probably partly man-made, incorporates a natural rock feature, and it is upon and behind this barrier that the actual ruins of the ancient city lie. Further ruins are also found on the hill which forms the eastern boundary. Beyond these hills lie the now silted agricultural areas, although some fields east of this region, irrigated by the Wadi Mihbadh, are still in use today. Shabwa's group of salt mines lie within the encircling hills forming the valley.

Three villages inside the confines of the site comprise the modern Shabwa, and the inhabitants live among the ruins and remains of ancient grandeur. Maiwan lies to the north, Mathna to the east and Hajar surmounts the hills on the eastern perimeter. It is clear that where the site has not suffered by erosion it has suffered at the hands of the local people who have incorporated any useful building material into the construction of their dwellings. Much of the re-used stone masonry is similar to the limestone blocks employed in the building at ʿUqla. These possess the same fine dressing on all faces and are marginally drafted with horizontal and vertical chiselling and pecked centre panels which link the work-

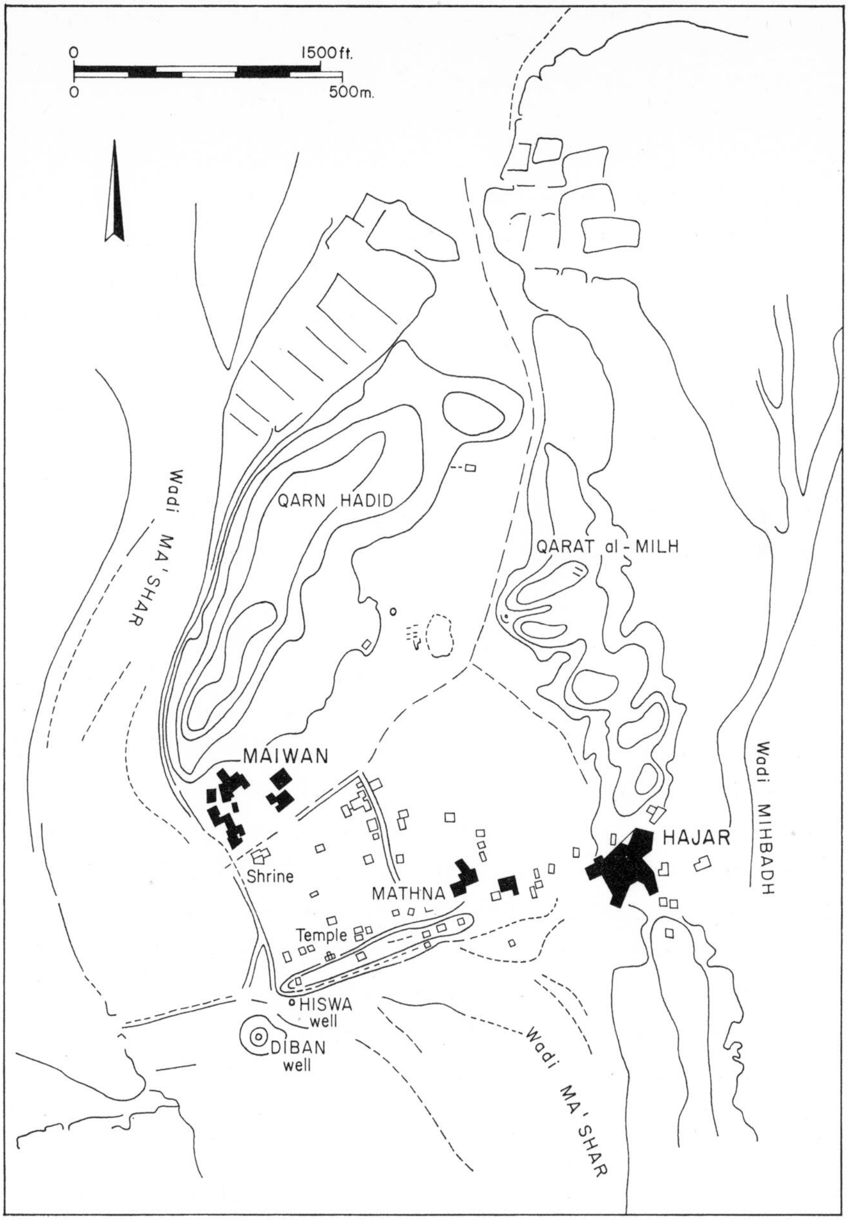

38 A sketch map of Shabwa, based on air photographs taken by the Royal Air Force as well as the plan by H. St John Philby, and the author's ground survey

manship with that styled as Type 2 by Van Beek.[205] The ashlar facing of a wall of the palace at Hajar which Van Beek mentions and was also photographed by Philby,[206] appears to be of similar construction.

'*From my site notes*

I approached Shabwa from the north, riding down the west bank of the Wadi Ma'shar until the little mosque or shrine of Maiwan came into sight and near it a large, rectangular building built of large and finely dressed masonry blocks, which clearly date from the pre-Islamic period. Crossing the wadi I passed between the Tiban well (for livestock) and the Hiswa well (for humans) and up to the massive natural rock bastion which seemed to be about forty feet high.

I was permitted to walk upon the dyke, or mound, from the open space before Hajar village and noticed many structures in which old masonry had been employed but I did not see any potsherd on the ground. One building, which I was not able to visit but which I photographed, was of exactly the same type of construction as the building on the rock of 'Anwadm at 'Uqla and a building at Naqb al Hajr. I was informed that this is the same building excavated by the late Lord Belhaven when he spent several weeks at Shabwa in 1938.

Plates 117, 118

I inspected the 'temple' site, which was described in great detail by Philby who was allowed to spend sufficient time at the site to take measurements of some of the buildings, and saw the limestone bases for the four circular columns which he mentions but did not find the 'holes for all the columns to sit on' – presumably the dowels. I also searched in vain for the remnants of columns, which could have been of stone and probably plastered smooth as is the practice in the Ḥaḍramaut today. The large plinth at the east side of the entrance was clearly visible, and I noticed recesses in the top for fixing a statue – perhaps of metal – or some similar feature. There was a companion plinth, also, at the opposite side of the entrance.

With a base of 2 feet 6 inches and a column diameter at base of about 2 feet the height of the entablature would have been less than twenty feet above the base and the effect of grandeur would only have been apparent from below the flight of steps. However, the use of circular columns was very rare in South Arabia, and here were probably the direct result of external influence.

It is of interest to speculate whether this portico formed part of the rebuilding of Shabwa, referred to by Yd''l Byn, king of Ḥaḍramaut, in his inscription at 'Uqla.'

L. P. Kirwan, the Director of the Royal Geographical Society, has very kindly made available Major The Honourable A. Hamilton's (later Lord Belhaven) actual site notes recorded during the excavation at Shabwa when he was a Political Officer in the Western Protectorate. He was the author of many publications and books on Southern Arabia, the best known being *The Kingdom of Melchior* and *The Uneven Road*.

We are extremely fortunate to have this first-hand report of the work in 1939. Obviously any account of actual finds is of intrinsic value, but it is unusual to be able to follow the story of how they were brought to light through the actual words of their discoverer.

'It was not found possible in the time and with the materials available to improve on or to enlarge Philby's map. The object of the small excavation undertaken was to ascertain the purpose of the large step-pyramid buildings, the number of which, while one cannot give it accurately because of their apparent intercommunication, is considerably over fifty. The greatest area lies to the west of the main temple. Here, without extensive excavation, the cost of which would be some thousands of pounds, it would be impossible to disentangle the complexity of inner and outer walls.

It can be said however that the type of structure is similar throughout the whole ruin. A steeply stepped side faces a street. Behind and to either side of this 'face' run lines and walls of galleries containing small rectangular chambers both windowless and doorless. The floors are of thin plaster and, when these are broken through, deep earth is found beneath. It is evident that these chambers are not meant for human habitation but are graves and one is led to the conclusion that Shabwa is a vast graveyard.

The site chosen for excavation is perhaps the least productive in the ruin, since not only has it been lived on in recent times, but it has obviously been much excavated and broken. Excavation was stopped when I could no longer afford to continue, but the vaults, while not startling, are interesting and should be helpful to the future excavator. For one thing they show clearly is that considerable funds will be required before any but meagre information can be obtained.

The most interesting discovery was that of the door with some of the wood in place. Within the chamber a large marble slab was found, neither a door nor a floor, which may, however, have fallen from above, as did the large stone window-sill. The floor of the chamber was unprotected earth. The next chamber is equally puzzling and an excavation to a depth of 19 feet, while revealing a cessation of careful building at 16 feet, revealed not even the purpose of the wall of any of the chambers; the door, with a paved slab of marble outside, is evidence of connection with the small temple, but, in later times, when the door was built, those passing through it cannot have been aware of the long excellently built walls or of the 'window' beneath their feet. It is suggested that these lower walls are much earlier structures, whose use ceased and which were used as foundations for the later step-pyramid building. No evidence of a wooden floor nor of wooden steps were found. Such would, however, have enabled the builders of the door to have access to the deep rooms beneath it, from which it is possible that access was had to the upper graves. The wall of the upper passage is vertically in line with the west wall of the lower chamber and this points to a similarity of purpose, or a central passage dividing the two main blocks of tombs. Thus, commencing 20 feet or more below ground level, the tombs may have been filled in and earth-covered until at last a small square single tomb crowned the edifice. The stone steps suggest that, either the building was higher, which again is borne out by the broken and incomplete frescoes and inscription or, and this is less likely, that the building was incomplete when it was abandoned.

No complete burial was found, nor in the disturbed state of the building was one to be expected. Grave I was the only grave found to have a floor and was uncovered.'

G. Lankester Harding made the following comments after his brief visit in 1959.

'At the junction of the north gate road and another running east is an eminence on top of which are the rooms excavated by Lord Belhaven; it is impossible to interpret the work now as the rooms have been cleared to well below floor level and no control has been left anywhere. The walls are well built of carefully dressed limestone blocks, the rooms are connected by door-ways, and one has a good flight of steps. Below these rooms in the south are some long narrow chambers, the south wall of which appears to have been the outer wall of some building destroyed by earthquake. Two courses of another building on the south side of the street from this wall have marginally drafted pecked masonry; it appears to belong to van Beek's Type 4 with wide upper and lower margins, but there was not time to examine in a great detail ... The site is clearly no city of the dead as Lord Belhaven deduces; his tombs contained no bodies or grave goods and are in fact ordinary rooms of ordinary houses.'[207]

However, Brown and Beeston say: 'These narrow cells were found packed with earth containing human bones and apparently also pottery and were sealed when complete with plaster. Lord Belhaven thought they were graves but no burial was found *in situ.*'[208]

It would appear, therefore, that only scientific excavation of this site could provide conclusive evidence as to which of these conflicting opinions is correct.

'Uqla

On the southern side of the Jabal 'Uqla, which is some ten miles west from Shabwa, is an insignificant group of rocks. They are, however, unique, for here the early kings of the Ḥaḍramaut and their followers commemorated a ceremony when titles were distributed to chosen guests. The smoother faces of the rocks are literally covered with inscriptions.

The central rock of the group is surmounted by a small stone building and is surrounded by a boundary wall on three sides with a ditch which levels out at the south-western side. Plate 119

The 'Uqla inscriptions seem to have been first seen and recorded by St John Philby during the tour he made of this area when visiting the Ḥaḍramaut in 1939.[209] A total of over 100 inscriptions have now been found on this rock,[210] although some contain only a few letters and several are either defaced or indistinct. Plate 120

It is thought that this place, known in ancient times as 'Anwadm, held great significance for the king and people of Shabwa, the capital of the Ḥaḍramaut, and it was here that rulers and nobles from the tribes and representatives from neighbouring kings came to hold their ritual celebrations. Many of the inscriptions refer to the King of Ḥaḍramaut by name and mention those who accompanied him to the crowning ceremony preceding accession to the throne. One inscription, that of Yd''l Byn, refers to the rebuilding of Shabwa, the completion of which was commemorated at 'Anwadm when a ritual hunt and banquet were arranged. No references are made in the inscriptions to deities nor to dedicatory offerings. Possibly the ceremonies held at 'Anwadm were purely temporal an the rocks themselves held no religious significance although it would be hard to prove either way.

The central rock is not square but, for simplicity, it is possible to refer to the east face, west face, etc. The nearest rock is to the southern side about 16 feet away.

The east face, which carried the important and clear inscriptions, also has two water cisterns or tanks, one rectangular at ground level and the other semicircular placed on a rocky ledge overhanging the other and the inscriptions. Both tanks are of rough masonry construction, roughly coursed and bedded in lime mortar with a rendering of lime plaster on the outside as well as within. It does not seem likely that these tanks are contemporary with the inscriptions, nor with the building on the top of the rock. Part of the lower tank wall, which is two feet thick, covers two inscriptions where it butts against (now cleared) the rock surface.

The building at the top of the rock is in a ruinous state but portions of the walls remain on all sides. It is approximately square with 16 feet 6 inch long walls. The northern side is placed at 125° and the eastern side at 220°. The south-east corner stands 5 feet 6 inches high and the north-east and north-west corners are 5 feet high. The walls are constructed with quoins on all faces and finely dressed limestone blocks of masonry, marginally drafted and pecked in the centre panel, bonded and laid dry. The lengths of the wall consist of coursed and bonded headers only of roughly hewn stone, all of a consistent size laid dry. These stones are of the same height as the cut stone quoins and therefore the courses are regular along the length of the walls.

It seems probable that at some later period the building was used as an observation post or fort and that the water tanks were provided for the benefit of those left in charge of it. Gradually it had been allowed to fall into disrepair, although the removal of quoins indicates certain wanton damage. What its original purpose could have been can only be surmised, but it is likely that it was linked with the celebration ceremonies of the royal house of Shabwa, and may have been a form of throne or retiring room for the ruler.

The masonry quoins were cut and quarried elsewhere, possibly at the same quarries which supplied Shabwa, for there many buildings were constructed of similar stone pecked and with drafted margins.

Eastwards from the ʿUqla group of rocks there lies a group of small stone erections which on first inspection appeared to be cairns but later turned out to be nothing more than modern sangars (stone breastworks) intended possibly for troops with small arms should the need arise.

Two of the more interesting inscriptions on the rock face are:

a. ʿUqla No. 12 = *Philby* 83 = RES 4910 = *Jamme* 921

1 ʾIlʿadhdh [ʾIlʿazz] Yalit King of Ḥa

2 ḍramaut son of ʿAmmdhakhar went

3 to the fortress ʾAnwadm in order to

4 to give titles.

b. ʿUqla No. 40 = *Philby* 84 = RES 4912 = *Jamme* 949

1 Yadaʿ ʾil Bayin King of Ḥaḍramaut son of Rabbšams of the freeman of Yuhabʾir, he who has altered and transformed the city Šabwat

2 and had rebuilt in stone the temple, put a roof [and] a pavement in the fortress when they [the temple and the fortress] had broken down because of a collapse, and they killed thirty-five oxen

3 and eighty-two young camels and twenty-five gazelles and eight leopards at the fortress ʾAnwadm.

Al-ʿAbr, Wadi al-Aqābih

The Wadi Al-Aqābih is situated about ten miles north-west of Al-ʿAbr, approximately one hour distance by vehicle. Although Raas Arghadd is given locally as a nearby feature, it was not known except to local inhabitants and is not marked on any published map. The most prominent feature of the wadi is the Jabal Aqābih, which dominates the rock cleft lying to the eastern side. Plate 121

This narrow pass is one of the main routes through the hills surrounding Al-ʿAbr, an oasis formerly the outer centre for the trade-route connecting the Wadi Ḥaḍramaut and its capital Shabwa lying across the sands to the south, with Najrān and the north. The sands blowing from the north-east have levelled out the northern end of the pass, where three levels are now visible. The raising of the floor is particularly noticeable where graffiti are to be found at ground level, and in a few places even below it. The total length of the pass is about 2,500 feet, the first section being a 1000 feet long narrow rock-cleft and averaging some 40 feet in width. The centre section, at a higher level, is about 600 feet wide, while the north-eastern section is level with the rock sides until the wadi opens into the sands. Plate 122

There is one well at the northern end of the first section of the pass which is still in use and from local evidence another, unusable, well exists at the end of the second section.

Plates 123, 124

On both sides of the pass the rock faces are covered with hundreds of inscriptions and drawings.[211] Many of them are unusual for there are drawings of hands with fingers and thumbs outstretched, accompanying a personal and sometimes a family name and usually contained within an encircling line. Some inscriptions carry as many as 12–17 drawings of hands, some only 4–6 drawings and many incorporate the marks known as 'water signs'. Some examples of these inscriptions are: HYB followed by 17 hands; YMD'L with 6 hands and three different water signs; MMRHMW with 6 hands; TB 'ṮY with 4 hands.

The meaning of the portrayal of a hand is not known but it could well have been intended as an indication of distance, or even the number of camels travelling in a particular caravan on this important route. In any case, the drawings of hands at this pass would appear to enhance the name with which it appears. A desert guide, Hamid, who was a native of this area, did not know the reason for the drawings although he obliged by pecking a small modern graffito of his own.

Plate 127

Fig. 39

The Jabal Aqābih, which overlooks the pass, is noticeable for the stone cairns lining its narrow ridge. These are clearly visible from both sides of the Jabal but it seems probable that they were intended to be seen against the skyline by travellers from the desert sands to the north. The cairns number thirty-three in all and are of a consistent size and shape. They stand about three feet high, are spaced five feet apart, and are carefully constructed of rough masonry laid flat with no mortar. An additional cairn stands at the north-west end of the ridge, and this is much larger than the others, measuring from four to five feet high and fifteen feet across. It is possible that at one time it contained a chamber which has now collapsed. A similar cairn was excavated and found to contain human bones. Many other cairns of this nature are to be found on mountain and hill ridges in the Al-'Abr area, the Wadi 'Irma and Wadi 'Idm south of Sāh,[212] where the larger cairns can be compared with the large one described above. A pill-box type of cairn is also found at Ruwaiq and 'Alam 'Abyad as mentioned by St John Philby,[213] but these latter types are obviously tomb groups whereas the single-line ridge cairns are likely to have formed part of a system indicating routes.

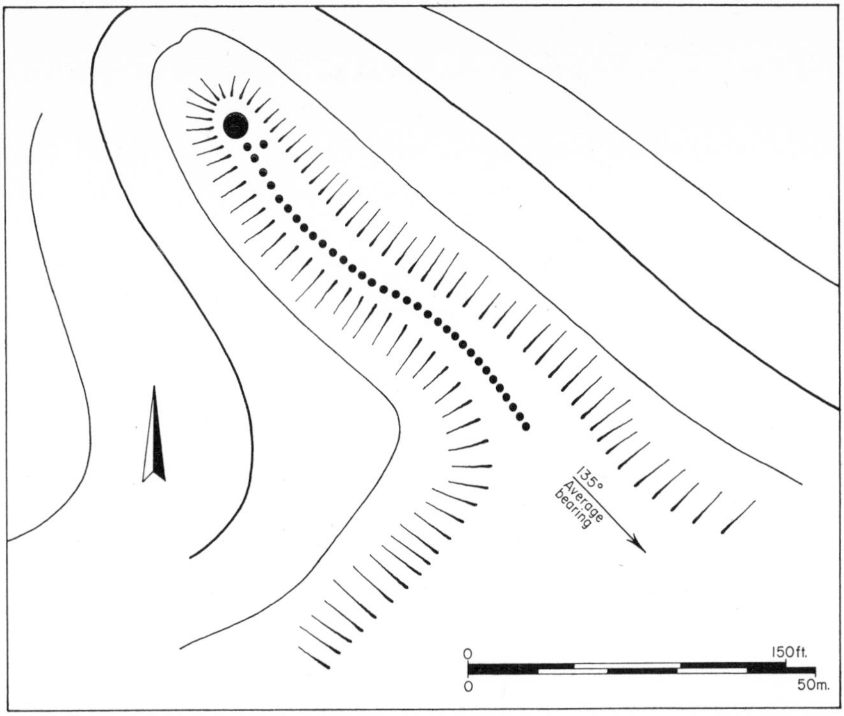

39 The line of small cairns leading from the main cairn on the flat summit of Jabal Aqābih. There are many such in the area

Cairns noticed by Philby on his journey south-east towards Al-ʿAbr seemed to indicate the better route. He says that after the cairn at Radm Al-ʾAmir and in a straight line towards Al-ʿAbr there are cairns at regular intervals of a few hundred yards, said to extend on a route known as Darb al-ʾAmir. However, this series of cairns, although along a probable ancient route, appears modern and was erected to mark the path to Al-ʿAbr.

Other lines of cairns noticed in the vicinity of Al-ʿAbr were to the west of the oasis and lying east of the modern track which winds away from Al-ʿAbr in a southerly direction to the level plains and the sands of Ramlat Sabatain, towards the rock outcrops of Tirbaq and Arain and the Wadi Shuqaiqāt down to Shabwa.

Ḥuraiḍah

The site consists of a temple and domestic buildings and tombs in the northern scree slopes, in the Wadi ʿAmd a few miles north-west of the town of Ḥuraiḍah. Under the direction of Dr G. Caton Thompson in

1937[214] it was the first controlled archaeological excavation carried out in Southern Arabia, or Southern Yemen as it is now called.

From inscriptions found on the site the temple was dedicated to the Moon God Sīn and the ancient name of this site is also given, it was Ma<u>dh</u>ābum.

THE MOON TEMPLE

Fig. 40

The earliest phase of building is identified as an oblong stone-paved platform about 40 feet 6 inches by 31 feet 10 inches resting on a series of boulders enclosed in a wall over 12 feet high. Little remains today of the superstructure, but there are remains of stone pillar bases and part of the partition walling of the second and third phases of building which divide the south-west area into forecourts and passages. Two flights of stone steps led up to the platform. Originally the walls were built of freestone-rubble blocks set in fairly regular courses. The blocks were trimmed into roughly oblong forms while the quoins were roughly squared. The masonry coping of the early phase of building was chisel-drafted on the margins, with pecked centre panels.

The temple platform rested on a series of boulders and rubble topped by a spread of limestone and sandstone pebbles with a gypsum plaster poured and trowelled over this. A complete length of pavement survives outside the north-west and south-east retaining walls. The earliest phase of building has been assigned to the fifth century BC.

The building had its corners orientated to the four cardinal points and the main façade is on the south-west side.

No *in situ* inscriptions were found inset in walling, although twenty-one archaic inscriptions were found re-used in the later work and are assumed to be contemporary with the earliest phase of building. No complete pottery was found in the temple but by comparison of sherds with the tomb pottery it was seen that the same forms were found in both places. Tomb pottery was generally hard and well fired with red or reddish brown slip.

Nearby, on the south-western side, is a series of shrines with altars and each is apsidal in shape. These were probably built to enable worship to continue after the destruction of the temple. There is a continuous line of stone skirting which lies parallel to the temple façade with sixteen slabs used in this length which seems to act as a boundary to the shrines.

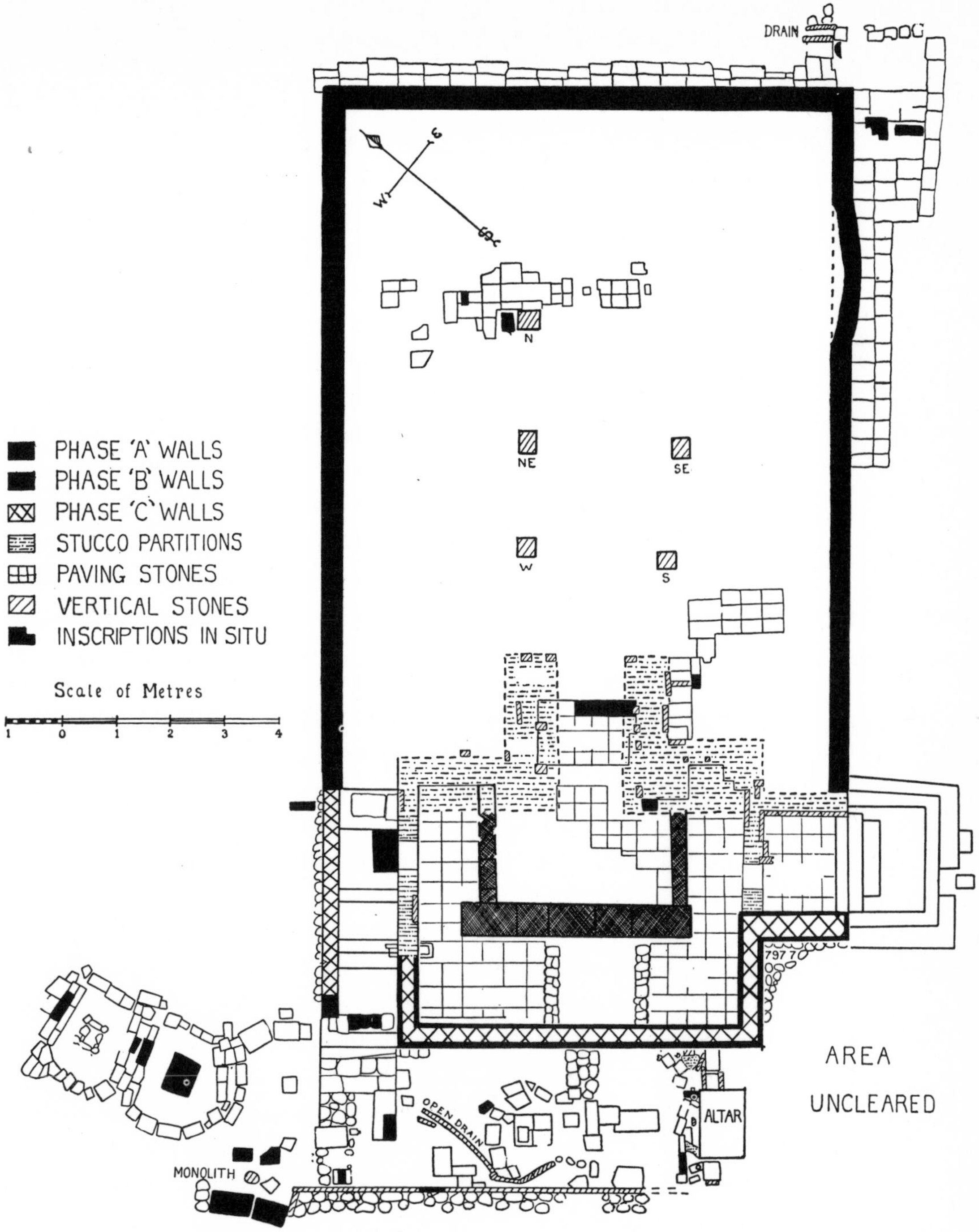

40 A plan of the temple dedicated to Sīn the Moon-god at Ḥuraiḍah, from the survey drawing of G. Caton-Thompson

Several limestone incense burners with four squared legs were found in the apsidal shrines and one in the temple area.

THE TOMBS

Several tombs lie in the lower scree slopes of the northern cliff face. Two of these were excavated and appear to be artificial caves for ossuary burials. A third, not completely excavated showed a series of empty wall niches. The entrance of one of the tombs was irregularly oval and had a maximum width of 9 feet 5 inches and a south-east outlook 132°. The actual chamber was excavated into the hillsides to a depth of about 26 feet and horse-shoe in shape while the walls were curved inwards to the roof over 7 feet 8 inches. The tombs yielded local unglazed pottery, some still complete, including some stemmed bowls, goblets and cups all found lying in irregular groups together with human skeletal remains on the floor.

Pedestal bowls with ledge rims were frequently found inscribed with early South Arabian characters. Stoneware bowls and unusual cups with spouts and flange handles were also discovered.

Several cosmetic palettes in cream alabaster with three short legs were the only pieces found of this material. Metal ornaments, probably of bronze, such as rings, pins and bangles, and necklace beads of carnelian, coloured glass bicones as well as perforated shells and faience discs were found with the burial groups. Obsidian microliths were found spread over the tomb floors.

The tombs are today much in demand as living quarters and stores.

THE FARMSTEAD

North of the temple site, lying nearly 150 yards away, is a mud-brick farm-house complex. The walls have no stone foundation and the mud bricks were laid in mud mortar and mud-plastered.

The floors were of hard mud and the roofs of rough rafters of local timber with an infill and cover of small branches or twigs and mud. Pottery fragments, a few pieces inscribed with early South Arabian letters, served to indicate that the buildings here were contemporary with the tombs.

Mashgha (Hidbat al Ghusan[215] and Dar al-Ghanimah)

Mashgha[216] is situated in the centre of the Wadi ʿIdm, a few miles northwest of the village of Sūnah, and its nearest town is Al-Rudūd.

This is an extensive pre-Islamic city site, measuring approximately 600 yards north to south by about 350 yards. It is located on silt well eroded on the east by the wadi flood-water and weather erosion leaving a series of isolated mounds which are topped by stone and mud-brick walls. Here the occupation debris has a depth of over 20 feet.

On the eastern side of the site a mud-brick wall about five yards high has been exposed by erosion and there is a high mound to the north-east with an exposed building of both different masonry styles and mud-brick walling.

Another mound to the north is surmounted with a large masonry building with a stretch of good stone walling on the south face.

On the west centre of the site is a building standing on a rectangular podium with a stone retaining wall and large limestone blocks. Beside it on the east is a roughly rectangular plastered floor.

Fragments of inscribed stones and remains of carved decorative building stones, fragments of sculpture and incense burners were found on the surface.

Potsherds are to be found spread widely over the site. Some fragments show definite all over burnishing, but all ware has a fairly thick slip. Incised wavy lines and raised bands of herring-bone pattern are popular decorative motifs. The depth of habitation-debris illustrates a long period of continued use which probably started about the eighth century BC.

Nearby and almost due north-west is a rock outcrop about 500 feet high close to the face of the wadi cliff. On the summit are the remains of a rectangular stone building. The top was reached by a masonry stairway which now extends only a short distance down the slope. Several stones in the vicinity were inscribed with early South Arabian names and from its orientation to the cardinal points the building may have been of religious significance.

At the foot of this rock on the southern side there are the remains of a small town with exposed masonry. The extensive ruin sites here are evidence of a large population in this part of the wadi.

Husn al-ʿUrr

This large spectacular stone fort stands on the summit of a commanding rock outcrop in the middle of the wadi, north of the flood course.[217] It is located between the towns of Qasam and al-Saum eastwards from the city Plate 130 *Fig. 41* of Tarīm. The foundations of the buildings are built directly on to the rock and the most prominent is the large rectangular structure some thirty feet in height which dominates the eastern end of the site. The walling of this building is of roughly cut stone blocks, averaging some two feet in length, laid dry and coursed.

The building is reached by a sloping path on the north side, passing the remains of a guard- and gate-house which straddles the path and overlooks a deep well at the end of a stone path extending on the north side. At this point the path winds sharply to the right and a four-line pre-Islamic inscription can be seen about half-way up the face of the north walling of the main building. The path continues to the summit where there is a large plaster-lined water cistern about twenty-three feet long and seven feet wide. Nearby on the southern side is a very deep pit in the natural rock, thought at first to be a well or cistern. There are several remains of masonry structures around the perimeter of the rock summit, but the main building has been used by the Ḥaḍrami Bedouin Legion and consequently the structure has suffered internal alterations and some external improvement. However, this was only the upper portion and on the south wall old window openings indicate the possibility of rooms at a lower level so far unentered.

Fine-cut limestone treads to steps created by the alterations looked as though they had been removed from an ashlar wall surface. However, although this fort seems to have been a utilitarian series of buildings, there are several portions of well-carved stones now preserved in the town of Mukalla which suggest these are later structures utilizing the foundations of more luxuriously decorated buildings; probably the whole group of structures on the summit were military and domestic quarters of a wealthy ruler who controlled the well-irrigated fertile wadi. There is one well-carved stone which is in the form of a Byzantine capital and depicts the ritual ibex hunt with horses and men. This was taken by Colonel van der Meulen from where it had been built into walling and is now in the Aden
Plates 3–5
Museum. Long stone sections of window or door architraves, carved with the grape and vine-leaf pattern with ibex and humans within the foliage were found lying on the floor and are now in the Mukalla Museum.

On the level area of the wadi and on all sides of the rock are many piles of stones, remains of a pre-Islamic irrigation system which utilized the flood-water from the main channel and controlled its supply with

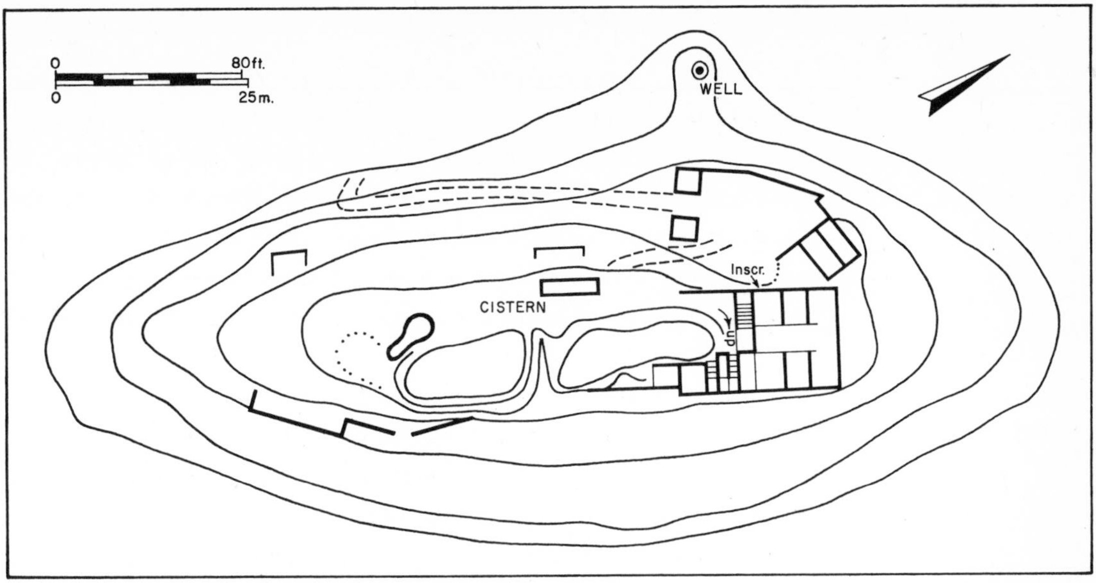

41 A sketch plan of Husn al-ʿUrr from the drawings of H. von Wissmann and H. T. Norris and from the author's ground survey

sluices to the fields that spread across the wadi area. The Husn al-ʿUrr was, therefore, probably the home of the local ruler and not always merely a fort guarding the Wadi Ḥaḍramaut from attack from the east, for this was then probably the task of the forces housed in the barracks and fort at Makainan.

Medieval town sites in the Wadi Ḥaḍramaut are to be found frequently on the lower shoulders and benches of the cliffs at the side of the wadi, usually with a prominent stone-built fort or *husn*. This suggests that the early Islamic period was one of insecurity. The design of forts on the wadi level often follows the Yafaʿ pattern.[218] This was probably the pattern of the earlier buildings on the level ground. This plan consists principally of a square building with nearly cylindrical bastions at the corners, hence the building was obviously designed for defence by enfilade fire. Buildings of this type do not usually remain occupied although the best example still used is the magnificent palace at Saiwūn. Later buildings were not designed with corner bastions, and during a long peaceful period the style became a clear rectangular or square plan, with more economical use of floor space. Abandoned houses and even small towns are to be found in the wadi as the inhabitants have left to live nearer to their fields, and it is not a rare sight to find a newer house built alongside a ruined fort.

Today the important towns and the centres of trade of the eastern part of the country apart from the port of Mukalla are Al-Qatn, Shibām, Saiwūn and Tarīm, all in the Wadi Ḥaḍramaut, and with the addition of Shiḥr on the coast and Ḥuraiḍah in the Wadi ʿAmd they also are the cultural centres where the historical documents and family histories are preserved in family and mosque libraries.

Saiwūn, the Kathīri state capital with its houses and market centre close to the enormous white-plastered palace in the shadow of the wadi cliff is typical of the town which has expanded into the surrounding country during a time of peace.

Shibām as a contrast is remarkable for its continued use of a walled site for many centuries. The skyscraper architecture at this Qaitiʿ centre is the result of the vertical expansion of mud-brick houses built to the defensive limits of the town walls, in some cases forming part of the walls. An island site, confined by the field areas and the wadi flood channel commanding the agricultural areas at the entrance into the wadi, it will be of great interest to the archaeologists of the future.

The First Governorate

THE ISLAND OF SOCOTRA

A description of some of the principal sites in South-west Arabia would not be complete without some information on the small island of Socotra.

Socotra[219], 72 miles long and 22 miles broad, is situated in the Indian Ocean some 350 miles from the mainland and about 500 miles from Aden. The capital town is Hadibu and the second town of importance is Qallansiya, on the western coast.

Hadibu, once known as Tamarida, a date-growing area on the north coast, lies at the western end of a large roughly semicircular fertile plain bound by mountains. The central range is known as the Haggier mountains, the granite pinnacles of which reach 5,000 feet.

At the eastern end of this Habidu plain is the small coastal town of Sūk, which was probably the early capital of Socotra. Here, in the year 1507, the Portuguese, after the conquest of Albuquerque, established a fort and later constructed a small church.

The plain is well irrigated from the regular rains in the mountains, and two main wadis bring fresh water for the palms and fields. Generally the south side of the island is uninhabitable through the shortage of good water and the presence of high impassable cliffs from the beach area.

The people of Socotra who live in the coastal areas are descended from those who came from the mainland between the twelfth and fifteenth centuries AD, when earlier inhabitants were driven inland to the mountainous regions. The present inhabitants of the mountainous interior, known by the coastal dwellers as the *bedus*, maintain a primitive existence and are mostly cave-dwellers, tending their herds of goats.

Ancient stone buildings and uninhabited ruins found on the island were probably built by the original inhabitants and the present-day cave-dwellers are possibly their descendants.

The Socotrans had an early connection with Christianity although few details of this part of their history are known. Before the birth of Islam, Christianity flourished for a short period in Southern Arabia, and its influence extended to the island.

St Thomas is traditionally supposed to have introduced Christianity to the people when he was shipwrecked there in the fourth century. From Ethiopia, Cosmos Indicopleustes visited Socotra in AD 524 and he found it to be subject to the Nestorian Catholikos of Babylon.

A report on Socotra before the time of the Portuguese attack was given by Ibn Mādjid, the famous pilot who guided Vasco da Gama from Malindi. From it we understand that Christians lived in Socotra. Ibn Mādjid also commented that once a woman ruled over them and that marriage was in the hands of the priest of the Christians who dwelt in the churches and managed the marriages according to her advice.[220]

Before Ibn Mādjid's arrival members of the ruling family from Mahrah had built a fort and had established their rule over the Socotrans. When one of these Mahrī was assassinated reinforcements of tribesmen came over from the mainland to avenge his death and Mahrah rule over Socotra was strengthened.

Later, when the island was visited by St Francis Xavier during his voyage to India in 1541–2, there were no ordained clergy and although the Office was recited publicly four times a day there were few traces of Christian knowledge. He found the Socotrans no longer practised baptism, although the sign of the cross was remembered.

The mosque and buildings, both at Hadibu and at the western end of the island at the port of Qallansiya, are mainly constructed of masonry roughly laid, bonded in mud, and lime-plastered. The designs have a distinctive plastic form to which the setsquare and plumb-line have contributed little. In both of these large mosques a large mud-brick dome covers the main court, and the whole building is dominated by a small though shapely minaret. The decorative motif of a continuous triangle pattern usually composed of flat mud bricks in a horizontal wall panel is used on the more important buildings.

Socotra was surveyed by Captain S.B. Haines of the Indian Navy, when he was commanding the survey ship *Palinurus* in 1834–5 and surveying the Indian Ocean shore of Southern Arabia. It was deemed advisable at one time to create a base there for the Bombay Government, as a coaling station for the new steam vessels sailing between Suez and Bombay. However, apart from the unfriendly seas for which Socotra was notorious, this island proved too unhealthy on the low ground for the troops and they were evacuated after a short period.

The first archaeological study of Socotra was made when the Oxford Expedition went there in 1956, and the archaeologist of the party, P. Shinnie was able to survey some of the ruined buildings. The main sites worked on or visited were in the Hadibu Plain, the fort of Jabal Hasun and the fort at Sūk, with small buildings nearby. The use of one of these buildings in the centre of Sūk, although described once used as a mosque, was probably the church. The large fort is now a pile of fallen masonry, plundered in the past by the inhabitants of Sūk, but the footings of the circular corner bastions and on the walls are clearly the remains of a large structure designed for defensive purposes. It is not unlike the design of old forts known as of the Yafaʿ pattern still to be found in the Ḥaḍramaut. The fort at Sūk is about 82 feet long by 66 feet wide and the alignment of this dimension is due north.

About 100 yards north-east of the fort lies the small platform site of the church. An earlier building may have existed here as two plaster floor levels have been found. The site is orientated on 35° and it may have been used by the Portuguese and later rebuilt with its columns of coral blocks as the Church of Our Lady of Victory.

Plates 131–133

The site consists of a low mound with a level rectangle of lime concrete trowelled smooth, 28 feet by 31 feet, with remains of perimeter walling only on the northern entrance front. The bases of the pillars, nine in number, are still to be seen, constructed of limestone masonry. These bases are of different designs, octagonal, circular and star-pattern, as a transition from the base-square to the presumably circular column. Other traces of the actual columns have disappeared and they may have been of roughly cut masonry with a plastered surface, long since utilized in the walls of the houses of Sūk. The entrance doorway and plastered side wall abutting the entrance patio still remain although the wall is only two to three feet high. In clearing the site imported medieval Chinese porcelain and glazed ware were found.

A drawing by the Portuguese made during the visit of Don Joam de Castro in 1541[221] gives documentary evidence of these buildings, and some idea of their appearance. The most interesting sketch noticed in the drawing shows the construction of the church, with its single open belfry over the entrance. It was built outside the defence walls of a fort, and so was probably intended for use by the people of Sūk as well as the Portuguese garrison.

About 200 yards south of the church, on an area of flattish limestone level with the ground surface, are drawings made by pecking at the surface. There are several patterns, but the predominant though fanciful design is that of the cross, usually with arms of equal length.

Sūk today is in appearance probably as the Portuguese had found it, with its palms and lagoon at the mouth of the wadi. The accuracy of the Portuguese artists is shown in the detailed portrayal of the rocks and mountains of the Haggier Range. The Jabal Hawāri which overshadows Sūk is still distinguished by its ancient white blown sand on the north-east face.

The fort on the rocks of Jabal Hawāri, which overlooks Sūk is not shown on the drawing. This is not surprising as it was well camouflaged. With the old town of Sūk also situated on the lower slopes of the hill, this position for a fort was ideal for all-round observation and protection. It is probable that this fort was the one attacked by the Portuguese in 1507 and later occupied by them.

On this drawing important buildings at Hadibu are also shown, although no fort on the symmetrically shaped hill Jabal Hasun south of Hadibu is apparent. This fort at the peak was solidly constructed with an inner fort and external perimeter walls which are approximately 60 feet long and 50 feet on the north–south orientation. The inner surface of the well-constructed central portion is lined with stucco and there are small openings on the northern face which may have been water-channels from the small catchment-patio in front; in which case this may have been the water cistern, probably open to the sky, for a superstructure in the open would have had supporting pillars. It is probable that this fort on Jabal Hasun was a walled enclosure rather than a fortress of several stories, although a small garrison would have been sheltered there.

The construction of the fort, presumably after 1541, with its clear field of view, seems to have been for the purpose of protection from the south from the inhabitants previously evacuated to the mountains away from the coastal plain. This garrison overlooking the Wadi Manufu could have given warning of attack to the small developing town of Hadibu, residence of the Mahrī ruler.

Another fort, situated in the interior at Feragey where a valley narrows, is triangular in plan with towers at the three corners of the walls. This fortress commanded a main route across the island and may therefore have been constructed at the time of the Mahrī invasion, to deny access to the Hadibu Plain from the interior.

Westwards from the Hadibu Plain is the cliff pass over the hills of Ras Hebak leading to the old R.A.F. station at Ras Kharma. On the flat tableland (Cemetery Hill) and on the plain below bordering the coast are circular buildings constructed of random stone walling. Those on the plain were not in such good condition as those on the hill. One circular construction in particular on the hill shows traces of stone columns for a roof and a hearth.

Further west is the Plain of Eriosh, where a naturally flat and level limestone 'pavement' area has attracted people, probably shepherds, to execute pecked graffito drawings. These often consist of the foot motif although there are the geometric designs and the cross. The drawings of ibex and South Arabian characters may show a direct link with the mainland in pre-Islamic times. This site is about a mile and a half inland and about three and a half miles east from Ghuba (Khor Dehagihan). The area is about 100 feet wide by about 750 feet long east to west, and a roughly constructed stone wall partly surrounds it.

Near the track from Ghuba to Qallansiya at a distance of some five miles south of the prominent Jabal Abalan there is a natural roughly circular depression in the ground about 30 yards in diameter. Masonry work consists of stones laid in concentric circles and in tiers. By its position in the valley on the lower slopes of the Jabal it appears to be connected with irrigation and water conservation.

It is near here and on the slopes of the hills leading westwards to Qallansiya that there are large well-laid 'square' fields with low stone walls around the perimeter.

During the survey of the island by Captain S.B. Haines in 1834 he reported on his map the ruins of buildings south of Ras Badu, close to the lagoon. These ruins are on high ground overlooking the coast and the lagoon, and are a complex of rooms and small buildings constructed of large roughly shaped blocks of local stone. The walls were in some cases about four feet high. No potsherds or other signs of habitation debris were seen.

Nearby is a much larger ruin-field which has not been recorded before. It lies on the nearest level ground to the southern slopes of the Ras Badu where the hill is known locally as Jabal Simār Quār. This ruin site is also known by the same name. It is 340° to the point of Ras Badu, 240° to Ras Shaab and 145° to the inland Jabal Shaab. It consists of walls of buildings, many about two to four feet high. Again the walls are constructed of random-size, roughly laid stone blocks of reddish brown sandstone. The total extent of the site which is in two main groups of buildings is about 300 feet south to north approximately.

A graveyard with remains of a small building is situated some 300 feet away to the north-west. Here the graves with stone slabs around the edges are in good condition although all aligned in different directions.

A small number of potsherds was collected but it is surprising that the site did not show more signs of occupation debris as it was clearly that of a small town or village.

The dating of this type of site, without any confirming materials is almost impossible but may be linked with the capture of the region by invaders possibly at the time of the Mahrī incursions. A small stone with two circular hollows and a geometric design on the front face was discovered here, and may have been a libation altar. The geometric pattern appears to have an affinity with early South Arabian characters.

Archaeological survey has also extended from Sūk and the Haggier Mountain area towards the eastern region of Ras Momi. Here there are many ruin sites of buildings, houses or farmsteads. They usually show the same design of random rubble walls laid dry with vertical stone monoliths to support roof timbers. Extensive alignments of boulder-walls are to be found across the eastern side of the island.

It is of interest to find the tradition among the present-day Bedu that Arabian Christians lived not only in the Haggier Mountains but also on the high plateau leading towards Ras Momi. So far no archaeological evidence can support this.

From a surface survey of a large part of the island in an attempt to gather information on its value in antiquity, two observations may be made. One is the lack of buildings of importance and the lack of any material of significance such as carved stonework, formal inscriptions in early South Arabian and potsherds which could be identified. The other evidence is the expanse of farmed land, the farm-houses and dwellings and the vast areas encompassed by alignments of stone walling. From the *Periplus of the Erythraean Sea*[222] it is known that the island was subject to the Kings of Ḥaḍramaut, and the nearest port on the mainland which exported frankincense and aloes was Qana'. The *Periplus* also says that the island was then farmed out under the Kings and was garrisoned. This suggests that it was considered a part of the Kingdom and guarded accordingly. Products from the island such as aloes and frankincense, known to have grown there, were shipped to Qana' and exported from there.

Notes

References preceded by *Bibl.* are numbered works cited in the Bibliography.

GENERAL

1 *Bibl.* 6a, 52–3.
2 *Bibl.* 2a, 120, also *BASOR* 78, 1940 8 ff.
3 *Bibl.* 5a, 231.
4 *Bibl.* 15b; 61e, 474, and notes 117, 118.
5 *Bibl.* 61c, 300.
6 *Bibl.* 32b.
7 *Bibl.* 61e, 492.

TOPOGRAPHY AND CLIMATE

8 *Bibl.* 15e; GASS, I.G., MALLICK, D.I.J., and COX, K.G. The Royal Society Vulcanological Expedition to the South Arabian Federation, *Nature* 205, 1965, 952–5; GASS, I.G., MALLICK, D. I. J. Jebel Khariz, *Bulletin Volcanologique* XXXII-I, 1968, 33–8.
9 *Bibl.* 30, 13.
10 Details were supplied by the Royal Air Force Meteorological Office at Khormaksar, Aden.

LANGUAGE

11 *Bibl.* 27, 70–71.
12 *Bibl.* 59a, 6.
13 *Bibl.* 25, 51.
14 *Bibl.* 22, 116–20.
15 *Bibl.* 4h.
16 *Bibl.* 43a, 88–103, and fig. 6.

RELIGION

17 *Bibl.* 3f, 534–7.
18 *Bibl.* 41a, 363–4.
19 *Bibl.* 6b, 133–6.
20 *Bibl.* 41a, 371–9.
21 *Bibl.* 55, 125–8.
22 *Bibl.* 8a, 65.
23 *Bibl.* 61b, 22; 61f, 39, note 8.
24 *Bibl.* 27, 48.
25 *Bibl.* 4c, 207–28.
26 *Bibl.* 34.
27 Philostorgius, *Historia ecclesiastica* III, 4.
28 *Bibl.* 61c, note 8; 11b, 150.
29 *Bibl.* 61e, 490.
30 *Bibl.* 61c, 319.
31 *Bibl.* 48, 322f.
32 *Bibl.* 60.
33 *Bibl.* 48, 320–325.

FRANKINCENSE AND MYRRH

34 BREASTED, J.H. *Ancient Records of Egypt*, Chicago, 1906. I, 161, Sahure of the V Dynasty; I, 360, 361, Pepi II of the VI Dynasty.
35 *Bibl.* 49, 121–2; 29, 7–9.
36 *Bibl.* 27.
37 *Bibl.* 49, 123.
38 *Bibl.* 26, III, 97; 44, XII, 68–70.
39 *Bibl.* 3e, 82–6.
40 *Bibl.* 3b, 146.
41 *Bibl.* 2a, 120.
42 *Bibl.* 44, XII, 52, 53.
43 *Bibl.* 44, XII, 54.
44 *Bibl.* 44, XII, 60–3.
45 *Bibl.* 26, IV, 42.
46 *Bibl.* 61c, 303–4.
47 *Bibl.* 44, XII, 85–7; 26, III, 107.
48 *Bibl.* 49, 285–6.
49 *Bibl.* 49, 30–2.
50 *Bibl.* 44, XII, 84.
51 *Bibl.* 39, 54.
52 *Bibl.* 27, 63; 60.
53 *Bibl.* 27, 66.

ARCHAEOLOGY

54 *Bibl.* 21b.
55 *Bibl.* 27, 51 (inscriptions found were in fact much more numerous. Arnaud 60, Halevy 685 and Glaser about 2000).
56 *Bibl.* 61a.
57 *Bibl.* 8a.
58 *Bibl.* 6a; 42; 9b.
59 *Bibl.* 33e.
60 *Bibl.* 25.
61 *Bibl.* 61g, 56–60; 15a, Report 1960–1 and Bulletin; Report 1961–3, 4.

THE MINAEANS

62 *Bibl.* 61c, 308 and note 67; 61e, 432.
63 *Bibl.* 44, XII, 53–6.
64 *Bibl.* 44, VI, 154–6.
65 *Bibl.* 59a, 3–9.
66 *Bibl.* 16a, 131, 'I found a first Himyarish legend of the desert written upon the cliff'; 2b, 15, note 31.
67 *Bibl.* 54, VII, 16, 4, 2 and 16, 4, 18.
68 *Bibl.* 54, VII, 16. 4. 4.
69 *Bibl.* 41c, 264–71.

70 *Bibl.* 44, VI, 156–9.
71 *Bibl.* 61c, 299–300.
72 *Bibl.* 14.
73 *Bibl.* 61c, 297–9.
74 *Bibl.* 16a, and see note 70, illus. facing pages 111–7 and 133. Also, ROBERTSON, D.S. *A Handbook of Greek and Roman Architecture*, Cambridge, 1943, p. 221.
75 *Bibl.* 2c, 20. Also, review of J. RYCKMANS, L'institution monarchique en Arabie méridionale avant l'Islam, in *J. Amer. Orient. Soc.* 73, 1953, 36–40.
76 *Bibl.* 6a, 295; 2b, 15.
77 *Bibl.* 2b, 10–1.
78 *Bibl.* 61c, 300–1, 307–8, notes 41, 42a, 42b.
79 *Bibl.* 61e, 447.
80 *Bibl.* 2b, 11, note 14.
81 *Bibl.* 44, VI, 161–2.

QATABANIANS

82 *Bibl.* 42, 123.
83 *Bibl.* 32c; 46.
84 *Bibl.* 2b, 5–15.
85 *Bibl.* 61e, 431–2.
86 *Bibl.* 61f, table 2.
87 *Bibl.* 61c, 432–4, notes 10, 13.
88 *Bibl.* 4f, 51.
89 *Bibl.* 61c, 442.
90 *Bibl.* 42, 220.
91 *Bibl.* 10, 199; 61e, 465.
92 *Bibl.* 44, XII, 63–5; 44, VI, 151–4.
93 *Bibl.* 4f, 47–8.
94 *Bibl.* 61e, 464, note 86.

ʾAUSĀN

95 *Bibl.* 41a, 346–8.
96 *Bibl.* 49, 28.
97 *Bibl.* 61b, 293–5.
98 *Bibl.* 11; 61e, 432, note 8 (RES 3858); 47c, (*Ryckmans* 116); 61b, 276–7, and note 5.
99 *Bibl.* 36, 6–8 (RES 454).
100 *Bibl.* 43b, 138–40, and Pl. XI.
101 *Bibl.* 61b, 288.

THE SABAEANS

102 *Bibl.* 27, 37.
103 *Bibl.* 27, 42.
104 *Bibl.* 54, VII 16, 4 19-20.
105 *Bibl.* 45b, 45–8.
106 *Bibl.* 6a, 215–39.
107 *Bibl.* 44, VI, 159–62.
108 *Bibl.* 61e, 430.
109 *Bibl.* 54, VII 16, 4 24; 61e, 435.
110 *Bibl.* 44, VI, 158–62.
111 *Bibl.* 33e, 318 (CIH. 140).
112 *Bibl.* 33e, 83 (*Jamme* 578); 61e, 451.
113 *Bibl.* 33e (*Jamme* 629) 128–30.
114 *Bibl.* 33e, 351–75.
115 *Bibl.* 61e, 493, note 176.

ḤAḌRAMAUT

116 Pliny refers to the Atramitae, and Eratosthenes refers to the Chatramotitae, but both names seem to survive in the name Ḥaḍramaut.
117 *Bibl.* 2b, 14.
118 *Bibl.* 44, VI, 154–6.
119 *Bibl.* 31b, 340.
120 *Bibl.* 62.
121 *Bibl.* 44, XII 50–3.
122 *Bibl.* 33f.
123 *Bibl.* 61e, 482, note 139; 33b, I, note 3; 2b, 14.
124 *Bibl.* 42, 306.

ART

125 *Bibl.* 45b, 49, figs 15, 16.
126 *Bibl.* 3c, 287, Appendix V.
127 *Bibl.* 3d, 269–73.
128 *Bibl.* 1b, 231.
129 *Bibl.* 1a, 25–38; 6a, 123.
130 *Bibl.* 1a, 28; 42, 256–7.
131 *Bibl.* 45b, 134.
132 *Bibl.* 25, 43–4, pl. XXXVII.
133 *Bibl.* 22, pl. XXVI, 2.
134 *Bibl.* 45c, fig. 11; 22, 213, fig. 97.
135 *Bibl.* 13, 36–47.
136 *Bibl.* 9a, 455–60.
137 *Bibl.* 33c.
138 *Bibl.* 45a, 246, photo 394–6. A similar statue to this is the Roman portrait statue of the Emperor Trebonianus Gallus who reigned from AD 251 to 253. This life-sized statue is in an act of exhortation and, apart from the drapery over the arm and the lace sandals, is uncannily like the Sanʿa statue. (In the collection of the Metropolitan Museum of Art, New York. Rogers Fund 1905. No. 05.30; ht. 7 ft 11 in.).
139 *Bibl.* 6a, 269, note 11; 283, photo 196–9.
140 *Bibl.* 51, 210; 6a, 155–78.
141 *Bibl.* 15c, 150–62.
142 *Bibl.* 15a and 15c; 25, 20.
143 *Bibl.* 8a, 115–31; 25, 28–32 and note on p. 12.
144 *Bibl.* 8a, 96.
145 *Bibl.* 4f, 48.
146 *Bibl.* 43b, 61–5.
147 *Bibl.* 56a, 623–6.
148 *Bibl.* 32a, 35.

149 *Bibl.* 44, XII, 83–4.
150 *Bibl.* 58, 157–82.

THE SITES

151 *Bibl.* 44, XII, 87–9.
152 *Bibl.* 15a, (60–61), 13; 15c, 161.
153 *Bibl.* 52c, 126–7.
154 *Bibl.* 61c, 305, note 60.
155 *Bibl.* 49, 32 para 26.
156 *Bibl.* 15e, 4; 15f, 7–9.
157 *Bibl.* 39, 102; 52c, 127.
158 *Bibl.* 15a, *Bull.* 7, 15.
159 *Bibl.* 52, 123.
160 *Bibl.* 61b, 307, plate I, 2.
161 *Bibl.* 19, 69.
162 *Bibl.* 15a, *Bull.* 7.
163 *Bibl.* 35, 108.
164 *Bibl.* 52c, 125.
165 *Bibl.* 15c, 161–2.
166 *Bibl.* 25, 20.
167 *Bibl.* 15a, (60–61) 11; 15c, 158.
168 *Bibl.* 49, 32 para 26.
169 *Bibl.* 44, XII, 69.
170 *Bibl.* 44, VI, 158.
171 *Bibl.* 61e, 439 and note 24.
172 *Bibl.* 33a.
173 *Bibl.* 61b.
174 *Bibl.* 4f, 51–2.
175 *Bibl.* 15a, *Bull.* 2; 61g, 68–77.
176 *Bibl.* 15a, *Bull.* 4; 61g, 77–89.
177 *Bibl.* 33a.
178 *Bibl.* 20, 425–9.
179 *Bibl.* 15a, *Bull.* 6; 15d, 31–8.
180 *Bibl.* 33e, 300; 15b, 191–8.
181 *Bibl.* 61e, 474.
182 *Bibl.* 25, 35; 61d.
183 *Bibl.* 4f, 46.
184 *Bibl.* 25, 33.
185 *Bibl.* 41a.
186 *Bibl.* 44, XII, 63–5.
187 *Bibl.* 6a, 199–207.
188 *Bibl.* 46; 31 c.
189 *Bibl.* 3a, 8.
190 *Bibl.* 3a, 10–13; 42, 170–3.
191 *Bibl.* 6a, 155-164.
192 *Bibl.* 6a, 183–193.
193 *Bibl.* 3a, 10; 6a, 191–2.
194 *Bibl.* 46; 31c, 278–92.
195 This text has been published by A.F.L.Beeston in *Qahtan. Studies in Old South Arabian Epigraphy*, London 1959.
196 *Bibl.* 6a, 186–8.
197 *Bibl.* 9b; 3a, 13–14.
198 *Bibl.* 42, 115 and illus. facing page 116.
199 *Bibl.* 3a, 14–7.
200 *Bibl.* 47b.
201 *Bibl.* 8b, 189.
202 *Bibl.* 63; 3f, 533–4.
203 *Bibl.* 25, 49 and illus. XXXIV and LI.
204 *Bibl.* 3f, 526–34, 543.
205 *Bibl.* 3c, 291.
206 *Bibl.* 41a, 84.
207 *Bibl.* 25, 38–9.
208 *Bibl.* 7, 43–62.
209 *Bibl.* 4b; 41a and Appendix.
210 *Bibl.* 33f.
211 *Bibl.* 33g, 47–50; 25, 57–9.
212 *Bibl.* 6b, 133–6.
213 *Bibl.* 41a, 373–9.
214 *Bibl.* 8a.
215 *Bibl.* 61b, 134.
216 *Bibl.* 25, 40–2; 3f, 537–9.
217 *Bibl.* 61b, 136–9; 25, 43–4.
218 *Bibl.* 52b, 157.
219 *Bibl.* 15a, South Arabian Notes, 1–5. Shinnie, P. L. *Antiquity*, XXXIV (1960), 100–110.
220 *Bibl.* 52b, 157–8, Appendix V.
221 *Bibl.* 52b, pl. 12.
222 *Bibl.* 49, 34 para 31.

Select Bibliography

The following short list gives some of the more general books of interest on Southern Arabia whilst the full Bibliography is keyed to the Notes.

BOWEN, R. Le Baron, and ALBRIGHT, F.P. *Archaeological Discoveries in South Arabia,* Baltimore, 1958.
HAMILTON, A. (later Lord Belhaven). *The Kingdom of Melchior*, London, 1949.
– *The Uneven Road*, London, 1955.
HARDING, G. Lankester, *Archaeology in the Aden Protectorates*, London, 1964.
INGRAMS, H. *Arabia and the Isles*, London, 1952.
MEULEN, D. Van der. *Faces in Shem*, London, 1961.
– *Aden to the Hadramaut*, London, 1947.
MEULEN, D. Van der, and WISSMANN, H. von. *Ḥaḍramaut*, Leyden, 1932, repr. 1964.
PHILBY, H. St John. *Sheba's Daughters*, London, 1939.
PHILLIPS, W. *Qataban and Sheba*, London, 1955.

Bibliography

Abbreviations

BASOR	*Bulletin of the American Schools of Oriental Research.*
BSOAS	*Bulletin of the School of Oriental and African Studies.*
CIH	*Corpus Inscriptionum Semiticarum IV, Inscriptiones Sabaeas et Himiariticas continens*, vols I–III, 1889–1927.
JRAS	*Journal of the Royal Asiatic Society.*
RES	*Répertoire d'Epigraphie Sémitique,* vols V–VIII, 1938–68.

References in the Notes preceded by *Bibl.* are to numbers in the following list.

1a ALBRIGHT, F.P. The Excavations of the Temple of the Moon at Marib (Yemen), *BASOR*, 128, 1952, pp. 25–38.
b – Excavation at Marib in Yemen, *Archaeological Discoveries in South Arabia*, Baltimore, 1958, pp. 215–39.
c – and BOWEN, R. Le Baron. *Archaeological Discoveries in South Arabia*, Baltimore, 1958.
2a ALBRIGHT, W.F. *From the Stone Age to Christianity*, Baltimore, 1940.
b – The Chronology of Ancient South Arabia in the Light of First Campaign of the Expedition in Qataban, *BASOR*, 119, 1950, pp. 5–15.
c – The Chronology of the Minean Kings of Arabia, *BASOR*, 129, 1953.
3a BEEK, G.W. van. Recovering the Ancient Civilization of Arabia, *Biblical Archaeologist*, 15, 1952.
b – Frankincense and Myrrh in Ancient South Arabia, *Journal of the American*

Oriental Society, 78, No. 3, July–Sept. 1958, p. 141–52.
c – Marginally Drafted, Pecked Masonry, *Archaeological Discoveries in South Arabia*, Baltiomore, 1958.
d – A new interpretation of the so-called South Arabian House Model, *American Journal of Archaeology*, 63, 1959, pp. 269–73.
e – Frankincense and Myrrh, *Biblical Archaeologist*, 23, 1960.
f –, COLE, G.H., and JAMME, A. An Archaeological Reconnaissance in Hadhramaut, South Arabia, A Preliminary Report, *Smithsonian Institution Report*, 1963, 1964, pp. 525–34.
4a BEESTON, A.F.L. *Sabaean Inscriptions*, Oxford, 1937.
b – The Philby Collection of Old-South-Arabian inscriptions, *Le Muséon*, 51, 1938, pp. 311–33.
c – The Oracle Sanctuary of Jār al-Labbā, *Le Muséon*, 62, 1949, 3–4.
d – Problems of Sabaean Chronology, *BSOAS*, 16, 1954, pp. 37–56.
e – *Epigraphic South Arabian Calendars and Datings*, London, 1956.
f – Epigraphic and Archaeological Gleanings from South Arabia, *Oriens Antiquus*, Rome, 1962, pp. 41–52.
g – and BROWN, W.L. Sculpture and Inscriptions in Shabwa, *JRAS*, 1–2, 1954, pp. 43–62.
h – *A Descriptive Grammar of Epigraphic South Arabia*, London, 1962.
5a BENT, J.T. *The Sacred City of the Ethiopians*, London, 1893.
b – *Southern Arabia*, London, 1900.
6a BOWEN, R. Le Baron, and ALBRIGHT, F.P. *Archaeological Discoveries in South Arabia*, Baltimore, 1958.
b – Burial Monuments of South Arabia, *Archaeological Discoveries in South Arabia*, Baltimore, 1958.
7 BROWN, W.L., and BEESTON, A.F.L. Sculptures and Inscriptions in Shabwa, *JRAS*, 1–2, 1954, pp. 43–62.
8a CATON-THOMPSON, G. *The Tombs and Moon Temple of Hureidha (Hadhramaut)*, Reports of the Research Committee of the Society of Antiquaries of London XIII, Oxford, 1944.
b – Some Palaeoliths from South Arabia, *Proceedings of the Prehistoric Society*, XIX, 1953, pp. 189–218.
9a CLEVELAND, R.L. Cherubs and the 'Tree of Life' in Ancient South Arabia, *BASOR*, 172, December 1963.
b – *An Ancient South Arabian Necropolis*, Baltimore, 1965.
10 COMFORT, H. Imported Pottery and Glass from Timna, in F.P. Albright and R. Le Baron Bowen, *Archaeological Discoveries in South Arabia*, Baltimore, 1958.
11a CONTI ROSSINI, C. *Chrestomathia arabica meridionalis epigraphica*, Rome 1931.
b – *Storia d'Etiopia*, I Milan, 1928.
12 COON, C.S. *The Races of Europe*, New York, 1939.
13 COONEY, J.D. An Early Christian Sculpture from Egypt, *The Brooklyn Museum Annual*, II and III, New York, 1960–62.
14 DIODORUS SICULUS, Bk. 11 50 (1) trans. by C.H. Oldfather, Loeb Classical Library, London, 1935.

15a DOE, D.B. *Department of Antiquities Reports 1960–66, Bulletins,* 1–7, Aden, 1961–7.
b – Husn al-Ghurāb and the Site of Qana', *Le Muséon,* 74, 1–2, 1961.
c – Pottery Sites Near Aden, *JRAS,* 3, 4, October 1963, pp. 150–62.
d – Ghanam Al-Kuffār in the wadi Ahwar, *Sonderdruck aus Archiv für Völkerkunde,* XIX, 1964–5.
e – *Aden in History,* Aden, 1965.
f – Die Stadt Aden in der Geschichte Südarabiens, *Bustan,* 2, 1964, pp. 7–9.
16a DOUGHTY, C.M. *Travels in Arabia Deserta,* London, 1888–1930.
b – *Wanderings in Arabia,* New York, 1908.
17 DOSTAL, W. The Evolution of Bedouin Life, *L'Antica Societa Beduina,* 1959, pp. 11–34.
18a – FAKHRY, A. Les Antiquités du Yémen, *Le Muséon,* 61, 1948, pp. 215–26.
b – *An Archaeological Journey to Yemen,* Service des Antiquités de l'Egypte, I–III, Cairo, 1951–2.
19 FARIS, N.A. *The Antiquities of South Arabia,* being a Translation from the Arabic with Linguistic, Geographic and Historic Notes of the Eighth Book of AL-HAMDĀNĪ's *al-Iklīl,* Princeton, 1938.
20 GHUL, M.A. New Qatabani Inscriptions, I, II, *BSOAS,* 1959, pp. 1–22, 419–38.
21a GLASER, E. *Die Abessinier in Arabien und Afrika,* Munich, 1895.
b – *Reise nach Marib,* ed. by D.H. Muller and N. Rhodokanakis, Vienna, 1913.
22 GROHMANN, A. *Arabien, Kulturgeschichte des Alten Orients,* Munich, 1963.
23a HAINES, S.B. Memoir, to accompany a Chart of the South Coast of Arabia from the Entrance of the Red Sea to Misenat, in 50° 43′ 25″ E, *Journal of the Royal Geographical Society,* 1839.
b – Memoir of the South and East Coasts of Arabia, *Journal of the Royal Geographical Society,* 1845.
24 HAMILTON R.A.B. Six weeks in Shabwa, *Geographical Journal,* 100, 1942.
25 HARDING, G. Lankester. *Archaeology in the Aden Protectorates,* London, 1964.
26 HERODOTUS. *Histories,* Bks II, III, IV, Loeb Classical Library, trans. by A.D. Godley, London, 1921.
27 HITTI, P.K. *History of the Arabs,* London, 1964.
28a HÖFNER, M. Die katabanischen und sabäischen Inschriften der Südarabischen Expedition, im Kunsthistorischen Museum in Wien II. *WZKM,* 43, 1936.
b – Eine qatabanische Weihinschrift aus Timnaʿ, *Le Muséon,* 74, 3–4, 1961.
29 HOURANI, G. *Arab Seafaring,* Princeton, 1951.
30 HUNTER, F.M. *An account of the British Settlement of Aden in Arabia,* London, 1877.
31a INGRAMS, H. From Cana to Sabbatha: The South Arabian Incense Road, Burton Memorial Lecture, *JRAS,* 1945, pp. 169–85.
b – *Arabia and the Isles,* London, 1952.
32a IRVINE, A.K. Some notes on Old South Arabian Monetary Terminology, *JRAS,* 1–2, 1964.
b – On the identity of Habashat in the South Arabian Inscriptions, *Journal of Semitic Studies,* 10, 2, 1965.
c – Homicide in pre-Islamic South Arabia, *BSOAS,* XXX, pt. 2, 1967.

33a JAMME, A. Les Inscriptions Rupestres de la Région de Mukeiras, *Bulletin de l'Académie royale de Belgique* (Classe des Lettres), 1951.
b – Pièces épigraphiques de Heid bin ʿAqil, *Le Muséon*, 30, 1952.
c – Inscriptions on the Sabaean Bronze Horse of the Dumbarton Oaks Collection, *Dumbarton Oaks Papers*, 8, 1954.
d – Inscriptions Related to the House Yafash in Timnaʿ, in Albright and Bowen, *Archaeological Discoveries in South Arabia*, Baltimore, 1958, p. 183.
e – *Sabaean Inscriptions from Maḥram Bilqis (Marib)*, Baltimore, 1962.
f – *The Al-ʿUqlah Texts*, Washington, 1963.
g – Preliminary Report on Epigraphic Research in North Western Wadi Hadramaut and at Al-ʿAbr. *BASOR*, 172, 1963.
h – *Notes on the Published Inscribed Objects Excavated at Heid bin ʿAqil*, Washington, 1965.
34 KENSDALE, W. E. N. *The Religious Beliefs and Practices of Ancient South Arabians*, Ibadan, 1953.
35 LANE, A., and SERJEANT, R. B. Pottery and Glass Fragments from Aden Littoral with Historical Notes, *JRAS*, 1948.
36 MARGOLIOUTH, D. S. Two South Arabian Inscriptions, *Proceedings of the British Academy*, XI, 1925.
37 MEULEN, D. Van der, and WISSMANN, H. von. *Ḥaḍramaut*, Leyden, 1932.
38 MILES, S.B., and MUNZINGER, W. Account of an Excursion into the Interior of Southern Arabia, *Journal of the Royal Geographical Society*, 41, 1871.
39 IBN AL-MUJAWIR, TARIKH AL-MUSTABSIR. *Descriptio Arabiae Meridonalis*, O. Löfgren edit. Leiden, 1951.
40 *Periplus of the Erythraean Sea*, trans. and annotated by W. H. Schoff, New York, 1912.
41a PHILBY, H. St John. *Sheba's Daughters*, London, 1939.
b – *The Background of Islam*, Alexandria, 1947.
c – *Arabian Highlands*, New York, 1952.
42 PHILLIPS, W. *Qataban and Sheba*, London, 1955.
43a PIRENNE, J. *La Grèce et Saba*, Paris, 1955.
b – *Le Royaume Sud-Arabe de Qataban et sa datation*, Louvain, 1961.
c – Le Rinceau dans l'Evolution de l'Art Sud-Arabe, *Syria*, XXXIV, 1957, fasc. 1–2.
d – Notes d'Archéologie Sud-Arabe I, *Syria*, XXXVII, 1960, Fasc. 3–4.
e – Notes d'Archéologie Sud-Arabe II, *Syria*, XXXVIII, 1961, Fasc. 3–4.
f – Notes d'Archéologie Sud-Arabe III, *Syria*, XXXIX, 1962, Fasc. 3–4.
g – Notes d'Archéologie Sud-Arabe IV, La déesse sur des reliefs sabéens, *Syria*, XLII, 1965, Fasc. 1–2.
44 PLINY. *Natural History*, Bks III–VII, Loeb Classical Library, trans. H. Rackham, London, 1945, 1947.
45a RATHJENS, C. Sabaeica I–II, Hamburg, 1955.
b – and WISSMANN, H. von. *Vorislamische Altertümer in Südarabien*, Hamburg, 1932.
c – Kulturelle Einflüsse in Südwest-Arabien von den ältesten Zeiten bis zum Islam, *Jahrbuch für Kleinasiatische Forschungen*, 1950.

46 RHODOKANAKIS, N. *Die Inschriften an der Mauer von Kohlan-Timnaᶜ*, Vienna, 1924.
47a RYCKMANS, G. Une Inscription Chrétienne Sabéenne aux Musées d'Antiquités d'Istanbul, *Le Muséon*, 59, 1946, pp. 167–70.
b – Inscriptions Sud-Arabes, *Le Muséon*, 62, 1–2, 1949, pp. 55–124.
c – Inscriptions Sud-Arabes, *Le Muséon*, 48, 1935, pp. 153–187.
48 RYCKMANS, J. *La Persécution des Chrétiens Himyarites au Sixième Siècle*, Istanbul, 1956.
49 SCHOFF, W.H. trans., *The Periplus of the Erythraean Sea*, New York, 1912.
50 SCOTT, H. *In the High Yemen*, London, 1947.
51 SEGALL, B. Sculpture from Arabia Felix, The Hellenistic Period, *American Journal of Archaeology*, 59, 1955, p. 210.
52a SERJEANT, R.B., and LANE, A. Pottery and Glass Fragments from the Aden Littoral with Historical Notes, *JRAS*, 1948.
b – *The Portuguese off the South Arabian Coast*, Oxford, 1963.
c – Notes on Subaihi Territory, *Le Muséon*, 66, 1953, pp. 123–31.
53 SHARAFADDIN, A.H. *Yemen, Arabia Felix*, Ta'izz, 1961.
54 STRABO. *The Geography*, trans. by H.L. Jones, Loeb Classical Library, London, 1930.
55 THOMAS, B. *Arabia Felix*, London, 1932.
56a WALKER, J. The Moon-God on Coins of the Ḥaḍramaut. *BSOAS*, 1952, p. 623.
b – A new Katabanian Coin from South Arabia. *Israel Exploration Society Journal*, Jerusalem, 1963.
57 WELLSTED, J.R. *Travels in Arabia*, London, 1838.
58 WHEELER, R.E.M. *Rome Beyond the Imperial Frontiers*, London, 1955.
59 WINNETT, F.V. The place of the Minaeans in the history of Pre-Islamic Arabia, *BASOR*, 73, 1939.
60 WINSTEDT, E.O. *The Christian Topography of Cosmas Indicopleustes*, Cambridge, 1909.
61a WISSMANN, H. von, and RATHJENS, C. *Vorislamische Altertümer*, Hamburg, 1932.
b – and HÖFNER, M. Beiträge zur historischen Geographie des vorislamischen Südarabien, *Akademie der Wissenschaften und der Literatur*, Mainz, 1952.
c – De Mari Erythraeo, *Sonderdruck aus der Lautensach-Festschrift, Stuttgarter Geographische Studien*, 69, Stuttgart, 1957.
d – Al-Barira in Girdan im Vergleich mit anderen Stadtfestungen Alt-Südarabiens, *Le Muséon*, 75, 1962, pp. 177–209.
e – Himyar Ancient History, *Le Muséon*, 77, 3–4, 1964, pp. 429–98.
f – *Zur Geschichte und Landeskunde von Alt-Südarabien*, Vienna, 1964.
g – *Zur Archäologie und antiken Geographie von Südarabien*, Istanbul, 1968.
62 WREDE, A. von. *Reisen in Hadramaut*, ed. by H.V. Maltzan, Braunschweig, 1870.
63 ZEUNER, F.E. Neolithic sites from the Rub al-Khali, Southern Arabia, *Man*, 209, 1954, pp. 133–6.

List of Illustrations

All photographs are by the author unless otherwise acknowledged.

Colour Plates

AFTER PAGE 112

I The temple at Timnaʿ. Photo courtesy of Sir Mortimer Wheeler.

II Building near the South Gate, Timnaʿ, Photo courtesy of Sir Mortimer Wheeler.

III Alabaster bull's head votive plaque. Aden Museum.

IV Alabaster statue of a king of ʾAusān. Aden Museum.

V Alabaster statue of a king of ʾAusān. Aden Museum.

AFTER PAGE 130

VI Group of alabaster statuettes. Aden Museum.

VII Group of necklaces.

VIII Rings and ear-rings.

Monochrome Plates

AFTER PAGE 32

1 Rectilinear carved limestone slab. Aden Museum.

2 Carved limestone architrave, from Husn al-ʿUrr. Mukalla Museum.

3, 4 Architrave with entwined grape decoration, from Husn al-ʿUrr. Mukalla Museum.

5 Architrave with vine leaf and grape decoration, from Husn al-ʿUrr. Mukalla Museum.

6 Acanthus leaf capital, from the Wadi Ḥarib.

7 Inscribed slab with crouching ibexes.

8 Stylized frieze of ibex heads. Aden Museum.

9 Decorative marble panel (a tympanum?), from Marib.

10 Marble frieze, probably from Marib.

11, 12 Decorative friezes with antithetical designs, from Baihān. Aden Museum.

13 Frieze with antithetical griffins. Aden Museum.

14 Temple of ʾIlumquh, Marib. Photo G. Popov.

15 Marib dam. Photo G. Popov.

16 Walls of the temple of ʾIlumquh, Sirwāh. Photo G. Popov.

17 Temple of al-Masajid.

18, 19 Alabaster heads from memorial stelae.

20 Female figure plaque.

21 Sculptured left hand holding a bird.

22, 23 Inscribed and carved plaques. Aden Museum.

24 Alabaster head of a female child. Aden Museum.

25 Alabaster female statuette, possibly from Marib.

26 Alabaster bearded male head.

27 Baihān-type bowls.

28, 29 Goblet and bowl from Al-Qaraw, Abyan.

30, 31 Qatabanian pottery, Wadi Baihān area.

32 Unglazed jar from the Wadi Jirdān.

33 Two handled jars from Bir Nasir.

34, 35 Green glaze pottery found near Shaikh ʿUthmān. Aden Museum.

36 Bronze statuette of the Lady Baraʾat, from Timnaʿ. Aden Museum.

37 Alabaster jars. Muncherjee Collection, Aden Museum.

AFTER PAGE 80

38 Male bronze standing figure. Aden Museum.

39 Cast bronze plaque from Timnaʿ. Aden Museum.

40 Bronze statue of Dhamar Ali, ht. 2.2 m. San'a Museum. Photo H.Webb.
41 Bronze cherub. San'a Museum. Photo H. Webb.
42 Bronze male portrait head. San'a Museum. Photo H. Webb.
43 Bronze head from San'a. British Museum, presented to George V by the Imam of the Yemen.
44 Southern Arabian coins and their Athenian originals. British Museum, specimens selected and identified by Dr A.K. Irvine. Photo John Webb.
45 The Red Sea and Gulf of Aden from Gemini II. Courtesy of NASA and the U. S. Information Agency.
46 Early engraving of Aden, Admiralty Chart, 1835.
47 Paved 'Turkish Road', Aden.
48 Small cistern, Tawīla Tanks, Aden.
49, 50 Pottery kilns and pots at Al-Mimdara, near Shaikh 'Uthmān.
51 Huweirib, west of Jabal Kharāz.
52 Husn Malisah.
53 Al-Anād. Dar al-Rias.
54 Excavation trench at Ṣubr.
55 Mid-Acheulean hand-axes from near Jabal Tala.
56 Bir Aḥmed, decorated house.
57 Inscription stone, Abyan.
58 Fort gate, Jabal Sarar, Abyan.
59 Jabal Am'abeath, Wadi Yeramis.
60 Stronghold of Raudha.
61 The ruins of the mosque at Al-Aṣṣallah.
62 Am-Shabuh. Audhilla.
63 Pre-Islamic graffito, Haid Laḥmur. Audhilla.
64 Graffiti and camel drawings, Wadi Doḥ.
65 The *Aqabat* Thira.
66 Jabal Rada' stone alignments.

AFTER PAGE 148

67–69 Cairn and graffiti near Al-Madhan, northern Yemen.
70 Aerial view of Am-'Adiya.
71 Building 'W', Am-'Adiya.
72, 73 Inscriptions from Am-'Adiya. Aden Museum.
74 The great dam wall, Wadi Shirjān.
75 Inscribed rock, Wadi Shirjān.
76 Graffiti inscriptions above the Wadi al-Ruqub.
77 Paved area, Dhul Faiyaq.
78 Alignments, Ghanām Al-Kuffār.
79 The wall of Qalat.
80 Inscription RES 2687, Qalat.
81, 82 *Husn* al-Ghurāb.
83–85 Mayfa'at.
86 Al-Ḥauta.
87 'Sultan's' Palace, 'Azzān.
88 Qarn Bā Ja'ash.
89 A fortress farmstead, La'abel.
90 Water channel in the Wadi Amaqīn.
91, 92 Painted drawings and graffiti, Wadi Yaṯuf.
93 Painted graffiti, Wadi Salmūn.
94–96 Hajar al-Barīra.
97 'Ayadh.
98 Al-Binā.
99, 100 Salt mines, Haid al-Milḥ.

AFTER PAGE 196

101, 102 Hajar Am-Nab.
103, 104 Jabal Raydān, Baihān.
105, 106 Aerial views of Timna'.
107 Forecourt of the temple, Timna'.
108 Inscribed stone, Timna'.
109–111 Hajar bin Humaid.
112, 113 *Aqabat* Najd Marqad.
114 Ḥaribat.
115 Frankincense bush.
116–118 Shabwa.
119, 120 'Uqla.
121, 122 Wadi Aqābih.
123–126 Incised and pecked graffiti, Wadi Aqābih.
127, 128 Cairns and detail on the Jabal Aqābih ridge.
129 Mushgha.
130 *Husn* al-'Urr.
131–133 Church in Sūk, Socotra.
134 Burial on Jabal Hawāri, Sūk, Socotra.

Figures

(Drawn by Miss Lucinda Rodd, after the author)

1 Map of South-west Arabia, p. 17.
2 Trade routes from Arabia to India, p. 51.
3 Sketch map of the Marib dam, p. 77.

4 Plan of the temple 'Awwām, Marib, p. 77.
5 Column capital, p. 78.
6 Plan of the Tanks of Aden, p. 126.
7 Plan of Jabal Malisah area, p. 128.
8 Plan of the Husn Malisah, p. 129.
9 Plan of Kawd Am-Sailah, p. 135.
10 Plan of a structure at Kawd Am-Sailah, p. 136.
11–13 Pottery from Ṣubr, pp. 139–141.
14 Bowl fragment from Al-Qaraw, p. 142.
15 Survey drawing of Jabal Al-ʿAḥabuš, p. 143.
16 Inscribed slab from Jabal Al-ʿAḥabuš, p. 143.
17 Plan of fortifications on Jabal Sarar, p. 144.
18 Sketch plan of fort on Jabal 'Am-Mʿabeath, p. 145.
19 Sketch plan of Raḥab, p. 165.
20 Inscribed stone from Raḥab, p. 166.
21 Survey drawing of Am ʿAdiya, pp. 170–171.
22 Sketch map of the Wadi Shirjān, p. 173.
23 Sketch plan of the Wadi Shirjān, p. 174.
24 Dam inscription, Wadi Shirjān, p. 175.
25 Alignments, site 1, Ghanām al-Kuffār, p. 177.
26 Alignments, site 2, Ghanām al-Kuffār, p. 178.
27 Cairn, site 2, Ghanām al-Kuffār, p. 179.
28 Inscribed stone, site 2, Ghanām al-Kuffār, p. 179.
29 Sketch map of Qana' p. 183.
30 Plan of Mayfaʿat, p. 187.
31 Plan of Al-Barīra, p. 191.
32 Sketch map of field system, Al-Barīra, p. 194.
33 Plan of Al-Binā, p. 213.
34 Sketch map of irrigation system, Al-Binā, p. 214.
35 Survey drawing of recent excavations, Timnaʿ, p. 216–217.
36 Plan of the temple, Timnaʿ, p. 219.
37 Plans of houses, Timnaʿ, p. 221.
38 Sketch of Shabwa, p. 229.
39 Plan of cairns, Jabal Aqābih, p. 237.
40 Plan of Moon God temple, Ḥuraiḍah, p. 239.
41 Sketch plan of Husn al-ʿUrr, p. 243.

Index

Abalan, J. 248
Abdali, State of, 18
Abraha, 29–30, 59
ʿAbrain, W., 134
Al-ʿAbr, 24, 66, 97, 180, 186, 227, 235–7
ʾAbšibām, 71
ʾAbukarib ʾAsʿad, 15, 80
Abyan, 16, 49, 53, 64, 71, 73, 79, 117; area of, 142–7; inscriptions from, 146–7
Abyssinia, 14, 19; Christian teaching in, 27–9, 74, 184
Abyssinian, 14–15, 58
Abyssinians, 29, 30, 59, 79
Acheulean hand-axes, 134, 227
Aden, (Eudaemon Arabia), 13, 15–17, 19, 20; church at 27, 49, 53, 55–8, 64, 76; coins found, 80; area of, 123–39, 182, 184
ʿAdiya, J. 173
Adulis (Zula), 55, 58
Afalil, 24
Africa, 13, 54–5, 67, 73–4, 148
Agatharchides, 55, 68
Al-ʿAḥabuš, J., 146
Aḥwār, 24, 73, 177
Aksum, 15, 28; Gadarat ruler of, 79, 100
Alabaster, 106–7, 115–6
ʿAlam ʾAbyad (ʾAbiad), 24, 236
ʿAlam ʾAswad, 24, 66
Albright, Prof. F.P., 77, 78
Albright, Prof. W.F., 62, 69, 71
Albuquerque, Alfonso de, 124, 224
Alexandria, 29, 56–7
ʿAlhān Nahfān, unified Sabaʾ, 79, 97
Am-ʿAdiya, 23, 102, 148, 166; site of, 169–73, 226
Amaqin, W., 52, 186
ʿAmd, W., 25, 193, 226–7, 237
ʾAmdān Bayin, 80
American Foundation for the Study of Man, 62, 104, 110, 220–1, 224
ʿAmm, (ʿm), 25, 223–4
ʿAmyathaʿ, 74
Al-Anad (Dar al-Rais), 129, 133
ʿAnbay, 25, 224
ʾAnwad (ʾAnwadm), 80, 99, 230, 233–5
ʿAqaba, Gulf of, 67
Al-Aqābih, W., 235, J., 235–6
Aqrabi, 123
Arabia, Christian teaching in, 27–9; camels introduced, 50, 54–5
Arabia Felix, 12
Arain, 237
Architectural design, 102–6
Arethas, 28, 29
Arghadd, Raas, 235
Arnaud, T., 60, 61
Artemidorus, 67, 76
Aryab, 166
ʿAshtart, 25
Al-Aṣṣallāh, *see* Mesalum
Assyrians, 32
ʿAtaʿan (ʿAthʿan), House of, 220, 222
Ataq, 195
ʿAtf, W., 228
ʿAthʿan, *see* ʿAtaʿan
Athena, head of, 119, 121
ʿAttar, 25, 218, 224
ʾAud, 73; people of, 147
Audhilla, plateau, 146, 147
Augustus, 62; coinage, 119
Aulaqi (lower State of), 147, 177
ʾAusān, Kingdom of, 14; variety of myrrh, 49, 53, 65, 70, 73, 74; statues from, 107, 148, 214
ʾAwwām, 26; temple of, 62, 76, 104
ʿAyadh, 191, 195–6, 214
ʿAzzān, 98, 180

Bab al-Mandab, 73, 123, 134, 184
Babylon, frankincense at, 32
Bādhān, 59
Badu, Ras, 249
Baid, W., 68
Al-Baidha, 53, 147
Baihān, W., 20, 26, 50, 53, 62, 70–1, 73, 76, 79, 102; pottery from, 116, 193; area of, 215–26
Baihān al-Qasab, 71, 79, 215–6, 222
Baish, W., 68
Bal Ḥāf (Haf), 16, 180
Balsamodendron myrrh, 32
Bana, W., 53, 142, 146
Banu Bataʿ, 65
Baraʾat, Lady, 109
Al-Barīra, Hajar, 52, 64, 186, 191–6, 214
Barnett, Dr R.D., 11
Beek, Dr G. W. Van, 11, 63, 103, 227, 229, 232
Beeston, Prof. A.F.L., 11, 22, 167, 223, 233
Beitwan Mugraf Saad, 195
Berbera, 49
Berenike, 54
Besse, M. and Mme., 11

Bilqis, *see* Queen of Sheba
Al-Binā, 64, 191, 193–6, 213–4
Bir Aḥmed, 123, 137
Bir ʿAli, 16, 29, 63, 64, 98, 182
Bir Naʿamah, 123
Boswellia Sacra, 32; – *Carterii,* 32
Brown, W.L., 233
Bury, Wyman, 63
Byzantium, 28, 29

de Castro, Don Joam, at Socotra, 247
Charibael (Karibʾil), 57, 62
Cholaebus, 57
Christianity, 15, 29; church at Najrān, 68, 108–9; on Socotra, 245–7
Cisterns (Aden Tanks), 125–6
Coins, 118–22
Cole, Dr G., 227
Comoro, Is., 58
Constantine, 27, 80
Constantinople (Byzantium), 27
Coptic art, 108
Coptos, 31
Cosmos Indicopleustes, 245
Crater, port of Aden, 125
Crete, 68

Dahas (Yafaʿ), 73, 79, 142
Damarʿaly Yuhabirr, 79
Dar al-Ghanimah, *see* Mashgha
Dar al-Rais (Al-Anad), 129, 133
Dar ʿAnad, 129
Darius, 32
Dathina (Datinat), 73, 147
Debai (Dedabae), 68
Dedān, inscriptions, 21, 69
Deir el-Bahari, 13, 31
Delos, 68
Demeter, 109
Dhahaban, W., 68–9
Dhala, 18, 19, 20
Dhat Ḥamym, 25
Dhat Ḥamym ʿAthtar Yagul, 109
Dhufar (Ḍufar, Ṣaphar Ẓufar, Ẓafar), 11, 13, 15–16, 20, 24, 32, 49–50, 52, 56–7, 67; frankincense from, 97, 100–1, 182, 184, 227
Dhu Ghaylān, 72, 99
Dhu Khalil, 79
Dhu Nuwas Yusef, 28–9
Dhu Raydān, 28, 66, 79
Diodorus Siculus, 68, 101, 123
Discorida (Socotra), 56
Dostal, Prof. Dr W., 11
Duan, W., 226

Egypt, 13; incense for, 30–1, 49; camels in, 50, 56–7, 78, 184; artifacts, 227
Egyptians, expeditions, 13; hieroglyphs, 21; garrisons and trade, 31, 54
Elath, 67
Eleazus, 57, 62, 100
Ella ʾAsbaha, 29
Empty Quarter, *see* Rubʿ al-Khali
Eratosthenes, 67
Eriosh, plain of, 248
Ethiopia, 28; trading colonies, 55, 76, 101
Eudaemon Arabia, *see* Aden
Euphrates, 13
Ezana, 28
Ezion Geber, 31

Fadhli, state in Abyan, 142, 145
Am-Fadjarah, Dar ʿAnad, 129
Fakhry, A., 63
Fartak, Ras, 20
Feragey, 248
Fertile Crescent, 31, 74; influence, 108
Fid Fada, Aq., 147
Frankincense, trade in, 13; use of, 30–2, 49, 52–3, 55–7, 182, 250
Frumentius, Bishop, 27
Futura Pass/Aq., 52

Gaʿar, 145–6
Gadarat, 79, 99
Gallus, Aelius, 12, 62, 69, 78, 119
Gatn (Qatn), *see* Riša, W.
Gaza, 13, 52, 67, 215
Gebbanitae, 70; *see also* Qataban
Gerrha, 50, 67, 80
Gesenius, H.F.W., 22
Ghanam al-Kuffār, 24, 177–80
Ghuba, 248
Ghūl, Prof. M.A., 175
Ghurāf, 226
Ghurfah, 227
Glaser, Dr E., 60–1, 67, 222–3
Glass, manufacture of, 134–7
Greek, influence, 22; sea trade, 54; purchases, 58; colonists, 68; dress, 107; craftsmen, 110; coinage, 119, 121
Gregentius, Bishop, 29
Groom, N. St J., 226
Guardafui, Cape, 54
Gurat, tribe, 65; dynasty, 79

Habarut, Fort, 227
Habašat, 14, 79
Habban, W., 186
Hadath, House of, 221
Hadibu, 244–8
Ḥaḍramaut (Hazarmaveth) Kingdom of, 14, 16, 19, 22, 24, 26, 28; frankincense, myrrh, 49–53, 62–7, 69; in Qataban, 72, 75, 80, 97–100, 117, 119, 180–4, 186, 214, 217; capital of, 228, 230, 233; on Socotra, 250
Ḥaḍramaut, W., 14, 16, 105; area, 226–7, 243–4
Hadramis, 25, 28, 52, 67
Haggier, Mts, 244, 247, 249–50
Haid bin ʿAqil, 71, 106, 225
Haines, Capt. S. B., 63, 125, 137, 185, 246, 249

Hainin, 227
Hajar, 228–9
Hajar al-Barīra, *see* Al-Barīra
Hajar am-Nab, 53, 73, 148, 214
Hajar bin Humaid, 72; mint of Ḥarib, 119, 215–7, 225
Hajar Henu Az-Zureir (Ḥaribat), 215, 225
Hajar Quḥlān (Koḥlān), *see* Timnaʿ
Hajr, W., 16, 52; mountains of, 97, 181
Hakar, J., 148; site of, 166–7
Halevy, J., 60–1, 67
Al-Hamdani, 107, 123, 129, 142, 144
Hamdanid (dynasty) Hamdan, 65, 79, 99
Hamilton, A. (later Lord Belhavan), 63, 230–3
Harding, G.L., 11, 63, 196, 227, 232
Al-Harejah, 216
Ḥarib, mint and Palace of Nabaṭ, 72, 99, 119, 216; *see also* Hajar bin Humaid
Ḥarib, W., 70, 99, 215
Ḥaribat, *see* Hajar Henu Az-Zureir
Harpocrates, 108
Hartley, B.J., 167
Hasan, W., 142
Hasun, J., 246–8
Hatshepsut (Queen), 13, 31
Al-Ḥauta, Laḥej, 18, 129, 137
Hawari, J., 247
Hawfiʿamm Yuhanʿim, 71–2
Hawila, 69
Hazim, 65
Hejaz, 67–8
Herodotus, 32, 55, 60
Hidbat al-Ghusan, *see* Mashgha
Himyar, new state, 14–15, 23, 27–30, 52, 53, 57–9, 65, 66, 69, 71–2, 74; era of, 78–80, 98, 180–1, 190
Hippalus, 56
Hiswa, near Aden, 137, well at Shabwa, 230
Höfner, Prof. Dr M., 11, 22, 167, 223
Holkat, Bay of, anchorage, 124–5
Homeritaes (Homerites, Himyar) 57, 74, 78
Hugh Lindsay, steam packet, 125
Huqqa, 62, 76, 103
Ḥuraiḍah, 25, 62, 102; jewellery from, 118; pottery from, 117, 193, 226; site of, 237–40, 244
Husn al-Ghurāb, 29, 56, 63–4; site of Qanaʾ, 98, 182–5
Husn al-Urr, 105, 108; site of, 241–3
Husn Malisah, 127
Huwairib (Huweirib), 127
Hyksos, 31

ʿIdm, (ʿAdim) W., 24, 193, 226, 236, 240
ʾIl, 25–6
ʾIlʿ add, *see* ʾIlʿazz Yalit
Ilasaros, *see* ʾIlšarah
ʾIlʿazz Yalit (Yalut) bin ʿAmm-dahar, 62, 80, 99–100, 184, 235
ʾIlšarah (Ilasaros), 62, 78
ʾIlšarah Yaḥḍib, 79–80
ʾIlumquh, 25, 62, 64, 105, 115
ʾIlyafaʿ Riyam, 69
ʾIlyafaʿ Yašur, 69
ʾIlyafaʿ Yathaʿ, 69
India, 13, 54–8, 67, 78, 99; Roman coinage, 120, 148, 184
Indus, Bishop Theophilus, 27–8, 80
Inge, C.H., 226
Ingrams, D., 63, 181
Ingrams, H., 63, 97, 181
ʿIrma,W., 180, 228, 236
Irvine, Dr A.K., 11, 121–2, 222
Isis, 107–8
Islam, South Arabians before, 25, 27, 59, 65, 180
Am Jabalain, 146
Jabal bin Hussain al-Audhali, Naib, 148
Jacobs, H., 63
Jamme, Prof. A., 11, 167, 175, 224
Al-Jauf, 66, 97
Jerusalem, 60
Jewellery, 118
Jews, 29
Jibb, J., 227
Jilʿah, 180
Jirdān, W., 24, 52, 64, 119, 186; area, 190–1, 193–6
Johnstone, Prof. T., 11
Judaism, 15, 28, 59
Jurundish, J., 173, 176

Kaʿbah, 27, 30, 68
Al-Kabir, W., 134
Kaḥad, people of, 147
Kane, *see* Qanaʾ
Kanin, 65
Karibʾil (krbʾl), 12, 75, 100
Karibʾil Bayin, 79
Karibʾil Watar, 70, 73, 75
Karibʾil Watar Yuhanʿim, 62, 100
Karish, 169
Karnak, 31
Kaur Range (Khaur), 73, 147
Kawd am-Sailah, 134, 137
Khanfer (Gaʿar), 145–6
Kharāz (Ḥarīz), J. 15, 72, 99, 127
Kharma, Ras, 248
Khaura, W., 73
Khormaksar, 127
Khor ʿUmaira (ʿUmairah), 127, 129
Khor Malik, 227
Khor Ruri, 49
Kinda, 80
Kirsh, 18
Kirwan, L.P., 167, 231
Koḥlān, Hajar, *see* Timnaʿ

Al-Kud, 142
Kuwait, inscriptions from, 21

Lahayʿat, House of, 169
Laḥej, 16, 18, 73, 123–4, 133–4
Lake, Col., 63
Lak͟habah, *see* Kawd am-Sailah,
Leuke Kome, 54
Liḥyanite, inscriptions, 21, 67, 69; script, 121
Limatah, W., 186
Little Aden, 123
Lodar, 147
Lukman bin Ad, 75

Maʿad Karib, statuette of, 111
Maʿadʾil Salhan, 74
Maʿafir, King of, 53, 58
Maʿan, 67
ʾAm-Mʿabeath, (Amʿabeath), J., 146
Al-Mabnaʾ, W. (Obne, Ubbene, Libna, Mabana), 52, 181
Mablaqa pass/Aq., 70, 72, 215, 225
Madaʾin Saliḥ (al-Ḥijr) 69
Mad͟hābum, 238
Madhij, 53
Ibn Mādjid, report on Socotra, 245
Maifaʿah, W., 16, 64, 72, 98, 180, 188
Maʿin, Kingdom of, 14; inscriptions, 21; variety of myrrh, 49, 53, 65–7, 69–70, 72, 74, 78, 97, 102, 182
Maiwan, 228
Maghaniymah, J., 175–6
Al-Mahfid͟h, 177
Mahrah, Mahri on Socotra, 245, 248–9
Maḥram Bilqis, *see* ʾAwwām
Makainan, 227, 243
Malao (Berbera), 49
Malik, 26
Malisah, J., 127
Maʿmala, 69
Al-Mansur, Caliph, 54
Manufu, W., 248
Marʾalqays bin ʿAmrū, 80
Marawaha (W. Al-Ruqub), 148
Marib, (Mariaba), 12, 26, 59, 61, 62, 64, 66, 74–5; dam and temple at, 76, 78, 80; collapse of dam 97, 102, 104; bronzes, 110, 146, 184, 215
Mark͟ha, W., 53, 73; bowls from, 116; area of, 214
Marṯadum, 65
Martawa, 73
Maryamah, 216
Maryamat, 100
Masailah, W., 16, 226
Maʿshar, W., 228, 230
Mashg͟ha (Mushg͟ha), 193, 226, 240–1
Al-Mat͟han, (Al-Mad͟han), 24
Mathna, 228
Mayfaʿat, 52, 53, 64, 98–100, 102, 180, 182, 186–190, 192
Mecca, 27, 29, 54, 68
Medina, 28, 54, 67, 80
Mesalum, white myrrh from, 49, 142, 144
Meulen, D. Van der, 63, 242
Midianite, attacks of, 50
Mihbadh, W., 228
Miles, Col. S.B., 63
Al-Milh, J. 195
Minaeans, 21–2, 25, 53, 65; territory, 66–70, 74, 75, 78
Minoans, 68
Miswar (Miswara), 53, 73–4, 148
Mithras, 120
Mocha, 56, 58, 76
Momi, Ras, 249–50
Mosc͟ha, (Moscha), 16, 49, 56, 182
Moses, 31
Mosyllum, 49
Muhammed, birth of, 15, 30
Muhammed al-Qurra, Shaikh, 181
Mukalla, 19; carving at, 108, 226, 242
Mukarrib, 26, 70, 71, 79
Mukeiras, 19, 20, 23–4; town and district, 147–8, 166–7, 169, 173
Mundus, 49
Munzir, J., 124
Musemeir, 18
Mushainiqa, 28
Muza, 28, 49, 53, 56–8, 76
Myos Hormus, 31, 54
Myrrh, 30–2, 49, 55–6

Nabataeans, 69
Nabaṭ Yuhanʿim bin Šahr Hilal, 72, 79
Nāʿit, 65, 79
Najd Marqad, 53, 70, 215
Najrān (al-Ukhdūd), 15, 28–9, 67–9, 78, 80, 186, 235
Naʿmān, 74
An-Namāra, 12, 80
Naqb al-Hajar (Mayfaʿat), 22, 52, 53, 63–4, 98, 102, 186–190, 192
Našq, (Našqm), 66, 78
Necho, Pharaoh, 54
Negrana, *see* Najrān
Nile, 13, 30–1, 54
Nineveh, 31–2
Nisāb, 73
Nisyin, J., 214

Okelis (Ocelis), 56, 57–8, 71, 123, 184
Oman, 27, 184
Ophir, 31, 69, 75
Oxford Expedition, 246

Palestine, 67
Palmyra, 99, 105
Peloponnesians, 68
Pemba, 73
Perim, 123
Periplus of the Erythraean Sea, 12, 49; ports, imports and exports, 56–8, 60, 73, 97, 100, 123, 138, 184, 250

Persia, Persians, 15, 28–30, 50, 59; incense, 32, 135–6, 184; weight standard, 119
Petra, 67, 69
Philby H. St John, 24, 29, 63, 67–8, 229–33, 236–7
Phillips, Dr W., 11, 62
Phoenicians, 21; traders, 31, 54
Pirenne, Dr J., 11, 23, 71
Pliny, 49, 51, 58, 60–1, 66, 68, 72, 78, 97, 99, 120, 142, 144, 217
Popov, G., U.N. Ecological Expedition in Arabia, 259
Pottery, 116–8; at Ṣubr, 137–8
Prion, river of, 52
Ptolemies, 54
Ptolemy Cl., 52–3, 60, 68, 70, 98, 100, 123, 142, 144
Ptolemy Philadelphus, 55
Punt, Land of, 13, 30, 31

Qalat, 52, 63, 98, 180–2, 190
Qallansiya, 244–5, 248–9
Qamr, Bay, 16, 58, 97
Qana', 13, 14, 29, 52, 56–7, 64, 76, 80, 97–100, 180–6, 190, 250
Qara, mountain range, 16–7, 49, 182
Al-Qaraw, 115, 117, 144–5
Qariyat al-Hussain Muhd, 173 176
Qarnāwu, 66–7, 69–70, 78, 97
Qarn Qaimah, 227
Qarn ʿUbaid, J., 225
Qasam, 241
Qataban, Kingdom of, 14; variety of myrrh, 49, 53, 62, 65, 70; rulers of, 71, 72; with 'Ausān, 73–4; with Himyar, 78–80, 99, 108, 182, 215, 217
Qatabanians, 22, 25, 67
Al-Qatn, 244
Qatn (Gatn) W., *see* Riša, W.
Qur'ān, 30, 60
Quseir (Cosseir), 31, 54

Rabšams, 100
Radaʿ, J., 148; site of, 167
Radm al-'Amir (Darb al-'Amir), 237
Raḥab (Reḥab), Wadi and site, 148
Raibun (Ghaibun) beads from, 118; pottery, 193
Ramlat Sabatain, 16, 24; salt mines, 50, 53, 59, 67, 76, 97, 226, 237
Rathjens, Prof. Dr C., 62–3, 105
Raydān, mint at, 79, 80, 119
Red Sea, 15, 20, 31, 53–4, 56, 59, 71, 79; coast, 97; Roman sea trade, 120, 134
Rhodokanakis, Dr N., 222
Riša, (Qatn), W., 191, 193
Rodiger, E.R., 22
Romans, purchases by, 58, 78, 120
Rubʿ al-Khali (Empty Quarter), 16, 17; artifacts, 227
Al-Rudūd, 240
Ruwaik, 24, 66, 236
Ryckmans, Prof. G., 226
Ryckmans, Prof. J., 11
'Rymn (Raymanitae), 62, 78

Saba', Kingdom of, 14, 23, 25, 49, 53, 55, 62, 65–6, 68–74, 78–9, 146, 182
Saba' and Dhu Raydān, Kingdom of, 14, 66, 79, 100; mint of, 119, 146, 184–5
Sabaean, 22, 23, 28, 29, 53, 61, 64; clans, 65, 66; graffiti, 227
Sabaeans, 25, 57, 65–7, 74–9; affluence of, 106
Šabʿan, House of, 220–2
Sabota, Šabwat, Sabbatha, *see* Shabwa
Sachalites, (S'kl), 49
Ṣaʿda, 191, 194–5
Ṣafaʿ, graffiti, 21
Sāh, (W. Idm), 236

Šahr Ghaylān, 71
Šahr Hilāl Yuhanʿim, 71, 220, 223
Šahr Hilāl Yuhaqbid, 72
Šahr Yagul Yuhargib, 69, 72
Šaʿirm 'Autar, 79–80, 100, 184
Saiwūn, 226; palace at, 243–4
Salaḥan (Slḥn), 146–7
Salalah, 19, 20, 49
Salima, J., 173, 177
Salmun, W. (W. Jirdān), 93
Samʿi, 65
Šammar Yuharʿiš, 80, 100
Sanʿa (Sanaʿa), 29, 62, 65; statue at, 110–1
Šarahb'il Yaʿfur, 97
Šarah'il, 100
Sarar, J., 146
Sargon, 75
Sarr, W., 23
Saua, (Maʿafir), 57
Al-Saum, 241
Sawara, 53
Schoenus, measure of about 5 miles, 52
Sculpture, 106–15, 222, 225
Semites, 30, 31
Sennacherib, 75
Serjeant, Prof. R.B., 11, 63
Shaab, Ras, Jabal, 249
Shabwa, (Šabwat, Sabota, Sabbatha), 11, 14, 24; temple at, 26, 28, 51–53, 57, 62–3, 66; capital of Ḥaḍramaut, 97–100, 182, 184, 186, 189, 226, 228–35, 237
Shaikh ʿUthmān (Sheikh Othman), 18, 134
Shariah, 146
Sheba, Queen of, 60, 75; Maḥram Bilqis, 76
Shibām, 14, 23, 226, 244
Shiḥr, 244
Shinnie, Prof. P., 246
Al-Shiqq, 191
Shirjan, W., 148; site of, 173–7

Shuqaiqāt, W., 237
Shuqrā (Shuqra), 144
Šibam 'Aqyān, 65
Šibam Kaukaban, 106
Sidara, 181
Simār Quār, J., 249
Sīn (Syn), 25, 119, 238
Sinai, mines at, alphabet, 21, 30–1
Sira, Is., 124
Sīraf, 136
Ṣirwāḥ (al-Khariba), 74, 103
Smithsonian Institution, 63, 227
Socotra, 55–6, 244–50
Sohar, church at, 27
Solomon, merchant fleet of, 31, 50, 60, 69, 75
Somaliland (Somalia), 13, 19, 30–1, 49, 53; coins found, 80; myrrh and frankincense from, 148
Stark, Miss F., 63
Statuettes and stelae, *see* Sculpture
Strabo, 60–2, 67, 69
Ṣubaiḥi (Aṣābiḥ), 123, 129; Banu Haṣbaḥ, 176
Ṣubr, pottery at, 117, 137–8
Suez, 30, 54, 246
Sumhurum, 16
Sumhu'alay (Smh'ly), 64, 146
Sumhu'alay Watar, 71
Sumyafa' 'Ašwa', 29, 184
Sūnah, 240
Sune, beads from, 118
Sūk, 244, 246–7, 249
Šuqr, 119

Tafid (Abyan), 73, 142
Tala, J., 134
Talh, Aq., 147
Tamarida, *see* Hadibu
Tarīm, 226–7, 242, 244
Temples, 26, 32, 70–1, 76–8, 97–8, 102–5, 218–20, 230, 237–40
Thamudic, graffiti, 21, 22, 134, 226
Tha'ran Ya'ūb Yuhan'im, 80, 99
Tha'ran Yuhan'im, 27, 80
Thira, Aq. (pass), 147–8, 166
Thomas, B., 24
Thomas, St, 245
Thomna, *see* Timna'
Thompson, Dr G. Caton-, 25, 62, 227, 237
Tiban, well, 230
Tiban, W. (Tubanaw), 123, 129
Tiglath Pileser I, 50
Tiglath Pileser III, 32; tribute by Saba'i, 75
Tihama (Tihamat), 28; variety of myrrh, 49, 80
Timna', temple at, 26, 53, 62, 70–1; destruction of, 72, 102–4; carvings, 108; bronzes, 111, 186, 215–25
Tirbaq, 237
Tubanaw (Laḥej), 73, 142
Tyre, 27

Al-'Ula, 21, 67, 69
'Urāsh, dam of, 133
'Urr, Aq., 53
Al-'Urr, Husn, 241, 243
'Urr Mawiyat (Husn al-Ghurāb), 182–5
'Uqla ('Uqlah), J., 99, 228, 233–5

Wad'ab Yaf'n, 102, 172
Wadd, 25, Wadd 'Ab (Wad'b), 68, 74, 224, 226
Wahab'il Yaḥuz, 79
Wahidi area, 180–1
Waqt (al-Waḥt), 134–5
Waraw'il Ghaylān Yuhan'im, 72
Webb, H., U.S. Consulate, Taiz., 260
Wellsted, Lieut. J.R., 63, 185, 189, 190
Winnett, Dr F.V., 67
Wissmann, Prof. Dr H. von, 11, 62, 63, 68, 72, 167
Wrede, Baron A. von, 63, 98, 181
Al-Wuste, 72

Xavier, St Francis, 245

Yada' 'ab Dhubyān, 71–2, 148, 222–3
Yada''ab Ghaylān, 72, 79, 99
Yada''ab Yagil, 71
Yada''il, 69, 79
Yada''il Bayin, Yd''l Byn, 79, 99, 230, 233, 235
Yafa' (Yafai'), 53, 72, 79; port of, 144; myrrh from 148; fort design, 243
Yaf'an, House of, 172, 220
Yafaš (Yafash), house of, 72; bronzes at, 111, 220, 224
Yamnat, 80, 98
Yarim, *see* Ẓafar
Yaṣduq'il Far'am, 74
Yaṣduq'il Far'am Šaraḥ'at, 74, 107
Yaṯa''amar Bayin, 71
Yatha''mar (Yt''mr), 12, 75
Yathrib (Yaṯrib), *see* Medina
Yaṯil (Yṯl), 66
Ya'zil Bayin, 80
Yemen, 16, 18–9, 60
Yeramis, W., 146

Ẓafar (of Dhu Raydān), 14, 27–9, 53, 58, 65–6; Himyar capital, 79–80; mint at, 119, 184
Zanzibar, 58, 73
Zara, 147
Zingibar, *see* al-Qaraw
Zoscales, 100